MEDIA AND MIGRATION

From images of the Afghan airline hijack in Britain and the movement of Roma asylum-seekers throughout Europe, to North African immigrants in France and the Elian Gonzalez affair played out in Washington and Miami, the media have helped shape and determine the knowledge, attitudes and behaviour of all those involved in contemporary migration processes.

Media and Migration explores the close and vital relationship between the contemporary media and immigration. Drawing on newspapers, film, television and photography, and using examples from a range of countries, *Media and Migration* illustrates how the media intervene to affect the reception migrants receive, how they stimulate prospective migrants to move and how they play a dynamic role in the cultural politics and cultural identity of diasporic communities.

Contributors: Giovanna Campani, David Forgacs, Alec Hargreaves, Ronald Kaye, Russell King, Lee Siew-peng, Nicola Mai, Christine Ogan, Karen O'Reilly, Bruno Riccio, Mireille Rosello, Roza Tsagarousianou, Nancy Wood.

Russell King is Professor of Geography and Dean of the School of European Studies at the University of Sussex. **Nancy Wood** is Senior Lecturer in Media and European Studies and Director of the Graduate Research Centre in Culture and Communication at the University of Sussex.

ROUTLEDGE RESEARCH IN CULTURAL
AND MEDIA STUDIES
Series advisors: David Morley and James Curran

MEDIA AND MIGRATION

Constructions of mobility and difference

Edited by
Russell King and Nancy Wood

London and New York

First published 2001
by Routledge
11 New Fetter Lane, London EC4P 4EE

Simultaneously published in the USA and Canada
by Routledge
29 West 35th Street, New York, NY 10001

Routledge is an imprint of the Taylor & Francis Group

Typeset in Galliard by Taylor & Francis Books Ltd
Printed and bound in Great Britain by University Press, Cambridge

British Library Cataloguing in Publication Data
A catalogue record for this book is available from the British Library

Library of Congress Cataloging in Publication Data
A catalog record for this book has been requested

ISBN 0–415–22925–1

CONTENTS

CONTENTS

CONTRIBUTORS

Giovanna Campani is a Lecturer in the Faculty of Educational Sciences, University of Florence

David Forgacs is Professor of Italian Studies at University College London

Alec G. Hargreaves is Professor in the Department of European Studies at Loughborough University

Ronald Kaye is Honorary Fellow in the Department of Politics, University of Durham

Russell King is Professor of Geography and Dean of the School of European Studies at the University of Sussex

Lee Siew-peng has recently completed a Ph.D. in the Department of Anthropology and Sociology, School of Oriental and African Studies, University of London

Nicola Mai is a D.Phil. student in Media Studies at the University of Sussex

Christine Ogan is Professor of Journalism at Indiana University, Bloomington

Karen O'Reilly is Lecturer in Sociology at the University of Aberdeen

Bruno Riccio has recently completed a D.Phil. in Social Anthropology at the University of Sussex

Mireille Rosello is Professor of French and Comparative Literary Studies, Northwestern University, Evanston, Illinois

Roza Tsagarousianou is Senior Lecturer in the Centre for Communication and Information Studies, University of Westminster

Nancy Wood is Senior Lecturer in Media and European Studies and Director of the Graduate Research Centre in Culture and Communication at the University of Sussex

PREFACE AND ACKNOWLEDGEMENTS

This book is a product of the creative interdisciplinary research environment at the University of Sussex. It has its origins in a Workshop on Media and Migration organised by the editors in their capacities as directors respectively of the Sussex Centre for Migration Research and the Graduate Research Centre in Culture and Communication (CulCom). The Workshop took place in November 1998 and most of the chapters in the book were first presented as papers to that event. A few chapters are invited contributions which were commissioned in order to broaden the focus of the book and also to extend somewhat its geographical coverage – which remains, nevertheless, predominantly European.

The Workshop brought together two fields – media studies and migration studies – both of which are richly interdisciplinary yet rarely placed together. The linking of media and migration is thus a relatively new and unexplored field of investigation; this book is the first to explore this creative linkage. The contributors are a mixed grouping of senior academics and younger researchers; they represent a wide range of disciplinary and interdisciplinary backgrounds including media studies, journalism, sociology, anthropology, geography, politics and literary studies. Most of the chapters are based on primary research. Chapter 5, by Mireille Rosello, is being published in a slightly modified version in her forthcoming book *Postcolonial Hospitality: The Immigrant as Guest*, Stanford University Press.

As we discuss in more detail in our overview of the field in Chapter 1, media may intervene in the migration process and in the individual and collective experience of migration in a variety of ways. Images transmitted by the destination countries may be a key source of information for potential migrants, and therefore act as an important factor stimulating migrants to move. Second, media images of the migrants may be crucial in determining the type of reception they are accorded – and hence the degree of social inclusion or exclusion they are likely to achieve. Media stereotypes of particular migrant groups often play an important role here. Finally, media emanating from the country of origin, such as satellite television, and new global distribution technologies such as the world wide web, are playing a dynamic role in the politics and cultural identity of diasporic communities.

We close these brief introductory remarks by thanking the contributors for providing their papers more or less on schedule and for being so willing to accept our editorial input and suggestions for revision. We also thank Jenny Money of the School of European Studies at Sussex for her editorial assistance and her role in bringing the manuscript to fruition in its final stages.

Russell King and Nancy Wood

1

MEDIA AND MIGRATION

An overview

Nancy Wood and Russell King

Introduction

Migration and media studies are two richly interdisciplinary fields of study. They overlap in various ways but the interconnections have rarely been explored. These linkages are not just a subject for academic research, but impinge on the consciousness of the ordinary European citizen on virtually a daily basis. This has been very evident in the British press in the recent past when events and issues such as the Afghan airplane hijacking at Stansted Airport, the arrival of Roma asylum-seekers and the British government's evolving policy for dealing with asylum claims have been reported, discussed, exaggerated and politicised to the extent that so-called 'illegal immigration' and so-called 'bogus asylum-seekers' are repeatedly claimed (by the British Conservative Party at least) to be major election issues alongside health and education. Exactly how the media influence, shape or determine the knowledge, attitudes and behaviour of British and European citizenry with respect to contemporary migration processes is one of the major lines of enquiry of this volume. What emerges from the analyses carried out by the contributors, of specific migration events and of the national contexts to which these relate, is a complex picture where perspectives and approaches may dovetail at times, but may equally stand in stark contrast to each other. In this introductory overview, we merely wish to draw the reader's attention to some of these salient points of convergence and divergence.

To be more systematic, we suggest that media may intervene in the migration process and in the individual and collective experience of migration in three main ways. First, images transmitted from the destination countries, or by the global media generally, may be an important source of information for potential migrants. Whether this information is accurate or not, it can act as an important factor stimulating migrants to move. Images of wealth and of a free and relaxed lifestyle in the 'West' or the 'North' are commonplace in the developing and transforming countries of the world, and the constancy of these images in global media – in films, television, magazines and advertisements – tends to reinforce their 'truth' in the eyes of the beholders. Often returning migrants

1

collude in strengthening the veracity of these images, partly to impress, and partly to deny any elements of failure, suffering or exclusion, both to their family and friends back home, and perhaps also to themselves.

Second, host-country media constructions of migrants will be critical in influencing the type of reception they are accorded, and hence will condition migrants' eventual experience of inclusion or exclusion. Often acting as the mouthpiece of political parties or other powerful groups, media discourses have been shown to be immensely influential in constructing migrants as 'others', and often too as 'criminals' or 'undesirables'. Such a focus on migrant criminality creates stereotypes which are very far from the truth and very hard to shake off. In Britain there are heavy hints and assumptions that all asylum-seekers are 'bogus' whilst the term 'economic migrant' has been invested with a new negative meaning. We pick up the issue of British newspaper coverage of recent migration events later in this chapter.

Third, media originating from the migration sending country, such as films, video and satellite television, as well as new global distribution technologies such as the world wide web, are playing a dynamic role in the cultural identity and politics of diasporic communities. There are interesting linkages here between media and the creation and maintenance of transnational communities whose members are able to function in two or more worlds, with varying degrees of comfort. Such media may help migrants feel 'at home' in their country of 'exile' but at the same time perhaps slow down their processes of integration and incorporation. A further development occurs when emigrant groups and ethnic communities produce their own media in the form of film, television and music. Such communicative art forms often reflect hybrid inputs from the countries of origin, the destination setting and influences from the global music or entertainment scene. As far as the future is concerned, increasing use will undoubtedly be made by migrant and diasporic communities of internet technologies; the importance of this medium has only just begun to be researched by migration scholars (Elkins 1997; Morton 1999).

These three types of linkage between media and migration by no means exhaust the kinds of interrelationship which exist. In the final part of this introductory chapter we relate how individual chapters of the book explore a myriad of connections. Before we do this, we examine how the 'media and migration' interrelationship has been investigated and understood within the respective fields of migration studies and media studies, and we present two fairly specific examples of media–migration analysis – a brief survey of recent migration issues in the British print media, and the use of photographs to document the migration experience.

Media in migration; migration in the media

The migration studies literature – which has been growing extremely rapidly in recent years – is curiously silent on the role of the media. A perusal of the key texts which have been published in the last few years reveals that practically no attention has been paid to media issues: most do not even have 'media' as an index entry, let alone as a theme for a chapter or a chapter subheading. Migration tends to be objectified as a time–space event or process which is largely to be explained in economic, demographic or sociological terms and linked to issues of employment, development, population redistribution, class formation and the creation of ethnic communities.[1]

The significance of the media lies beneath the surface of these processes and its role is almost never made explicit by migration scholars. Where migration is modelled as a behavioural or decision-making process based on available sources of information to the potential migrant about the 'place utilities' of various destinations, the question is never really asked: what *are* these sources of information? How *do* potential migrants receive knowledge or impressions about places they might think of relocating to? To put the question in the specific jargon of the migration behaviourists, how do people construct 'information fields' about areas and places which then become their 'migration fields'? (White and Woods 1980: 30–4). For sure, these channels of information are many and varied – word-of-mouth, letters and other communications from friends and relatives who have already migrated, data from employment agencies and other bodies. But there must also be other sources of information and imagery which are received by the migrants but rarely studied by migration researchers. Hence we do not know what the precise roles are of newspapers, television or films in shaping the perception of migrants about places which enter into their migration fields. And we also do not know exactly to what extent these media-related images contribute to an accurate or (more likely) a distorted and exaggerated picture of the reality migrants eventually discover for themselves – at the same time as they discover their own delusion.

From the other side of the media–migration relationship, while the literature on media studies has been slow to engage with migration as a distinct phenomenon, it is fair to say that media and film studies have none the less been attentive to the migration experience in more oblique ways. As we have indicated above, if migration scholars are only now recognising the role that the media play in the migrant's behaviour or decision-making processes, media scholars have long been concerned with precisely the question of media 'effects'. Several of our contributors explore this vexed area of enquiry: in one case considering how coverage of immigration issues may have affected voting behaviour, in another looking at host-country representations that may have stimulated the desire to migrate. However, as with all studies of the infinitely complex relation between images and their alleged 'effects' on human psychology or behaviour, conclusions must be provisional and cautious.

A number of media scholars has also used ethnographic research methods to investigate the use of media in the everyday life experience of recent or more settled migrants. Marie Gillespie's pioneering work on how generational relations and conflicts amongst young Punjabi Londoners were negotiated in

3

the course of daily television viewing (Gillespie 1995) has paved the way for further studies of how migrants might use global media, host-country media, media transmitted from the country of origin or media produced by migrant communities to come to terms with their new lives and to make sense of their migration experience.

Finally, if it is in the broader domain of 'post-colonial' theory that notions like 'diasporic', 'hybrid' or 'transnational' identities have been explored, elaborated and debated, these terms are certainly ones that both media and migration scholars have invoked to characterise the multiple identities that geographical displacement tends to produce, especially among younger generations of migrants. Again, media and film theorists have been particularly concerned to identify the role that images and sounds originating from media sources might play in the 'identity politics' of migrant communities. To take just one striking example, in France, the term *'beur'*, proudly adopted by French youth of North African origin to celebrate their 'hybrid' identity (and in defiance of a deeply rooted prejudice against them), is now used in common parlance. It has also come to designate a distinct cinematic genre (*'beur'* cinema) and a national radio station bears the name 'Radio Beur'. Rap music coming from North Africa, especially Algeria, or produced by *beur* youth, now tops the French charts. Whether *beur* media merely gave expression to this identity politics or helped to bring it into being is precisely the kind of question which media and film studies are concerned to address. But however positive and uplifting this example, it cannot be taken for granted that such multiple, hybrid or 'diasporic' identities should be celebrated for their own sake; indeed, as we have already suggested, they might equally express a failure to adapt to new lives and an acute sense of alienation and exclusion. This is why, when analysing how the media articulates or engages with this new politics of identity, media scholars need to turn to the insights of migration studies for a more differentiated account of the migrant experience.

Issues of migration as constructed in British newspapers

Probably the largest volume of research on media–migration interactions has been carried out on the representations of migrants, migration events and migration issues in the printed media. Here we briefly review some of this research and provide a preliminary commentary on recent migration events as portrayed through the British press.

From a theoretical and methodological point of view, pioneering research on the analysis of media text has been carried out by Teun van Dijk, although his work tends to focus on media discourses of racism rather than on the process of migration (see especially van Dijk 1991; also 1987, 1992, 1993). Earlier work on racism in the mass media in Britain had been carried out by Hartmann and Husband (1974) and by Gordon and Rosenberg (1989). On a wider front, immigration and racism have received intense coverage in the media of most

European countries, particularly since the late 1980s, with numerous reports and features in the popular and serious press and programmes on television (Solomos and Wrench 1993). The broader social and political context of migration partly explains this – and the media itself has contributed to this more prominent social–political debate, as media and politicians conspire to create 'a dangerous tautology between two supposedly separate realms: that of representation and that of policy-making' (Rosello 1998: 137). Meanwhile writers such as Balibar (1991), Bovenkerk *et al.* (1990) and Miles (1993) have portrayed the development of a new kind of 'European racism' which has come about, at least in part, from the fact that the construction of a 'European identity' inevitably involves an explicit or implicit pattern of exclusion of 'the other' – notably immigrants, refugees, Muslims, black people, etc. At the national and local level, this exclusion reaches the level of relentless victimisation and demonisation of certain immigrant groups, as several studies have shown (Brosius and Eps 1995; Kaye 1998; Rosello 1998; ter Wal 1996). More complex cross-currents of media representation are evident in countries such as Switzerland and Belgium, which are multi-ethnic societies of long standing. In Belgium for instance, the francophone public media tend to highlight any expression of racism in Flanders – typical of the media's exaggeration of negative aspects on the 'other' side of the Belgian ethno-linguistic divide (Martiniello 1997: 292).

A good example of a scholarly analysis of the media portrayal of a single migration-related event is Jessica ter Wal's (1996) examination of the discourse surrounding the occupation by, and eventual eviction of, more than a thousand immigrants who were squatting in an abandoned factory, called La Pantanella, in Rome in 1991. Even though her analysis concentrated on the representation of the issue by a single newspaper (the broadly centre-left *La Repubblica*), ter Wal shows how the paper's articles and comments served to build a consensus in favour of the eviction of the immigrants from the building. Above all, *La Repubblica* gave extensive coverage to the views of local inhabitants who wanted to keep the immigrants out of 'their' neighbourhood. Press reports stressed the alleged links between the immigrants and the criminality, urban degradation and climate of 'fear' which were said to be characteristic of the area. Within the factory, overcrowding, filth and inter-ethnic conflict between the many migrant groups present were constantly referred to. Only after the eviction had taken place was there some attempt at a more balanced representation of the immigrant populations involved.

There is an interesting parallel between the police's storming of the Pantanella in Rome and the eviction of a group of *sans-papiers* (undocumented immigrants) from the church of Saint-Bernard in Paris in 1996. Rosello's (1998) analysis of the Saint-Bernard case embraces TV and cartoon representations as well as the press, and here it seems that the greater immediacy and impact of the visual narratives on television screens served, if anything, to delegitimise official actions and to arouse public sympathy for the evicted migrants, some of whom had been on hunger strike. This creation of sympathy for the plight of the *sans-papiers* amongst a French public supposedly hostile to immigrants forced the government to revise its own policies towards immigration, breaking down the cross-party consensus that deportation was a suitable response to the phenomenon of illegal immigration (Rosello 1998: 148–9). Further commentary on this issue of the expulsion of the *sans-papiers* is provided by Alec Hargreaves in the next chapter.

By contrast, Kaye's (1998) analysis of the UK media's portrayal of refugees and asylum-seekers during the period 1990–95 deploys standard quantitative techniques for monitoring the occurrence of prejudicial language, focusing on such terms as 'phoney' and 'bogus' when applied to asylum-seekers. Kaye's survey of the first half of the 1990s, updated to 1998 in his contribution to the present volume (see Chapter 4), sets the scene for the following commentary on the UK press coverage of migration issues in the first seven months of 2000. Several specific events are commented on, together with the more general and ongoing debate over the UK's asylum policy.

Four main 'stories' occurred – the Afghan hijack at Stansted Airport, the Elian Gonzalez affair, 'gypsy beggars', and the fifty-eight Chinese migrants found dead in the back of a lorry at Dover. Each excited the press in different ways, with variable connections made to the UK asylum debate and to wider European and global processes of refugee movement and economic migration.

What was surprising about the Stansted hijacking, which took place in February, was the slowness with which the media – or any other public commentator – grasped the asylum-seeking purpose of the whole event. Partly this was because of the lack of information given by the police during the early stages of the hijacking, but partly too it was a reflection of the fact that the common perception of a hijack (one or a few 'terrorists' taking a large number of people hostage for some personal or political end) blinded the media to the possibility that this was, in reality, a mass request for asylum – a petition which was, given the harshness of the UK's asylum regime and the country's uncompromising attitude towards hijackers, destined to fail for the majority of the plane's passengers (MacAskill *et al.* 2000; Sengupta 2000).

The case of Elian Gonzalez, the 6-year-old Cuban boy who survived a shipwreck in which his mother and ten other people died, received widespread UK media coverage, although obviously not as much as in the United States, where his survival and subsequent tug-of-war gave him almost mythical individual appeal as well as making him a pawn in Cold-War and diaspora politics. Several points are interesting in the coverage of the Elian case by the UK media (or by those parts of the American media selected for use in the UK). First the media seemed uncertain where the sympathy should be placed (apart from, obviously, on the boy himself): whether on the Miami relatives who wanted to keep him, or on the boy's father in Cuba. Second, there are the differential, and in some cases unintended, interpretations of some of the media images that were presented of the boy. When Elian was staying with his Miami relatives he was featured daily on television and in newspaper photos, playing with new toys and going on trips to amusement parks; at the same time, the pictures of him playing in the garden of the house where he was staying showed him behind a high wire fence which evoked images of him being imprisoned. Later, in a stage-managed media event where, speaking jerkily into the television cameras, he renounced his father, one did not have to be a child psychologist to see the confusion and tension he was suffering, nor to suspect the authenticity of what he was saying. And then, in the case's watershed moment, when government officials snatched him at dawn from the house where he was staying, images of the boy being grabbed at gunpoint were flashed around the world; yet public opinion (at least outside the Cuban community in the United States) was less condemnatory than might have been expected and, if anything, moved against the relatives whose constant attacks on Fidel Castro backfired. Instead the case coincided with improving relations between Cuba and the United States. Interestingly, when Elian flew back to Cuba with his father in June 2000, seven months after the rescue, the reaction in Havana was muted, Castro having decreed that there would be no big public celebrations or world media coverage. Hollywood, however, will probably have the last say.[2]

The arrival of Roma (gypsies), mainly from the Czech and Slovak Republics, had already provoked intense media debate in 1997 and 1998 (see Chapters 2 and 4 of this book). A further media splurge in the press occurred in March 2000 over the 'gypsy begging' issue. Objectively, the news story was small – the sentencing of a Romanian gypsy woman for begging with her child – but the event unleashed a tirade of tabloid invective and brought the topic of asylum-seekers once again to the top of the media agenda. The *Sun* and the *Daily Mail* led the attack with a string of sensationalist headlines and several accounts of 'gypsy scroungers milking the benefits system'. According to the *Sun* (14 March 2000),

> The beggars are taking us for a ride. They earn more from an hour's begging on the streets of London than the average Romanian makes in a week. And they're using it – and their social security which is paid for by YOUR taxes – to build marble palaces for the rest of the scroungers back home.

Paul Johnson in the *Daily Mail* (11 March 2000) somehow managed to link the conviction of a single Romanian woman to an emotive discourse about the supposed threat to Britain of billions-strong global migration, taking the most crudely stereotyped sideswipes at several other migrant nationalities along the way:

> The pool of potential beggar criminals ... is deep. A generation ago, it was just the Republican Irish and the West Indians. They have been

joined by the West Africans. ... East Africans, too, are coming in growing numbers. There are potentially millions more from the Balkans, the Caucasus, Ukraine and Russia. Then there are Pakistan, Bangladesh, Sri Lanka and, above all, India, with a billion people. Some of them have not yet heard of Britain. But they will, they will.

A week or so later, *Guardian* columnist Francis Wheen (2000) reflected on the *Sun*'s 'monstering' of the Romanian gypsies in Britain. He drew attention to the *Sun*'s front page of 9 March which carried the huge headline 'FLEECED'. In a blatant display of 'guilt by association' the *Sun* carried a photograph of a gypsy beggar alongside text which alleged that 'scroungers are fleecing Britain of £15 billion a year in lost taxes'. The word 'gypsies' was prominently displayed in order to mislead the reader into believing the identity of the culprits. In fact, the 'lost taxes' story was not about Romanians or gypsies at all, but about rich individual and corporate tax-dodgers (of whom, Wheen could not resist pointing out, the owner of the *Sun* is a prime example). Subsequently, the *Guardian* published long documentary articles by acknowledged authorities on Roma history and culture which exposed some aspects of the reality of life for Eastern European gypsies in the post-Communist era and which contrasted the intensification of their persecution in their 'home countries' with their slim chances of gaining asylum in the 'West' (Bowers-Burbridge 2000; Fonseca 2000). Later articles covered the International Romany Union's congress in Prague which called for the declaration of a gypsy nation with its own parliament.[3]

The fourth 'migration event' which we wish to highlight was undoubtedly the most tragic and costly in human terms. This was the discovery, just before midnight on Sunday 18 June 2000, of fifty-eight bodies of Chinese illegal immigrants in an airtight container lorry in the docks at Dover. The stark human horror of the tragedy led to a fundamental redirection in the nature of the debate on immigration in the British press. No longer were asylum-seekers and economic migrants the main target for tabloid vitriol: the attack shifted instead to the traffickers who perpetrated such crimes on the migrants, now seen as the victims. According to a leader in the *Sun* (20 June 2000),

> Some will blame the asylum seekers. Some will blame the European governments. Some will blame the British authorities. But the real villains are the organised criminals behind this illegal cargo.

However, a *Guardian* leader the same day pointed out the fragility of the apparent change of rhetoric:

> Everybody across the political spectrum expressed sympathy for the victims. ... Yet, had the 58 immigrants survived and been exposed in the back of the truck, there would have been nothing but condemna-

tion for the 'bogus asylum-seekers' and calls from both left and right for their deportation as quickly as possible. Why does it take deaths on such a gruesome scale to evoke the correct response?

In two other respects, the press offered new and important angles on the interpretation of international migration. In the days that followed the Dover tragedy the broadsheets offered a stream of information-rich articles about recent Chinese migration to Britain and Europe. In the absence of academic literature on the subject, good investigative journalism provided useful details about the migrants' origins in Fujian province in southern China, the 'snakehead' gangs which control emigration from this region worldwide, maps of the most commonly used routes, and insights into the 'Chinatown' informal economies in London and other big European cities which are easily able to absorb new arrivals.[4]

The second change in the press discourse following the Dover disaster was a greater appreciation of the economic and social benefits of immigration. After years of debate on asylum-seekers' claims for residence in Britain which tended so often to 'blame the victim' (see Kaye, Chapter 4 of this volume), many newspapers, including those on the political right, started to highlight the positive aspects of increased immigration. For instance, a leader in the *Daily Telegraph* (19 June 2000) stated:

> Whatever the social strains immigration produces, the economic basis for absorbing these people is a strong one. The arrival of a 'flood' of East African Asians a generation ago effectively saved the corner store. If they must work to live, most of them will, and this is good for our prosperity.

Alan Travis, Home Affairs correspondent for the *Guardian*, developed a more wide-ranging pro-immigration argument (Travis 2000). He pointed out that 'those who flee tend to be the most motivated and most hungry for success' and then adopted the social Darwinist argument by suggesting that 'those who survive the worst journeys ... should be rewarded with a job and legal status in their chosen country'. Quoting IMF estimates that the global value of remittances sent home by migrant workers ($65 bn a year) exceeds by $20 bn the annual global overseas aid effort, Travis concluded that migration 'proves [to be] a far more potent and effective way of helping the developing world than official overseas aid policies'.

Even before the Chinese tragedy, many British newspapers had started to carry articles which argued the case for more migration. The *Guardian* published a series of lengthy pieces by distinguished migration scholars such as Saskia Sassen and Nigel Harris, as well as airing the views on migration of seasoned journalists such as Peter Preston and Martin Woollacott. Sassen (2000) debunked the notion that the West is threatened with mass invasions of migrants; according to her, most contemporary migrations are likely to be temporary phenomena, with many migrants eventually returning home. Harris (2000) argued that immigrant workers make the host country richer not poorer, hence 'increased migration is an immense opportunity to advance the world'. In May *The Economist* also deployed powerful economic and demographic arguments, although from a somewhat different ideological perspective than Sassen and Harris, to argue for increased immigration into Europe. The cover shouted 'Go for it. Europe needs more immigrants'. Inside, some demographic facts were spelled out: the EU would need to import 1.6 million migrants a year simply to keep its working-age population stable between now and 2050.[5] Of course, demographers' projections are frequently proved wrong, and Preston (2000) and Woollacott (2000) crossed swords precisely on this issue.

In conclusion, what is clear is that migration continues to exercise the British print media on virtually a daily basis. It is equally clear that, on the migration issue, newspapers have the power both to reflect and to shape public opinion, and there are clear links to political parties and ideologies of various types.

Migration and photography

One obvious omission in this volume is any sustained discussion of the role of still photography. It might be countered that this is because migration is essentially a mobile, 'narrativised' experience – i.e., it is the story of a journey that begins in the home country, region or locale and, assuming the migrant is successful, ends in the chosen destination (whether a new country, region or city). Even when the journey is interrupted by tragedy or detection, there is the ensuing drama of death, arrest or deportation. Thus, it is those modes of media – television, film, the newspaper article – that can tell the unfolding 'story' which are considered best suited to rendering the migrant experience. However, such an assumption is not only facile; it neglects an important medium of representation which has already done much to shape public perception and understanding of migration issues.

For a start, most of the newspaper coverage of migration issues, like those just cited, will be accompanied by a still photograph. After all the ink has been spilled on the judicial, political and emotional tug-of-wars to which he was subjected, it will be the heart-rending smile-cum-grimace of Elian Gonzalez that will probably remain in many a newspaper reader's mind. And images too shocking to be shown – the bodies discovered in the Dover lorry for example – will none the less haunt the imaginaries of a public accustomed to the trade in stereotypes of the 'cunning' asylum-seeker.

The enduring quality of such images aside, it should not be forgotten that photographic technology is at the forefront of new surveillance techniques deployed by the authorities of destination countries to detect illegal immigration. Radioscopic cameras, modelled on the machines which x-ray airport baggage, can now outline the silhouettes of a lorry's occupants. Infrared night-vision devices on board helicopters help customs patrols to spot illegal migrants travelling at night – whether across the treacherous seas of the Strait of Gibraltar or the sweltering desert of the Mexico–California border. Photography, then, whether as documentary support for 'migration narratives' or as technological support for surveillance and detection, is very much implicated in the phenomenon of migration.

But can the still photograph tell us something in its own right about the migration experience? The conviction that photography can articulate a distinct and powerful discourse on contemporary migration underpins the recent work of Sebastião Salgado. While this is not the place to fully discuss and evaluate his latest project – an exhibition and catalogue entitled 'Migrations' – it is worth drawing attention to the intervention that Salgado intended this project to be.[6]

The 'Migrations' project can be seen as both testimony to the plight of migrants and refugees and a call to political action on their behalf. It embraces four main thematics: 'the flight of migrants, refugees, and displaced persons in different parts of the world; the unique tragedy of Africa; the rural exodus, land struggle and chaotic urbanisation in Latin America; and images from Asia's new megacities' (Salgado 2000: 8). Salgado acknowledges that the images in each section will inevitably resonate with each other – confirming the truly global nature of the 'convulsion' we are witnessing – but he also specifies that this thematic division is also a way of ensuring that the specific conditions and consequences of each migratory phenomenon will not merge into a single, undifferentiated whole.

Salgado's 'Migrations' project took place over a period of six years and took him to forty countries. It was financed primarily by the advance fees paid by major magazines (*New York Times*, *Rolling Stone*, *Stern*, etc.) for photographs that were used as reportage of events then in the news spotlight: the war in Bosnia, followed by Kosovo, the massacres in Rwanda and Burundi, and the uprising of Mexico's landless peasants. It is not surprising, then, that many of the photographs conform to the conventions of the genre of photo-journalism: by Salgado's own admission, they are images which attempt to 'capture the tragic, dramatic, and heroic moments' in the lives of migrants. However, what is also evident from other photographs in this exhibition is that after such pictures are taken, when other photo-journalists would have left the scene, Salgado remains and continues to photograph the aftermath of these moments. From his image sequences, therefore, one can construct 'migrant narratives' that often manage to tell us more about their subjects' lives than the more seamless flows of other media discourses.

Take the striking photograph of the child who stands in the foreground of an image perfectly bisected by a path which divides the fields of chunky earth to either side of him, and which leads the spectator's eye to the train in the hazy background which traverses the image horizontally (Figure 1.1). Apart from a perfect composition of all its constituent elements, the image has rich symbolic

Figure 1.1   Picture of a migrant story untold: eastern Croatia, 1994

value: a path which seems to come from nowhere and lead nowhere, the train – one of the enduring tropes of migration – which is nonetheless stationary, and the poignant image of the child himself, rubbing his eye with his small fist as if fighting back tears as his accusing gaze meets that of the spectator. This reading is supplemented by a text in the exhibition catalogue which explains that the train, in the east of Croatia, is home to 120 refugees of mostly Bosnian Muslim origin. These people, alleges Salgado, are the 'forgotten refugees' of the war in Bosnia who had not 'earned the right to migrate' because they had fled before the wave of atrocities had reached their communities. They are stranded in every sense, 'going nowhere, reminded daily of their fate' as other trains crammed with passengers, many of them refugees on their way to new homes, whizz by them. These are refugees whose plight will never be told by television news reports; their situation lacks the dramatic accoutrements that capture televisual attention.

This theme of what happens *after* wars end, how these unwilling migrants try to pick up their lives, is a central thematic in the 'Migrations' project. Salgado remains to photograph, for example, the hundreds of thousands of Rwandan Hutu refugees who are marooned in eastern Zaire in spring 1997, fearing retribution by Rwandan Tutsi should they return home, yet ordered out by Zairian rebels (Salgado 2000: 208–19). After all the grisly images of this conflict that we have already seen, and the 'compassion fatigue' to which we have allegedly succumbed by their constant repetition, how is it that Salgado's images manage to reawaken some sense of the novel and truly horrific dimensions of this catastrophe? It is certainly the case that his compositional prowess manages to elicit the mass nature of this population displacement: a deep-focus shot of a long line of young boys, sitting on a disused railway track, invites the viewer to imagine the line stretching interminably beyond the photographic frame (his caption tells us that these are young orphans who have been told to line up and wait for food – that never arrives); his wide-angle shot of a food distribution area for 120,000 refugees seems to encompass every last one of these hapless individuals within the tight confines of the frame. But the individual victim is featured as well: the close-up portrait of a little boy in a refugee column who is so weak he needs to walk with two canes; a rear-view shot of two men carrying a stretcher bearing a young child's corpse (the caption notes that these refugees were not even allowed to stop for the time it would take to bury their dead). From this powerful series of images emerge two seemingly paradoxical themes: the imperative imposed on these refugees to keep moving at all costs, and the interminable activity of waiting when they do stop their marching – waiting for food or water, for medicine, to be given their next marching orders, or simply for their own deaths.

Even from this brief description, it is clear that there is a fundamental tension in Sebastião Salgado's photographs of migrants, refugees and exiles. These images, which aim to evoke the anguish, hardship and precariousness of those displaced by poverty, repression or war, are very aesthetically pleasing. Indeed, it has been a common criticism of Salgado's past work that his images are aesthetically achieved to the point of coldness and sterility. His defenders, by contrast, argue that photo-journalists like Salgado who wish to move their viewers to action need to develop an aesthetic strategy that 'makes it possible to look at the unlookable' rather than to close their eyes or turn the page (Wroe 2000).

However, what both critics and defenders of Salgado tend to overlook is that these images are not intended to stand alone: in the exhibition, and to a much greater extent in the catalogue, Salgado has provided a detailed accompanying text which ensures that the tension between aesthetic pleasure and political contextualisation is not sacrificed in favour of the former alone. Though each image is striking by its subject matter and composition, we are prevented from merely admiring the photographic virtuosity on display by a text which interrupts our viewing, thwarts our visual pleasure, and imposes the task of digesting considerable information about the context and circumstances of the image's production. This is especially true of the sequence on the Rwandan refugees cited above. For the passive television spectator, the warring factions in Rwanda became blurred to the point where one could not distinguish between Hutu and Tutsi, victim and persecutor. Salgado spells out in great detail the circumstances by which former aggressors came to be victims in their turn, and by which uninvolved civilians on both sides came to constitute the greatest mass of displaced and persecuted persons. So while it is possible, as his critics claim, to pass in awe from one striking photograph to the next and to be left with the homogenised image of an 'Ur-Migrant' imprinted in one's visual memory, it is not Salgado who is responsible for this effacement of each image's context, but the abdication of responsibility on the part of the viewer. Salgado's aesthetic strategies compel us to look at his images rather than to avert our gaze, but it is the image/text relationship which defies us to claim 'compassion fatigue' and to remain indifferent to the migrant's plight.

An overview of the book

Despite the caveats noted earlier in this chapter concerning media 'effects', most of us readily attribute to the contemporary media considerable powers of influence over our informational and imaginative landscapes. In Chapter 2 Alec Hargreaves advocates caution when we attempt to gauge the extent of that influence, especially in the field of ethnic relations. As he rightly points out, media scholars have for some time now been arguing that the study of 'media effects' is a highly problematic and contentious terrain, and that the reputed effects of media images of sex and violence on human behaviour are not as direct and unequivocal as psychology and popular opinion assume. This is no less true when it comes to ascertaining the effect of media coverage of immigration and race issues on viewers' attitudes and, more precisely, their electoral behaviour. Hargreaves traces over the last decade the electoral fortunes of France's far-right party, the *Front National* (FN), a party known for its aggressive anti-immigrant stance and racist predilection, and attempts to correlate the party's electoral rise (and subsequent decline) with the amount and type of media coverage accorded to the FN on the one hand, and more general media coverage of immigration issues on the other. His conclusions suggest that the terms of the debate on immigration in mainstream political discourse played a greater role in the FN's electoral success than direct media exposure and that extensive media coverage may have even worked to the party's eventual disadvantage. In any event, Hargreaves argues that the problem is not one limited to exposure or censure of anti-immigrant views, but the fact that on French television, treatment of ethnic relations more broadly speaking tends to be relegated to news and political programmes alone. He contrasts this situation with British television where ethnicity is a far more familiar feature of the viewer's broadcasting experience across a range of television genres.

For Giovanna Campani (Chapter 3), the interests of media and political power in Italy are so inextricably intertwined that the type of coverage immigration receives by the media will *necessarily* be dictated by the prevailing political agenda. Indeed, while one can find major politico-economic interests behind most national media ventures, Campani maintains that Italy constitutes a special, 'abnormal' case where 'all the information is ideologically controlled through implicit choices and depends on economic and political paymasters'. Precisely for this reason, the media treat migration only in its most superficial and negative manifestations without considering how these are structurally related to the Italian system more generally. Thus the links between migration

14

and criminality which the media are so fond of emphasising – a theme which has reached, in Campani's view, the proportions of a 'national obsession' – are treated as an effect of migration itself rather than as a phenomenon which has its main origins in Italy's huge informal labour market, long-established system of organised crime and of entrenched official corruption. Moreover, if the immigrant-as-criminal is the prevailing (male) stereotype, Campani also shows that images in the Italian media cast migrant women primarily in the role of maid or prostitute, but in both cases as victims of their circumstances. Campani does not doubt for a moment the exploitation of these migrant women but questions whether there is not some degree of agency in their choices and actions that ought to be acknowledged and represented.

Given the dominance of the visual dimension in the global media landscape, the role of print media is often underestimated. In Chapter 4 Ronald Kaye attempts to rectify this omission by examining the language in which refugee and asylum issues have been couched by the print media and which he believes has found wider currency in other media and in popular rhetoric. In particular, he undertakes a quantitative and qualitative analysis of the terms 'bogus' and 'phoney' in British press coverage of refugee and asylum topics, taking as his main case study the period coinciding with the arrival of Czech Roma to Britain seeking political asylum. His quantitative analysis reveals the extent to which these expressions are used by specific daily newspapers and it is perhaps no surprise that Kaye finds they make their most frequent appearance in the popular and conservative press. Kaye's qualitative analysis considers the 'context of use' – i.e., whether the terms are used in reporting in order to criticise their application or to report criticism of their usage. Here Kaye's findings again confirm the political leanings of the respective newspapers. However, Kaye does not hold to a strict divide between the popular and quality press in one important respect: it is his contention that even when criticising terms like 'phoney' and 'bogus', the progressive quality papers do not sufficiently distance themselves from their perjorative connotations nor do they attempt to legitimise alternative terms like 'economic migrants' or 'economic refugees'. Thus the reader is implicitly 'socialised' in the very language the newspaper explicitly rejects. Kaye argues that the effect of this lack of linguistic vigilance is to demote the term 'asylum-seeker' altogether and, by implication, the suffering of those who seek haven under this appellation.

The 'economic migrant' or 'economic refugee' is the ostensible subject of the film discussed by Mireille Rosello in Chapter 5, *La Promesse*. As Rosello notes, 'the undocumented immigrant ... has become one of the most visible political icons' in the European public sphere, and cinema in particular has become a vehicle of political militancy pleading the cause of '*les sans-papiers*'. *La Promesse* clearly supports this political agenda and its own narrative is a searing indictment of those who traffic in immigrant labour but take no responsibility for the fate of their work force. When an illegal African migrant is killed accidentally on a building site near Liège, his employer and the employer's son,

Igor, bury the body to avoid exposure of the father's illegal dealings. The worker's wife, Assita, embarks on a search for her missing husband accompanied by a guilt-ridden Igor who assumes an increasingly protective role given the dangers to which she is now exposed. However Rosello's analysis complicates a reading of the film centred only on the tragic fate of the immigrant and his abandoned wife and the redemptive guilt of the employer's son and instead shows how the film solicits a different and profound type of reflection on the meaning of 'hospitality'. At stake in Igor's 'belated revelation' to Assita about her husband's tragic fate is not the spectator's moral outrage but an identification with Igor's 'split consciousness' as he learns what it means to truly assume the role of the 'host'.

An illegal African immigrant is also the centre-piece of the Italian film *Pummarò*, analysed by David Forgacs in Chapter 6. Forgacs salutes the film as one of the first attempts to highlight the plight of African migrant workers in Italy in the 1980s and the corruption, violence, racism and exploitative labour relations to which they were (and still are) exposed. Like *La Promesse*, *Pummarò* was made by a white production team about the experience of a black migrant. Thus, like Rosello, Forgacs is concerned to elucidate the politics of identification which the film solicits but his analysis concludes that the 'cross-race identification' sought by the film in fact tends to reproduce 'some of the very racist categorisations which on a conscious level it sought to repudiate'. Forgacs concentrates his critique on the film's orchestration of the spectator's 'look', which oscillates between encouraging vicarious and sympathetic identification with the main black character and turning him into an erotic object of the spectator's gaze. All films must of course negotiate this play of looks but Forgacs argues that despite – or perhaps because of – its liberal intentions, *Pummarò* polarises them, allowing the objectifying look to gain the upper hand all the while disavowing the inter-racial desire that such a look implies.

So far, this overview has highlighted the relationship between media and migration primarily in terms of the media's representation of the figure of the migrant and of immigration issues, or of the language and rhetoric through which these are articulated and understood. However, another axis of our enquiry is the way in which the media are used by migrants, either in the diaspora or in their home communities.

When the Czech Roma arrived on British shores in late 1997, most media coverage cited a Czech documentary extolling the virtues of the British welfare system as the 'cause' of the influx. As Hargreaves points out (Chapter 2), it is unlikely that any media event would have such a radical impact on behaviour unless there was a 'predisposition' to migrate in the first place. In Chapter 7 Nicola Mai takes the example of an earlier and larger mass migratory movement, that of Albanians to Italy in the early 1990s, to explore both sides of this equation: the ways in which Italian television might have shaped the 'migratory project' of these Albanians on the one hand, and the features of Albanian society which predisposed these would-be migrants to be swayed by the messages they received from Italian television on the other. Of the many debilitating features of the society subjected to Enver Hoxha's particular brand of totalitarianism, two features are treated by Mai as especially pertinent to the Albanian 'migratory project': Albania's high degree of self-enforced isolationism and the regime's 'stigmatisation of pleasure'. Not surprisingly, the response to the regime's attempt to keep all allegedly corrupting external influences at bay was precisely an intensified desire to be exposed to such forces, and the cross-border VHF signals which transmitted Italian television gladly obliged. Consequently, Mai argues, the monotone that had passed for cultural life in Hoxha's Albania was no longer a match against the showy vulgarity which was the hallmark of Italian entertainment television. Mai does not argue that Albanians naively embraced this image as the 'real Italy', but nor does he deny that television's ostentatious appeal to consumerist pleasures had a role to play in the decision to emigrate; instead his analysis seeks to show that the economic aspirations which allegedly fuelled the desire to emigrate cannot be separated from the migrant's quest for new forms of subjectivity – political and personal – in which pleasure must be accorded its proper place.

The figure of the migrant-as-criminal highlighted by Campani in Chapter 3 is given concrete form in Bruno Riccio's discussion of Senegalese street traders on Italy's Rimini coast (Chapter 8). Here frictions arising from economic coexistence between local shopkeepers and the Senegalese 'trading diaspora' have escalated to the point where there is a conflation of problems of irregular trade with the phenomenon of migration itself, from which, Riccio shows, it is only a short step to the depiction of the migrant as both economic *and* sexual predator. However, Riccio's analysis then takes a novel turn by considering how the Senegalese reverse this mirror of the migrant 'other' and negotiate their migrant experience in relation to Western media self-representations. Contrasting themselves with the parochial, socially irresponsible Westerners they see on television and in films, Senegalese migrants vaunt their travels as a source of knowledge, training and enhanced economic status, thereby creating an empowering self-image of migrants as the 'new national heroes'. While this strategy undoubtedly serves to challenge the racist images with which they are constantly confronted in host societies, Riccio wonders whether this strategy risks producing an 'essentialist rendering of the West' – a form of 'ethno-occidentalism' that can serve as a defence against a more positive engagement with external cultural flows.

The reception and use of satellite television by Europe's migrant communities is a subject that now commands the urgent attention of media and migration scholars alike. For it is clear that with the demise of state monopolies over broadcasting throughout the 1990s, and the proliferation of (mostly private) satellite channels, Europe's broadcasting landscape has been radically reconfigured. While politicians and cultural critics worry about the effects of deregulation, and especially the importation of American television fare, on nationally produced output, satellite reception has made programming from their countries of origin available to Europe's diasporic communities. Indeed, the mushrooming of satellite dishes amongst ethnic minority households has tended to be regarded with suspicion on the grounds that if, for example, the programming originates in Islamic countries, it will necessarily work against the assimilationist aims and expectations of host societies. Elsewhere, in a study of satellite television usage amongst France's Maghrebi community, Alec Hargreaves refuted this assumption and showed that the extent to which home-country programming was desired or viewed was dependent on generational, rather than religious factors (Hargreaves and Mahdjoub 1997). His study revealed that while the older generation of Maghrebi viewers tuned in to home-country programming to keep abreast of what was going on, or to enjoy television reception in their native tongue, most younger Maghrebi viewers wanted access to extra stations not to view home-country channels, but to watch American-style channels such as MTV that are popular with youth worldwide. Such findings at the very least remind us that we still know very little about how satellite television is received by Europe's ethnic minority communities – a situation which it is hoped further ethnographic fieldwork will rectify.

Satellite has also transmitted back programming originating in the diaspora. In Chapter 9 Christine Ogan discusses one such instance of the latter: the 1998 satellite broadcasting from Amsterdam of an annual celebration sponsored by the Milli Görüş – a group representing that part of the Turkish diaspora whose aim is to establish a more Islamically oriented Turkish state. The event was attended by 40,000 people and was transmitted live to Turkey and Europe simultaneously. In this sense, Ogan characterises the celebration as a 'media event' where television is not only a disseminator of, but a key actor in the event. According to Dayan and Katz (1988), 'media events' are typically used by state authorities to celebrate and reaffirm an official consensus. However, Ogan shows how the media event orchestrated by Milli Görüş was designed precisely to forge a new consensus based on the recognition of Islam as a legitimate political and religious movement in Turkey. Not only was this the message conveyed in the event, but it was incarnated in its very means of transmission – i.e., a private satellite channel which circumvented traditional forms of state control over the means of mass communication. Ogan's analysis shows how Islam, politics and the mass media have become inextricably intertwined in Turkey, in Europe's Turkish diaspora, and especially amongst young people who find in the communication activities promoted by Milli Görüş 'a sense of collective identity and belonging that has not been felt in relation to the host society'. Ogan's example of a use of satellite programming aimed explicitly at heightening Islamic consciousness, especially amongst minority youth, contrasts sharply with that of Hargreaves cited above, though Ogan is careful not to make premature judgements about the 'effects' this kind of media might have, either on the political behaviour of Turkish youth or on their prospects for eventual integration into Dutch society.

Another 'media event' – the satellite television coverage of Hong Kong's 'handover' or 'return' to China – is also at the centre of Lee Siew-peng's study of media use amongst Hong Kong Chinese who have settled in Britain (Chapter 10). In order to understand the responses to this momentous historical event, or *'wooi-gwai'*, it is necessary to appreciate the distinctive experiences of settlement undergone by different generations of Chinese migrants: those who arrived as young adult primary migrants in the period between the 1950s and 1970s (some of whom are now quite elderly); the children of these original immigrants (most of whom are now adults and parents of the 'third generation'); and an older generation still who arrived in Britain sponsored by their adult children (the primary migrants) who needed their behind-the-scenes help to run their catering businesses. For instance, whilst the older Hong Kong Chinese with whom Lee Siew-peng shared the television-watching event generally seemed pleased that Hong Kong was reverting to China, younger British-born Hongkongers were not so keen to be associated with mainland China. However many other subtleties of reaction to *wooi-gwai* and of hyphenated British, Chinese and Hong Kong identities are noted by Lee Siew-peng, dependent on birthplace, age at migration and length of time in Britain. The data are perhaps suggestive rather than conclusive, but they do point to ways in which the complexity of Hong Kong Chinese identities in Britain can be highlighted by a specific media event.

Consumption of media by diasporic communities is also the subject of Chapter 11 by Roza Tsagarousianou – this time the groups studied, by audience interview and focus-group methods, are the Greek Cypriot and the more heterogenous South Asian communities in London. Tsagarousianou explores the ways in which members of these ethnic communities utilise transnational media flows, as well as local media products, as resources in the construction of their everyday lives, helping them to create a space where they feel 'at home'. Intergenerational differences are contrasted: younger, more cosmopolitan respondents are generally more critical of these programmes, whereas older respondents, typically first-generation immigrants, are comforted by the intimacy and 'structured nostalgia' (Herzfeld 1997) which promotes a sense of an harmonious community rooted in 'home'. In reality, consumers of such media are involved in participating in a process of reimagining their national community at a deterritorialised, transnational level. Moreover, the harmonious image is not universal: Greek Cypriots complained of the growing influence of material and broadcasters from Greece, and inter-ethnic tensions emerged also from Tsagarousianou's South Asian interviewees – for instance allegations of a pro-Indian, anti-Muslim bias in some programmes.

Finally, in Chapter 12 Karen O'Reilly turns her attention to another migrant group neglected until recently by migration scholars: retirement communities living abroad. Yet the demographic significance of 'international retirement migration' is considerable and has resulted in a situation where some European countries which were once countries of emigration have, partly under the impact of retirement migration, become countries of immigration. This is the case for Spain's Costa del Sol, a region which has played host to a large retirement population from across Europe, but most notably from Britain. The popular image of the 'Brit in Spain' is familiar enough: that of 'expatriates searching for paradise, living an extended holiday in ghetto-like complexes, participating minimally in local life or culture, refusing to learn the language of their hosts, and generally recreating an England in the sun'. O'Reilly argues that the media are primarily responsible for constructing this one-dimensional portrait and that such stereotypes, while having some basis in reality, betray their own class and moral prejudices, and a negative view of migration more generally. Members of the British retirement community whom O'Reilly interviews refute this collective representation of their lifestyles and choices and insist on the positive benefits of their migration experience for the host country and migrant alike.

Notes

1   This is not the place for an extensive review of this literature. For some important texts see Boyle *et al.* (1998); Castles and Miller (1998); Cohen (1987, 1995); Faist (2000); Gorter *et al.* (1998); Hammar *et al.* (1997); Harris (1995); Jackson (1986); Massey *et al.* (1998); Papastergiadis (2000); Skeldon (1997); Weiner (1995); White and Woods (1980). None of the works in this list makes any mention of the media, let alone critically engages with the media's (mis)representations of migration. Indeed, in the case of Weiner's *Global Migration Crisis* one could argue that the very title of this book serves to contribute to an exaggerated portrayal of the drama and negativity of the multifaceted phenomenon of contemporary international migration, an impression which is further bolstered by the cover photograph of a rusty ship packed solid with migrants and refugees.

2   The coverage of the Elian Gonzalez story was fairly constant in the UK news between November 1999 and June 2000. For retrospective overviews of the case see the two long articles in the *Guardian* (Borger and Ellison 2000; Campbell 2000).

3   Such a nation would not involve the conventional creation of a territorial state but be a diasporic concept, supported by EU assistance. See Connolly (2000); Huggler (2000); Younge (2000).

4   For examples of such articles see Gittings (2000a, 2000b); Kelso (2000); McCrystal and McLeod (2000); also Williams (2000) on the educational and business achievements of the Chinese ethnic communities in Britain.

5   See *The Economist*, 6 May 2000.

6   As this book was going to press, Salgado's touring exhibition was showing at the Maison Européenne de la Photographie in Paris, entitled '*Exodes*'. It is expected to come to London in due course.

References

Balibar, E. (1991) 'Es gibt keinen Staat in Europa: racism and politics in Europe today', *New Left Review* 186: 5–19.

Borger, J. and Ellison, M. (2000) 'After months of protests, pleas and passion, Elian flies quietly home', *Guardian*, 29 June.

Bovenkerk, F., Miles, R. and Verbunt, G. (1990) 'Racism, migration and the state in Western Europe', *International Sociology* 5, 4: 475–90.

Bowers-Burbridge, J. (2000) 'On the road to nowhere', *Guardian (Guardian Society)*, 7 June.

Boyle, P., Halfacree, K. and Robinson, V. (1998) *Exploring Contemporary Migration*, London: Longman.

Brosius, H. B. and Eps, P. (1995) 'Prototyping through key events: news selection in the case of violence against aliens and asylum seekers in Germany', *European Journal of Communication* 10, 3: 391–412.

Campbell, D. (2000) 'The long goodbye of the boy next door', *Guardian*, 29 June.

Castles, S. and Miller, M. J. (1998) *The Age of Migration: International Population Movements in the Modern World*, London: Macmillan.

Cohen, R. (1987) *The New Helots: Migrants in the International Division of Labour*, Aldershot: Avebury.

—— (ed.) (1995) *The Cambridge Survey of World Migration*, Cambridge: Cambridge University Press.

Connolly, K. (2000) 'Europe's gypsies lobby for nation status', *Guardian*, 28 July.

Dayan, D. and Katz, E. (1988) 'Articulating consensus: the ritual and the rhetoric of media events', in Alexander, J. C. (ed.), *Durkheimian Sociology: Cultural Studies*, New York: Cambridge University Press.

Elkins, D. (1997) 'Globalization, telecommunication, and virtual ethnic communities', *International Political Science Review* 18, 2: 139–52.

Faist, T. (2000) *The Volume and Dynamics of International Migration and Transnational Spaces*, Oxford: Clarendon Press.

Fonseca, I. (2000) 'The truth about gypsies', *Guardian (G2)*, 24 March.

Gillespie, M. (1995) *Television, Ethnicity and Cultural Change*, London: Routledge.

Gittings, J. (2000a) 'Snakeheads keep stranglehold on worldwide trade in people', *Guardian*, 20 June.

—— (2000b) 'China steps up policing after Dover deaths', *Guardian*, 5 July.

Gordon, P. and Rosenberg, D. (1989) *Daily Racism: The Press and Black People in Britain*, London: The Runnymede Trust.

Gorter, C., Nijkamp, P. and Foot, J. (eds) (1998) *Crossing Borders: Regional and Urban Perspectives on International Migration*, Aldershot: Ashgate.

Hammar, T., Brochmann, G., Tamas, K. and Faist, T. (eds) (1997) *International Migration, Immobility and Development: Multidisciplinary Perspectives*, Oxford: Berg.

Hargreaves, A. G. and Mahdjoub, D. (1997) 'Satellite television viewing among ethnic minorities in France', *European Journal of Communication* 12, 4: 459–77.

Harris, N. (1995) *The New Untouchables: Immigration and the New World Worker*, Harmondsworth: Penguin.

—— (2000) 'Racists are so blind', *Guardian*, 2 May.

Hartmann, P. and Husband, C. (1974) *Racism and the Mass Media*, London: Davis-Poynter.

Herzfeld, M. (1997) *Cultural Intimacy: Social Poetics in the Nation-State*, London: Routledge.

Huggler, J. (2000) 'Gypsy leader demands EU help', *Independent on Sunday*, 30 July.

Jackson, J. A. (1986) *Migration*, London: Longman.

Kaye, R. (1998) 'Redefining the refugee: the UK media portrayal of asylum seekers', in Koser, K. and Lutz, H. (eds), *The New Migration in Europe: Social Constructions and Social Realities*, London: Macmillan.

Kelso, P. (2000) 'Lies, dreams and washing up in Chinatown', *Guardian*, 21 June.

MacAskill, E., Ward, L. and Kelso, P. (2000) 'Surprise as 72 hostages fly out', *Guardian*, 14 February.

Martiniello, M. (1997) 'The dilemma of separation versus union: the new dynamic of nationalist politics in Belgium', in Wicker, H. R. (ed.), *Rethinking Nationalism and Ethnicity*, Oxford: Berg.

Massey, D. S., Arango, J., Hugo, G., Kouaouci, A., Pellegrino, A. and Taylor, J. E. (1998) *Worlds in Motion: Understanding International Migration at the End of the Millennium*, Oxford: Oxford University Press.

McCrystal, C. and McLeod, C. (2000) 'As Dover counts the cost, a village in China says goodbye to its men', *Independent on Sunday*, 25 June.

Miles, R. (1993) 'Race and racism in contemporary Europe', in Solomos, J. and Wrench, J. (eds), *Racism and Migration in Western Europe*, Oxford: Berg.

Morton, H. (1999) 'Islanders in space: Tongans online', in King, R. and Connell, J. (eds), *Small Worlds, Global Lives: Islands and Migration*, London: Pinter.

Papastergiadis, N. (2000) *The Turbulence of Migration*, Cambridge: Polity.

Preston, P. (2000) 'We're growing old. We need more immigrants', *Guardian*, 8 May.

Rosello, M. (1998) 'Representing illegal immigrants in France: from *clandestins* to *l'affaire des sans-papiers de Saint-Bernard*', *Journal of European Studies* 28: 137–51.

Salgado, S. (2000) *Migrations*, New York: Aperture.

Sassen, S. (2000) 'Home truths', *Guardian*, 15 April.

Sengupta, K. (2000) 'The grounding of Mr. Straw', *Independent on Sunday*, 13 February.

Skeldon, R. (1997) *Migration and Development: a Global Perspective*, London: Longman.

Solomos, J. and Wrench, J. (1993) 'Race and racism in contemporary Europe', in Solomos, J. and Wrench, J. (eds), *Racism and Migration in Western Europe*, Oxford: Berg.

ter Wal, J. (1996) 'The social representation of immigrants: the Pantanella issue in the pages of *La Repubblica*', *New Community* 22, 1: 39–66.

Travis, A. (2000) 'Open the door', *Guardian*, 20 June.

van Dijk, T. (1987) *Communicating Racism*, Newbury Park CA: Sage.

—— (1991) *Racism and the Press*, London: Routledge.

—— (1992) 'Discourse and the denial of racism', *Discourse and Society* 3, 1: 87–118.

—— (1993) *Elite Discourse and Racism*, London: Sage.

Weiner, M. (1995) *The Global Migration Crisis: Challenge to States and to Human Rights*, New York: Harper Collins.

Wheen, F. (2000) 'The *Sun*'s gypsy curse', *Guardian*, 22 March.

White, P. and Woods, R. (eds) (1980) *The Geographical Impact of Migration*, London: Longman.

Williams, P. (2000) 'Meet the UK's highest fliers', *Independent on Sunday*, 6 February.

Woollacott, M. (2000) 'We don't need immigrants to pay for our pensions', *Guardian*, 23 June.

Wroe, N. (2000) 'Man with the Golden Eye', *Guardian*, 10 June.

Younge, G. (2000) 'A nation is born', *Guardian*, 31 July.

2

MEDIA EFFECTS AND ETHNIC RELATIONS IN BRITAIN AND FRANCE

Alec G. Hargreaves

Introduction

The role of the mass media in shaping the incorporation of minority ethnic groups within different national contexts is a complex and in many ways controversial issue. The media are undoubtedly a powerful force in the creation and/or dissemination – the distinction is as important as it is problematic – of public images of the 'imagined community' that is the nation (Anderson 1983). The extent to which immigrants and their descendants are portrayed by broadcast and print media as part of – or apart from – the national community may significantly affect attitudes among the majority population towards minority groups. Access to information flows and to decision-making processes within the media may in turn affect the capacity of minorities to successfully mobilise in support of ethnically oriented goals. There has so far been very little comparative research on the influence of the media in shaping ethnic relations within different national contexts. This is perhaps hardly surprising in view of the many obstacles to productive research within this field. 'Media effects' are one of the most contested areas in media studies, with opposing camps advancing claims and counter-claims over the possible role of the media in inducing audiences to behave in particular ways. Controversy frequently rages, for example, over the role of television violence in allegedly stimulating violent behaviour among viewers (Barker and Petley 1997). When the methodological complexities and hazards of cross-national comparisons are added to such quarrels, it would be a bold researcher indeed who dared to advance a comprehensive theory for understanding the role of the media in shaping ethnic relations. The aims of the present chapter are more modest. It aims, first, to set out a typological framework for the analysis of media effects in the field of ethnic relations, second to explore the implications of this with particular reference to the rise of the *Front National* (FN) in France, third to consider whether any useful lessons can be learnt from the British media in their approach to minority ethnic groups, and finally to draw together my main findings by way of some concluding remarks on the recent decline in support for the FN.

A typology of media effects

Some of the complexities and ambiguities surrounding the relationship between the media and minority ethnic groups are apparent in coverage of a recent upsurge of asylum-seekers from central and eastern Europe entering Dover and other nearby British ports.[1] In December 1998, Kent police threatened to bring criminal charges against a number of newspaper editors over their coverage of these events. The police were concerned, for example, by an editorial in the *Dover Express* which stated: 'Illegal immigrants, asylum-seekers, bootleggers and scum-of-the-earth drug smugglers have targeted our beloved coastline. We are left with the back-draft of a nation's sewage and no cash to wash it down the drain.' As a consequence of this and other articles accusing asylum-seekers of criminal patterns of behaviour, the group editor of the *Dover Express* and other local newspapers, Nick Hudson, was warned by the police that he risked being charged with inciting racial hatred. In response, Hudson claimed: 'I'm merely reflecting my mailbag. I don't think we are making news, we are merely reflecting it.' Hudson's denial of any causal effects resulting from articles published in his and other newspapers was flatly contradicted by a police spokesman, who said: 'There has been a lot of inflammatory coverage which has raised tensions among communities and attracted members of far-right organisations.'[2]

In contrast with disputed claims such as this, an earlier episode involving a sudden increase in the number of Roma, or gypsies, from eastern Europe seeking asylum at Dover in 1997 offers an unusually clear-cut instance of a behavioural effect linked to a particular media event. Scores of Roma in the Czech Republic sought asylum in Britain shortly after seeing a film report on Czech television in which a family of Roma asylum-seekers from Prague spoke enthusiastically about the welcome they had received in Dover. Within a few weeks of the film being broadcast, more than 200 Roma landed in Dover requesting refugee status (Goldman 1997).[3] A similar upsurge in applications had been reported by the Canadian authorities a few months earlier after a documentary film broadcast on Czech television had painted an idyllic picture of the lives of Roma asylum-seekers admitted to Canada from the Czech Republic.

There is little doubt that Roma asylum-seekers would not have presented themselves in such numbers in Canada and Britain had the two television films – both made by the same reporter, Josef Klima – not been seen in their home country. A Czech Minister said the rush to Canada had been 'triggered by a single TV documentary' (Sliva 1997). Yet it would clearly be far too simple to attribute these flows of asylum-seekers solely or even principally to the broadcasting of Klima's reports. 'People think that it was us [Klima and his film crew] who made the Romanies [*sic*] want to leave,' Klima stated. 'But we didn't do it. We just mapped out the situation and presented it to our viewers.'[4] Roma viewers in the Czech Republic would clearly not have reacted as they did had they not been predisposed to seek a more conducive place in which to live. Beyond the immediate impact of the TV broadcasts at least two sets of prior conditions must therefore be taken into account in explaining the number of Czech Roma seeking refugee status in Canada and Britain: widespread hostility among the majority Czech population towards Roma, and the feelings of insecurity which this has engendered among the latter, leading them to seek a better life elsewhere.

This is not to say, of course, that the media's role in these events was necessarily confined to the 'trigger' effect of Klima's films. The media may also have contributed to the formation of prejudice and hostility among the majority population towards the Roma minority. From an analytical point of view we need, therefore, to distinguish between two basic levels on which media effects may operate in the field of ethnic relations: immediate behavioural effects and long-term attitude formation. The complaints voiced by British police over press coverage of asylum-seekers focused mainly on short-term trigger effects: newspapers were accused of heightening inter-ethnic tensions (which were assumed to have already existed at lower levels) and of attracting the attention of extreme-right militants (whose basic attitudes also pre-dated these events). At the same time, it is reasonable to suppose that consistently negative media representations of asylum-seekers over a sustained period are liable to create or reinforce basically unsympathetic attitudes among the public. It should be noted that while some effects may be attributable to reasoned arguments presented via the media, others may work primarily through emotive processes. Combining these factors, we may distinguish three main types of media effect. The trigger effect, seen at work in the response to Klima's reports, occurs when media consumers are prompted by a particular media event to take certain actions in conformity with attitudes or goals which they already held before this event. Long-term attitudinal effects, a second type of media effect, are a consequence of structural aspects of media production and content, which may include ongoing bias or imbalances in the representation of minority groups. A third type of effect lies in the persuasive power of individual media events to change the attitudes of viewers, listeners or readers, either by emotive impact or by reasoned argument.

This last type is probably the least common form of media effect. It would be surprising if a single media event were sufficiently powerful to change opinions if there were not already doubts or uncertainties in the minds of the audience clouding their existing views. Where readers or viewers have built up a strongly-held opinion over a sustained period of time, they are unlikely to be persuaded of the contrary position by a single argument or reportage, no matter how emotive.

The limited effects of a single piece of media coverage can be seen in the mixed public reaction to a particularly emotive episode during the 1996 sit-ins in Paris by African *sans-papiers*, undocumented immigrants seeking regularisation. Graphic television images of a police operation in which immigrant families were expelled from a church in which they had taken refuge partially backfired against the centre-right government of Alain Juppé. The authorities had hoped to end the long-running sit-in by a decisive intervention demonstrating to public opinion that they were on top of the situation. In an opinion poll carried out immediately after the police operation, 46 per cent of those questioned said they felt sympathetic towards the *sans-papiers*, compared with 36 per cent expressing hostility. Some 53 per cent disapproved of the police action, while 42 per cent supported it. Yet in the same survey, 68 per cent of respondents said they wanted to maintain or strengthen the Pasqua laws, which had created the circumstances against which the *sans-papiers* were protesting; only 23 per cent wanted to relax or abolish those laws (Ipsos 1996). While television viewers had apparently been upset by images of women and children being dragged off by the police, the emotive impact had not been sufficient to produce a change of heart on the basic principle at stake in the *sans-papiers'* demand for regularisation: 67 per cent of those interviewed were in favour of deporting them as illegal immigrants, with only 27 per cent favouring regularisation.

A possible example of a more significant effect generated by a relatively brief but prominent piece of media coverage may be found in the 1992 British general election. During the campaign, opinion polls consistently indicated that Labour was set to win. When the Conservatives retained office, there was much debate over the apparently misleading findings of pre-election polls. It was frequently suggested that respondents had lied to pollsters about their voting intentions. Another common argument was that there had been deficiencies in sampling techniques. An alternative hypothesis was advanced by Billig and Golding (1992). Drawing on a systematic analysis of media election coverage, they argued that a late swing (undetectable in pre-elections polls) may have occurred as a result of scare-mongering a few days before the election by leading Conservatives, whose warnings of an influx of immigrants in the event of a Labour victory were given front-page coverage in the largely pro-Tory tabloid press. Billig and Golding noted that 'those who followed the General Election in the quality papers, and on the television news, may have missed the ferocity with which the race card was played at the end of the campaign' (Billig and Golding 1992: 162). It was in tabloid newspapers such as the *Daily Express*, the *Sun* and the *Star* that a barrage of front-page scare stories, editorials and opinion columns warned of an uncontrolled 'flood' of immigrants in the event of Labour coming to power. Bearing in mind the mass circulation of these newspapers and the narrowness of the Conservative victory, Billig and Golding observed:

> The combined readership of the Tory tabloids is roughly seventeen
> million. Maybe half the electorate were exposed to such lurid 'fear' sto-

ries, playing on racist feelings at the latest stage of the campaign. ...
Even if only two in a hundred electors were swayed by the immigration
scares in the Tory tabloids, the effects would have been profound: such
a late swing would have been sufficient to give the Conservatives their
overall majority.

(Billig and Golding 1992: 163)

The available evidence is insufficient to determine with certainty whether such a
switch occurred as a result of this press coverage, and if so whether it merely
triggered a small but critical increase in the Conservative vote in response to
pre-existing fears about immigration or whether, as seems less likely, it
persuaded readers to adopt a new attitude towards immigration and with it a
change in party allegiance. As a general rule, it is far more likely that the media
contribute to attitude formation by repeated patterns of representation –
significant aspects of which may impact in unconscious ways – rather than
through spectacular one-off high-impact events. The absence of minority ethnic
groups in certain media spaces (such as television sitcoms or game-shows,
characterised by a convivial atmosphere) may be just as significant as over-
exposure elsewhere (notably in news and current affairs programmes, focusing
primarily on societal problems). As I will argue below, the popularity of racist
parties such as the FN in France may indeed owe more to long-term imbalances
in the representation of immigration and ethnic minorities than to the direct
media exposure enjoyed by such parties.

The media and the *Front National*

The debate over media effects in the field of ethnic relations has often been at
its most heated in connection with the access of racist and xenophobic
politicians to the press, radio and television. In the run-up to Denmark's local
government elections in November 1997, for example, anti-racists complained
that the extreme-right Danish People's Party was being favoured by imbalances
in television broadcasting, fostering anti-immigrant attitudes among the
electorate. Xenophobic statements by the DPP's leader, Pia Kaesgaard, were
alleged to be receiving excessive exposure on news bulletins, with insufficient
coverage of opposing views, while extensive reporting of violent and criminal
acts by youths of immigrant origin was said to be creating an overwhelmingly
negative picture of minority ethnic groups (Hussain 1997a, 1997b). In the UK
during the 1997 general election and again during the 1999 European
elections, anti-racist groups protested against the decision to allow a television
election broadcast by the British National Party, fearing that it might have a
trigger or persuasive effect on the voting intentions of viewers. Similarly, in
France, there have been periodic calls for the openly racist leader of the *Front
National*, Jean-Marie Le Pen, to be banned from television, in the belief that
this might reduce popular support for the party. In an opinion poll conducted

in 1997, only 26 per cent thought that media coverage had no significant effect on the fortunes of Le Pen and his party. Even allowing for 'don't knows' (9 per cent of the sample), a substantial majority were convinced that support for the party was affected by the media, though there was disagreement about the nature of their impact. Some 51 per cent considered that coverage of the FN tended to work in its favour, while 14 per cent (foremost among whom were FN supporters) said the media were basically harmful to the party (SOFRES 1998: 80).

Between 1984 and 1998, the FN consistently scored between 10 and 15 per cent of the vote in nationwide elections, making it the most electorally entrenched extreme-right party in Western Europe. With 15 per cent of the vote in the first round of the 1995 presidential elections, Le Pen was only five points behind the eventual winner of the second ballot, centre-right candidate Jacques Chirac. Politicians and political analysts have been deeply divided concerning the most effective means of fighting the FN. Taguieff (1995) has distinguished seven main strategies: demonisation, silence, fellow-travelling, non-alliance, republican frontism, intellectual harassment and socio-economic intervention. Three of these revolve primarily around different views of the volume and types of discourse which are best suited to combating Le Pen's party. Those who demonise Le Pen believe that by maximising alarmist discourse about the FN with the aid of the media, they will succeed in turning the electorate away from the party. By contrast, those who argue in favour of saying nothing about Le Pen do so on the grounds that any publicity works to his benefit. Those who favour intellectual harassment put their hopes in reasoned arguments designed to demonstrate to the public that the FN's ideology and policy platform are fatally flawed.

Each of these three positions makes important and in some cases conflicting assumptions about media effects. The demonisers believe that the emotive power of the media can be a powerful weapon in the fight against right-wing extremism. Those who favour silence fear that, when relayed by the media, the devil has the best tunes. Unlike the other two camps, the proponents of intellectual harassment seek to use the media as a rational tool against racist ideology.

No systematic research over a sustained period has yet been undertaken into the possible correlation between the amount and type of media coverage accorded to the FN and the party's electoral scores. The arguments which have raged around this question have been informed mainly by anecdotal evidence and/or gut feelings on the part of journalists and political analysts. Empirical evidence against which to test rival views is both fragmentary and mixed.

On the one hand, an opinion poll conducted shortly after one of Le Pen's first major television appearances, in February 1984, indicated that electoral support for the FN had doubled, reaching 7 per cent compared with 3.5 per cent before the broadcast (Simmons 1996: 79); the party went on to score 11 per cent of the vote in the European elections held a few months later. On the other hand, opinion polls also show sharp falls in the popularity of Le Pen and his party after massive media coverage of certain statements appealing to racist sentiments. This was the case, for example, in the autumn of 1987, when Le Pen described the holocaust as a 'point of detail'. A similar drop was registered a year later, after he made a pun about the gas chambers out of the name of a Jewish minister and in 1989 when he claimed that a 'Jewish international' was at work in the media and elsewhere (SOFRES 1993).

Although precise quantitative data have not been computed, there is general agreement that, in the run-up to the 1993 parliamentary elections, the FN received considerably less publicity than in any nationwide election since 1984 (Oriol 1995). Yet the party increased its share of the vote to 12.4 per cent, compared with 9.7 per cent in the two previous parliamentary elections, when it enjoyed a much higher media profile.

There is clearly no direct correlation between the sheer quantity of media coverage accorded to the FN and the level of popularity enjoyed by the party. In seeking to illuminate that relationship, other factors also have to be taken into account. Since 1984, opinion pollsters have accumulated a run of data at regular intervals on the popularity of the FN and its leader. These indicate that support for Le Pen's ideas peaked in October 1991, when 32 per cent of those questioned said they agreed somewhat or completely with him (SOFRES 1993 and 1997). With printed and broadcast news outlets dominated during much of the previous year by the Gulf War and its aftermath, Le Pen had enjoyed relatively little media coverage in the months leading up to this poll. Shortly before it, however, leading figures in other parties had hit the headlines with inflammatory statements about the 'problem' of immigration (Perotti 1991; Perotti and Thépaut 1991). In June 1991, Chirac complained about the smells generated by an 'overdose' of immigrants. The following month Socialist Prime Minister Edith Cresson spoke of organising special charter flights to speed up the deportation of illegal immigrants, an idea first tried as a publicity stunt by the previous centre-right government. In September, the former centrist President Valéry Giscard d'Estaing likened immigration to an 'invasion'. Shortly after this series of highly publicised statements, support for Le Pen's ideas hit an all-time high, despite the fact that the FN leader had been largely out of the limelight during the preceding months. This implies that media coverage of immigration, fuelled in many cases by the discourse of mainstream politicians, is at least as important as, if not more important than, direct exposure for the party in generating support for the FN.

Le Pen's electoral breakthrough, beginning in 1983, was driven primarily by anti-immigrant propaganda, and his electoral base has remained dominated, more that of any other party, by voters troubled by immigration and associated feelings of insecurity (Mayer 1995; SOFRES 1998: 49–83). At various times, other party leaders have sought to counter Le Pen's electoral appeal by stealing his anti-immigrant clothes. As Le Pen himself has observed, this has been a largely unsuccessful tactic: faced with a choice between the original and mere copies, voters attracted by peddlers of anti-immigrant propaganda have preferred what they perceive to be the 'real thing'. Thus it was that Le Pen emerged in the autumn of 1991 as the principal beneficiary of a string of racially tainted statements fed to the media by figures on the left, the centre and the right of the mainstream political spectrum.

Three important features are apparent in these events. First, although the FN has gained more than any other party by appealing to racist sentiments, it is by no means alone in helping to generate them. Second, it would be no less over-simplistic to attribute solely to the media the antipathy towards immigrants on which Le Pen has so successfully capitalised. While the media have undoubtedly contributed to the propagation of racist attitudes, the mainstream politicians whose words they have reported have also played an essential role, and it is indeed extremely difficult to say precisely where their responsibility ends and that of the media begins. Third, the articulation of hostility towards certain minority groups, even when the FN is given little air time or press space, is of greater benefit to the party than intensive media coverage of its leader's pronouncements against other ethnic groups.

The three instances cited earlier of reductions in support for Le Pen all came in the wake of intensive media coverage of anti-Semitic remarks. His popularity has surged when the media have focused on anxieties aroused among the majority population by the presence of Arab and Third World immigrants, without the FN necessarily being at the forefront of these stories. This was the case, for example, during the first Islamic headscarf affair in 1989, which culminated in the FN winning a parliamentary by-election in the town of Dreux, to the west of Paris, with 61 per cent of the second-round vote. The FN played a relatively minor role in the intensively reported – if not indeed media-created – headscarf affair (Gaspard and Khosrokhavar 1995), in which the main voices relayed by the media were those of mainstream politicians and intellectuals who took up opposing positions on what all agreed to be the 'problem' of how to regulate the emergence of a new Muslim minority within French society (Berris 1990). Similarly, when Chirac, Cresson and Giscard d'Estaing played on public hostility towards 'immigrants' – which in the French context is shorthand for minorities of Third World, and more particularly Arab, origin – the raw nerve on which they touched, amplified by the media, played directly into the hands of Le Pen.

Le Pen first came to prominence in the media during local election campaigns held in 1983, in which immigration was highlighted as a key issue (Amirouche 1983). While public anxiety in this area has been exploited by the FN more successfully than by any other party, it neither created immigration as an electoral issue nor controlled the processes through which overwhelmingly negative images of minority ethnic groups had already been constructed by the media. Detailed research by Seguret (1981), Hames (1989) and Bonnafous (1992) has shown that over a long period prior to Le Pen's breakthrough, there were serious imbalances in media images of Third World immigrants, revolving primarily around criminality, economic dependency and religious extremism. In each respect, immigrant minorities were portrayed as alien or disruptive forces in relation to the behavioural norms of the national community. In seeking to capitalise on those images, mainstream politicians on both the right and the left of the political spectrum played the 'race' card in well-publicised ways at various points in the late 1970s and early 1980s, paving the way for the FN's subsequent electoral successes as the party promising to put anti-immigrant measures at the top of the policy agenda (Schain 1985: 78–83; Wihtol de Wenden 1988).

If the media have undoubtedly contributed to the formation of harmful ethnic stereotypes, it would be wrong to suggest that they work solely to the advantage of racist parties. As already noted, heavy media coverage of anti-Semitic remarks has damaged Le Pen's standing on more than one occasion. SOFRES pollsters have asked respondents at regular intervals whether they regard the FN as a threat to democracy. When the question was first asked, in October 1983, only 38 per cent saw Le Pen's party in that way, while 43 per cent did not consider it dangerous. During the next four years, there was a steady rise in those regarding the FN as dangerous, reaching 66 per cent in December 1988, while those taking the opposite view fell to 25 per cent. Since then, the proportion disinclined to see the FN as a threat to democracy has remained at about that level, while those considering it dangerous have grown in number, standing at 73 per cent in 1999 (SOFRES 1998: 69, 1999). It seems likely that the relatively low percentage regarding the FN as a threat to democracy in 1983 arose in part from the fact that the general public knew little about Le Pen's party at that time. In the absence of such information, respondents had little reason to regard the FN as dangerous. In 1983, 19 per cent of those interviewed expressed no opinion in response to this question. Five years later, this figure had fallen to 8 per cent, and by 1999 it stood at 3 per cent. The simultaneous increase in those considering the party to be a threat to democracy is almost certainly due in part to the fact that they were better informed about the FN as a result of extensive media coverage. In this respect at least, information flows provided by the media appear to have worked against Le Pen.

It nevertheless remains true that since the late 1980s, about a quarter of interviewees have been disinclined to see the FN as dangerous, and for almost a decade and a half – between 1984 and 1998 – the party consistently enjoyed between 10 and 15 per cent of the vote in nationwide elections. As noted earlier, FN voters are obsessed by anti-immigrant attitudes linked with deep-seated feelings of insecurity, and there can be little doubt that these attitudes are at least partly sustained by imbalances in media representations of minority ethnic groups. The latest locus around which negative stereotypes have been focused by the media lies in the *banlieues* (literally, 'suburbs'), which in the French context has a similar resonance to 'inner-city' areas in Britain (Hargreaves 1996). In the 1970s, a team of researchers led by Stuart Hall showed how media representations of British inner-city areas encouraged the public to conflate immigration, criminality and poverty (Hall *et al.* 1978). Almost identical processes were at work during the 1990s in high-profile media representations of the French *banlieues*, fuelling anxieties about immigration on which the FN's political base was built.

The British experience

What, if any, lessons can be drawn from the British context in considering possible changes in media policy with a view to improving the state of ethnic relations in France and elsewhere? Some fifteen years before the rise of Le Pen, British 'race' relations were thrown into turmoil by Enoch Powell's adoption of a stridently anti-immigrant discourse, voiced most notoriously in his widely publicised 'rivers of blood' speech, predicting wide-scale inter-ethnic violence if nothing was done to reverse recent inflows of Third World immigrants. Much of what Powell said then could readily be repeated today almost word-for-word by Le Pen, with the simple substitution of Arabs and Africans for West Indians and Asians. Powell was soon marginalised by the political establishment, and extreme-right parties which sought to capitalise on racist rhetoric in Britain – notably the National Front, and more recently the British National Party – have never achieved a level of electoral support remotely approaching that won by Le Pen in France.

It would be far too simple to suggest that the spectre of the extreme-right in Britain was conjured away by a flick of some media switch or more substantive public policy measures such as the Race Relations Acts of 1965, 1968 and 1976. If the NF and BNP have remained marginal political forces, one of the reasons for this may be that their positions have been incorporated in some degree by right-wingers visible to the electorate within the Conservative Party, which has thus served as a conduit for anti-immigrant votes. It would also be a mistake to imagine that ethnic relations in Britain are necessarily more harmonious than in France. Official figures on racially motivated attacks on both sides of the Channel suggest that there is no room for complacency in either country (Hargreaves and Leaman 1995). It is nevertheless possible to identify at least three types of initiative relating to the British media which have worked in favour of improved 'race' relations: measures to ensure more balanced media content, a greater presence of minority ethnic professionals in at least some media sectors and journalistic codes of practice designed to avoid ethnic stereotyping.

The institutional framework of terrestrially based television – by far the most pervasive single medium in Britain, as in France – is much more open to ethnic diversity in the UK. While Le Pen was enjoying blanket media coverage in France amid the FN's electoral breakthrough in 1983, British viewers were becoming acquainted with a new television station, Channel 4, launched the previous year with the specific remit of catering for minority groups of all kinds. Among these were groups of recent immigrant origin, for whom Channel 4 created a Multicultural Programmes Unit. On a more modest scale, BBC2 had also targeted various minorities since its creation in the late 1960s, and it significantly increased its programming for ethnic minorities during the 1980s. Britain's most popular TV channel, ITV, has a strong regionally based structure, which makes it possible to reflect regional concentrations of ethnic minorities in programme outputs. News and other programmes on the BBC's most popular channel, BBC1, also include significant regional variations. Many programmes originally aimed at ethnic or regional minorities have subsequently gained cross-over audiences, entering into 'mainstream' schedules. This applies, for example, to sitcoms such as Channel 4's *Desmond's*, the eponymous hero of which is a West Indian immigrant in London, and BBC2's comedy sketch show *Goodness Gracious Me*, featuring second-generation Asians. In France, by contrast, five of the six terrestrially based channels are heavily centralised, and neither they nor the only station with a significant regional dimension, F3, have any specific responsibility for addressing the needs of immigrant minorities. Programmes for or about those minorities are consequently few and far between (Hargreaves 1997).

The BBC operates an equal opportunities policy which has significantly increased the proportion of minority ethnic professionals across the whole structure of the corporation, and commercial channels have also made considerable efforts to recruit minority ethnic presenters, particularly but by no means solely in news and current affairs programmes. These and other measures have helped to strengthen the presence of minority ethnic groups in an increasingly wide range of programmes, in stark contrast with the situation in French television, where it is still rare to encounter people of minority ethnic origin other than as 'problems' in news and current affairs programmes (Hargreaves and Perotti 1993). Across all six French terrestrial channels, there is still only a single minority ethnic newsreader to be seen presenting national news bulletins. Although Algerian-born Rachid Arhab regularly anchors F2's lunchtime bulletin, it should be noted that this has a much smaller audience than the main evening news. With the exception of Arhab, and one or two reporters on the regionally based F3, it is rare to see any minority ethnic journalists in the main news programmes of any French channel. In Britain, by contrast, minority ethnic presenters and reporters feature regularly in the national news broadcasts of all the main channels. West Indian-born Trevor MacDonald, for example, became the most popular newsreader in Britain as the anchor of ITV's *News at Ten*. On both the BBC and ITV, regional news broadcasts in areas such as London and the Midlands, where there are high concentrations of minority ethnic groups, are often presented by minority ethnic journalists. In many other programme sectors, from soaps and game-shows to children's TV and drama, minority ethnic groups are far more in evidence in Britain than in France. Their virtual exclusion from prime-time representations of everyday life in the national community implicitly suggests that minority ethnic groups are not a 'normal' or 'natural' part of French society.

A rare area in which there have been similar initiatives within both the British and French media concerns codes of practice in the reporting of news stories featuring members of minority ethnic groups. Since 1975, the British National Union of Journalists has operated a code of practice, periodically updated, designed to ensure that the 'racial' or ethnic origins of people featured in news stories, particularly those of a criminal nature, are not mentioned unless these are in some demonstrable sense germane to the events in question (van Dijk 1991: 255–7). In France, the Centre de Formation et de Perfectionnement des Journalistes (CFPJ) has fostered a similar code of practice in training courses for journalists, which appears to have had a perceptible effect on reporting techniques (Anstett 1996). Just as the British media no longer feature stories on 'black muggers', it is now increasingly rare for French newspapers to run headlines about 'Arab thiefs' or 'Maghrebi drug-dealers', as if ethnicity were somehow the cause of criminality.

There are still serious imbalances in media coverage of ethnic relations, and these generally remain more pronounced in France than in Britain. A study of British media coverage of 'race' issues in the six months prior to the 1997 general election found that almost three-quarters of the news items surveyed conveyed a broadly anti-racist message (Law *et al.* 1997). Although no directly comparable data were compiled during the run-up to the 1997 elections in France, it is most unlikely that a similar balance would emerge from such a survey. Moreover, while improvements in the handling of news and current affairs may be reducing some of the worst features of media stereotyping, the general public is unlikely to perceive minority ethnic groups as full citizens in the national community until they are integrated in the whole range of media ouputs, including comedy, drama and light entertainment. The French still have a lot of ground to make up in this respect.

Conclusion

The end of the 1990s brought a sharp fall in support for the FN. In opinion surveys conducted since 1984, support for Le Pen's ideas had never fallen below 16 per cent and had usually stood at at least 20 per cent or considerably more. In May 1999 the figure plummeted to 11 per cent (SOFRES 1999), and in the European elections held the following month the party won less than 6 per cent of the vote. As there had been no substantive change in media policy towards the party or its pet theme, immigration, it is unlikely that the media were in any direct sense responsible for the decline in the FN's fortunes. The party's poor showing in the 1999 European elections appears to have been due primarily to economic and political changes which had taken place over the previous two years.

Huge self-inflicted damage had been caused by a split within the FN which led Le Pen's number two, Bruno Mégret, to set up a breakaway party, the *Mouvement National* (MN), at the beginning of 1999. The abuse heaped upon each other by Le Pen and Mégret did nothing to inspire public confidence in either of their parties. In the European elections, even the combined vote of the FN and the MN – 5.7 and 3.3 per cent respectively, making 9 per cent in all – fell well short of the 15 per cent won by Le Pen and his party in the presidential, parliamentary and regional elections of 1995, 1997 and 1998.

Significant changes had also taken place in the wider political and economic situation. After more than twenty years of almost constantly rising unemployment in France, the trend was at last reversed in the autumn of 1997, when a modest but steady decline began. The FN had been the main political beneficiary of anxieties generated by high levels of unemployment among voters blaming economic and other forms of insecurity on the presence of foreigners. A general improvement in economic confidence, apparent by the beginning of 1999, was clearly unhelpful to the party.

It may also be significant that since the election of a Socialist-led government in 1997 the discourse and policies of mainstream politicians on issues relating to immigration had taken a more moderate turn, with even opposition right-wingers such as Pasqua supporting an amnesty for the *sans-papiers*. Along with the improved economic climate, this change in the discourse of political elites may have helped to engender the more sympathetic attitudes towards immigrants – including the *sans-papiers* – registered among the general public at the end of the 1990s (CSA 1998, 1999). Whatever its causes, this reduction in public discontent concerning immigration – the key ingredient on which the FN's electoral machine had successfully fed – was bound to weaken Le Pen's appeal.

One other factor should also be mentioned: the victory of France's multi-ethnic football team in the 1998 World Cup. While the 'feel-good' effect of this triumph may prove ephemeral, prominent media coverage of the role of minority ethnic players in securing the French victory – half the national squad were born outside metropolitan France or of immigrant parents – undoubtedly helped to generate a more favourable image of immigrants and their descendants. The media did not of course create the French victory any more than they were responsible for falling unemployment, infighting within the FN or changed mainstream political postures in relation to immigration, but they played an essential role in disseminating information about these events to the general public. Moreover, while the electoral fortunes of anti-immigrant parties such as the FN appear to be determined primarily by wider economic and political factors, it is abundantly clear that the media play a significant role in shaping public attitudes towards minority ethnic groups. The evidence from France and Britain suggests that if more balanced media coverage can help to create less negative images of minorities, this may also reduce the reservoir of racism and xenophobia on which extremist parties are able to draw.

NOTES

1 For a more detailed analysis of the media treatment of this episode see Ron Kaye's chapter in this book.
2 See the article 'Warning to Editors on "racist" reports', *Independent*, 17 December 1998.
3 See also the articles 'Dover overwhelmed by Gypsy asylum-seekers', *The Times*, 20 October 1997; and 'Gypsies left to face chilly winds at the Cliffs of Dover', *Independent*, 21 October 1997.
4 See 'Sun, seaside and singing for TV's Romany exiles', *Guardian*, 21 October 1997.

References

Amirouche, K. (1983) 'L'extrême droite et les autres', *La Semaine de l'Emigration*, 10 March.
Anderson, B. (1983) *Imagined Communities*, London: Verso.
Anstett, S. (1996) 'Ni diabolisation, ni angélisme', *Migrance* 11–12: 98–102.
Barker, M. and Petley, J. (eds) (1997) *Ill Effects: The Media/Violence Debate*, London: Routledge.
Berris, D. (1990) 'Scarves, schools and segregation: the *foulard* affair', *French Politics and Society* 8, 1: 1–13.
Billig, M. and Golding, P. (1992) 'Did the race card tip the balance?', *New Community* 19, 1: 161–3.
Bonnafous, S. (1992) 'Le terme "intégration" dans *Le Monde*: sens et non-sens', *Hommes et Migrations* 1154: 24–6.
CSA (1998) Opinion poll data in *Le Monde*, 21 November.
—— (1999) Opinion poll data in *Le Monde*, 25 March.
Gaspard, F. and Khosrokhavar, F. (1995) *Le Foulard et la République*, Paris: La Découverte.
Goldman, T. (1997) 'Roma refugees arrive in Dover', article relayed by ERAM electronic mailing list, 19 October.
Hall, S., Critcher, C., Jefferson, A., Clarke, J. and Roberts, B. (1978) *Policing the Crisis: Mugging, the State and Law and Order*, London: Macmillan.
Hames, C. (1989) 'La construction de l'islam en France: du côté de la presse', *Archives en Sciences Sociales des Religions* 68, 1: 79–92.
Hargreaves, A. G. (1996) 'A deviant construction: the French media and the "*banlieues*"', *New Community* 22, 4: 607–18.
—— (1997) 'Gatekeepers and gateways: post-colonial minorities and French television', in Hargreaves, A. G. and McKinney, M. (eds), *Post-Colonial Cultures in France*, London/New York: Routledge.
Hargreaves, A. G. and Leaman, J. (1995) 'Racism in contemporary Western Europe: an overview', in Hargreaves, A. G. and Leaman, J. (eds), *Racism, Ethnicity and Politics in Contemporary Europe*, Aldershot: Edward Elgar.
Hargreaves, A. G. and Perotti, A. (1993) 'The representation on French television of immigrants and ethnic minorities of Third World origin', *New Community* 19, 2: 251–61.
Hussain, M. (1997a) 'Neoracism', article relayed on ERAM electronic mailing list, 21 October.

—— (1997b) 'Media and minorities in Denmark', article relayed on ERAM electronic mailing list, 2 November.

Ipsos (1996) Opinion poll in *Le Monde*, 27 August.

Law, I., with Svennevig, M. and Morrison, D. (1997) *Privilege and Silence: Race in the British News During the General Election Campaign*, London: Central Books.

Mayer, N. (1995) 'Ethnocentrism and the *Front National* vote in the 1988 French presidential election', in Hargreaves, A. G. and Leaman, J. (eds), *Racism, Ethnicity and Politics in Contemporary Europe*, Aldershot: Edward Elgar.

Oriol, P. (1995) 'Les immigrés dans les urnes', *Migrations Société* 7, 42: 17–41.

Perotti, A. (1991) 'Le programme de Valéry Giscard d'Estaing sur l'immigration', *Migrations Société* 3, 18: 65–73.

Perotti, A. and Thépaut, F. (1991) 'Immigration: le fracas dans le discours, la contradiction dans les faits', *Migrations Société* 3, 16–17: 93–116.

Schain, M. (1985) *French Communism and Local Power: Urban Politics and Political Change*, London: Pinter.

Seguret, P. (1981) 'Images des immigrés et de l'immigration dans la presse française', Montpellier: Université Paul Valéry, unpublished *thèse de 3e cycle*.

Simmons, H. G. (1996) *The French National Front: The Extremist Challenge to Democracy*, Boulder, Colorado: Westview Press.

Sliva, J. (1997) 'Czech Gypsies plan to move to Canada', Associated Press report, 14 August, quoted on ERAM electronic mailing list, 21 October.

SOFRES (1993) *L'Etat de l'Opinion*, Paris: Seuil.

—— (1997) Opinion poll data in *Le Monde*, 20 March.

—— (1998) *L'Etat de l'Opinion 1998*, Paris: Seuil.

—— (1999) Opinion poll data in *Le Monde*, 4 May.

Taguieff, P.-A. (1995) 'Antilepénisme: les erreurs à ne plus commettre', in Martin-Castelnau, D. (ed.) *Combattre le Front National*, Paris: Editions Vinci.

van Dijk, T. A. (1991) *Racism and the Press*, London: Routledge.

Wihtol de Wenden, C. (1988) *Les Immigrés et la Politique*, Paris: Presses de la Fondation Nationale des Sciences Politiques.

3

MIGRANTS AND MEDIA

The Italian case

Giovanna Campani

Introduction

This chapter deals with the image of migrants in the Italian media, with special attention paid, towards the end of the chapter, to the images of migrant women. Recently the issue of the portrayal of migrants in the Italian media was raised at the *Consulta* on immigration – a consultation structure set up by the Minister of Social Affairs, Livia Turco. It was pointed out that there is a serious problem of stereotyping and a lack of specific radio and TV programmes directed to immigrant audiences. The only existing programme is *Un mondo a colori* ('A world in colours'), shown at 10.30 on weekday mornings from Tuesday to Friday on RAI 2 in the RAI educational slot. The programme presents different life-stories and experiences, highlighting the difficulties migrants encounter in Italy but also showing the positive aspects of integration.

Very little research has been carried out on the theme of media and migration in Italy. The most important work has been carried out by Massimo Ghirelli (1990a, 1990b) who denounces the stereotypes and prejudices the media use to represent migrants. Ghirelli has also established an Archive on Immigration, which collects together all the video production on migration. Also worthy of mention is the recent issue of the journal *Studi Emigrazione* devoted to the theme of 'mass media, ethnic conflict and immigration' (Cotesta 1999). Amongst other things, this research shows how, via a strategy of anticipation, newspapers have spread pre-formed images of foreigners, well before the Italian population as a whole could have a direct experience of them (Cotesta 1999: 496).

In spite of this developing work, the Italian critique of mass media and the immigration question has yet to analyse the structure of the Italian media's response to immigration and the specificity of the images of migrants in the Italian context. Another dimension which is missing is any comparison with how migrants are portrayed in other national media, for instance in Europe or North America. In other words, is there a specificity to the stereotyping produced in the Italian media, or do we just encounter a general, transnational practice of conveying common negative images of migrants and minority groups?

Following the pioneering work of van Dijk (1994), we know that:

- the dominating group (which usually means the 'white' majority) and the elite support an information system which legitimises their power and their dominant position, and which creates prejudices against members of ethnic minorities;
- the media reproduces power in general and can produce racism in particular, by proceeding actively to the construction of a negative social representation of ethnic minorities and by spreading such a representation in the public arena.

This general discourse has to be applied to each specific context in order to be heuristic. A further step is represented by the analysis of the role the media play inside the relations of power existing in each society. The media reflect the multidimensional relations of power (historical, political, economic etc.) and each topic, such as immigration, has to be understood in relation to them. Hence migration into Italy represents an issue in the specific power relations between the parties and economic groups in the country. For example, during the war in Kosovo, when the image of the Albanians in Italy up to that point was very negative in the media, the picture was completely transformed in a few weeks in order to construct solidarity with the Albanians (both in Kosovo and in Albania) and to generate approval of the government's engagement in the war. The media responded to the general strategy of the politicians – to obtain popular support for the war effort.

The chapter is in four parts. First, I will try to analyse the role of the Italian media in connection to the power blocs that they represent, stressing the uniqueness of the Italian situation compared to other Western countries. Second, I will explore the general discourse on the phenomenon of immigration as projected by the Italian media in relation to the evolution of migration across three periods. Third, I will describe the creation of stereotypes in relation to the three migratory phases, and finally I will comment more specifically on the images of migrant women in the Italian media. We will see that, whilst the media's stereotyped images of immigrants are expressions of racist mentalities, lack of professional ethics or, sometimes, just plain ignorance, such images are also part of political battles and the fight for specific power interests.

The Italian media

In order to understand the role of the media within the structures and relations of power in Italy, it must be made clear that what might be called 'autonomous journalism' – that is to say a journalism based above all on the quality of the information and on the objective of trying to obtain the support of the audience through the quality of information provided – is very much the exception in Italy.[1]

If in virtually every country the existence and slant of the media depend on the support and orientation of powerful financial consortia, in Italy this phenomenon reaches extremes which would be unacceptable, even unthinkable, in other Western countries. This is because of the close ties which link the business empires to the political powers. The four so-called national newspapers which have the largest circulations and which are read all over the country – *Il Corriere della Sera*, *La Repubblica*, *La Stampa* and *Il Giornale*[2] – all are dependent upon large financial groups which are all, in turn, deeply involved in politics. This engagement in politics is often an instrument to obtain material economic benefits for the industrial group in question. The Berlusconi group owns *Il Giornale*, the weekly review *Panorama* and three television stations – Italia Uno, Canale Cinque and Retequattro. Silvio Berlusconi is president of the political party Forza Italia and was head of the national government in 1994. The Agnelli group (which runs the powerful Fiat empire) owns *La Stampa*, the Rizzoli group owns *Il Corriere della Sera*, whilst *La Repubblica* is under the control of the De Benedetti group, which also controls the weekly magazine *L'Espresso*.

It is true that the reader does sometimes have the impression of being presented with 'autonomous journalism' in newspapers like *La Stampa* or *La Repubblica*, and there are, of course, some excellent journalists, but their freedom is ultimately limited by the industrial empires that own the newspapers. For example, during the Kosovo war, *La Stampa* had a much more critical attitude than the other newspapers, because this was also the general orientation of the Agnelli group, which had investments in Serbia. In fact NATO had bombed a Fiat joint-venture there. But there are contrasts to be drawn. I would say that Carlo De Benedetti (*La Repubblica* and *L'Espresso*) represents the best that capitalism has produced in Italy in terms of 'intelligence', innovation and morality; while Silvio Berlusconi (*Il Giornale, Panorama*) represents the worst in terms of the corruption and exploitation of the state for his own personal interests.[3] Inevitably, this contrast is reflected in the quality of the newspapers and magazines controlled by the two groups.

This 'abnormal' situation (abnormal in relation to the rest of the Western world – in fact Italy can be compared to the South American democracies as far as the media situation is concerned) can partly explain the arrogance with which the recent head of government, Massimo D'Alema, behaved towards journalists. He treated them as servants, as *valets de chambre*. In no other country would this be possible to such an extreme. Witness the rigorous grillings to which British TV and radio journalists have subjected their prime ministers and other political leaders in recent years!

What of the other Italian newspapers? With local and regional newspapers, the situation is not very different: they depend on local business interests which are often tied to the larger national consortia.[4] The local consortia are often more reactionary than the national ones, and this is reflected in a social and political orientation of these newspapers that leans more to the right than towards the left. The political parties' newspapers, on the other hand, survive thanks to public money, that is to say with subventions from the state, as well as the support of the parties themselves. These newspapers include *Il Popolo* (the paper of the Popolari, the 'old' Christian Democrats), *Il Secolo d'Italia* (Alleanza Nazionale, the so-called post-fascists), *Liberazione* (Rifondazione Comunista, the 'old' Communists) and *L'Unità* (Left Democrats, formerly PCI, the Italian Communist Party).

Somewhat exceptional is *Il Manifesto*, a left-wing newspaper, which survives through state money, the low wages of its journalists, who are organised in a co-operative, and occasional donation-subscriptions from the readers. *Il Manifesto* is very sensitive to new social and economic processes in Italy and to new cultural trends, as well as to the international dimension. The journalism can often be excellent, thanks also to the printing of articles from international journalists who cannot otherwise be read in Italy; for instance, *Il Manifesto* has a regular collaboration with *Le Monde Diplomatique*. *Il Manifesto* has a very ideological point of view: it is still a 'communist daily paper'. The Communist tradition makes the difference with *Le Monde Diplomatique*; the common opposition to the neo-liberal global economy of the two newspapers starts from different analyses of the processes taking place in civil society. *Il Manifesto* often tries to defend the Communist tradition, and this can sometimes be very harmful to the quality of the information in controversial contexts – the Balkan wars, for instance, or the changes in Eastern Europe and China.

So, to conclude this section, we do not find in Italy the equivalent of the French newspaper *Le Monde*. There is no means of providing high-quality information which is not influenced, to a greater or lesser extent, by the interests of the major economic groups or by the political parties. In practice, in Italy all the information is ideologically controlled through implicit choices and depends on economic and political paymasters. This extends to the management of the media as a whole, which does not give an image of world affairs and national issues that is divorced from the ownership of those media channels.[5] The extreme case is that of Berlusconi, where it is possible to speak of a sort of soft totalitarianism through the media, using the media to promote a political career and to hide the scandals (the biggest of which is of course the ownership of the country's largest private media empire by a powerful politician who at one time was the prime minister). Hence Berlusconi's media are used to convey propaganda for Forza Italia, the party he founded, and to attack and insult the other parties.

Moreover, the media which belong to the big financial and political groups are somehow considered as completely 'inside the system' (here I am referring to the 'Italian system' which is an anomaly in the European context) in the sense that the dominant point of view – the one of the ruling elite – is represented both in the left and in the right parties which are sharing political and economic power. In Italy the only opposition to such common values, common ideas and a deep acceptance of the system as it is, comes from the extremes. On the one side are the 'old' Communists, who express their positions in the pages of *Liberazione* and *Il Manifesto*. On the other side are the secessionist Lega Lombarda, which is openly xenophobic[6] and which has a small-circulation newspaper called *La Padania*, and a small fascist party which polls only 1–2 per cent of the electorate and does not express itself in the mass media.

Immigration and migrants

The discourse on immigration reflects first of all the degree of support for or opposition to the government's policies on this issue, and/or a general vision of the field of international relations. The image of the migrants which is projected by the media can support the general discourse and policy on immigration. If the migrant is presented as a poor victim or refugee, borders can be half-opened; if the migrant is regarded as a dangerous criminal, the borders must be closed. The discourse on immigration – both on the part of government and of the media – has changed over the years according to the development of the migratory flows and types. We will first consider the various periods of migration into Italy; then we will see how the phenomenon of immigration is presented in the media now and in the past, paying particular attention to the role of stereotyping. In the final section of the chapter, we will focus more specifically on the images of the migrant woman, trying to understand what role is played by gender.

In spite of its relatively short history, immigration into Italy has already passed through different phases, varying according to the origin and character-istics of the migrants, the sectors of employment they enter into in Italy, the migratory policies put in place (but often not operationalised) by the Italian authorities, and the attitudes and perceptions of Italian society (Campani 1999a; Melchionda 1993). Three main periods can be identified.

The first starts at the beginning of the 1980s and closes with Law 39, the so-called Martelli Act, in 1990. This period is characterised by:

- lack of legislation (the first law on immigration was voted through in 1986 but only Law 39 represents a serious attempt to establish a general legal framework);
- migratory flows coming mainly from the global South (Africa, Asia, Latin America) for reasons of work, finding employment in rather specific eco-nomic sectors (domestic service, street-vending, agriculture) and therefore in specific parts of the country (cities, tourist resorts, areas of intensive agriculture);
- slow change in public opinion towards immigrants from tolerance and curiosity to fear, intolerance and the first acts of racist violence.

At the beginning of this period, the phenomenon of immigration was largely ignored by the Italian population; an atmosphere of disinterested or vaguely curious tolerance prevailed. In the mid-1980s the Italian sociologist Franco Ferrarotti (1988) theorised Italian social tolerance in the face of the first incursions of mass immigration and wrote of a multicultural, multiracial Italian society. From the mid-1980s, this context begins to change. The killing of a black immigrant, Jerry Masslo, in 1989 represents a turning point (Andall 1990; Balbo and Manconi 1992).

The second period is characterised by changes in the origin and typologies of the migratory flows (more refugees arrive, mainly from the Balkan region, among them many gypsies), by the growing intolerance of the Italian population, and by changes in the internal political context with the collapse of the Christian Democrats and the Socialists in the *mani pulite* ('clean hands') corruption scandals and the emergence of new parties hostile to immigration (Lega Nord and Alleanza Nazionale). The fall of the Berlin Wall and the economic and political crisis of the Eastern European countries are at the origin of new flows from this region, of which the Albanian exodus of 1991 is the most spectacular example, followed by the refugees from the break-up of Yugoslavia. Both the Albanian crisis and the war in the former Yugoslavia oblige the Italian government to implement new measures and laws, like the humanitarian permit for former Yugoslavs. Italian public opinion shows solidarity for the first wave of Albanian refugees, but then quickly turns to hostility (Zinn 1996). By the early 1990s Albanians and people from the former Yugoslavia (especially Roma) become the main victims of intolerance and racism (Lapov 1998).

The third phase starts with the Dini Decree in 1996, which represents the first attempt to implement a new migratory policy since the Martelli Law of 1990. This attempt to create a new policy regime is concluded by Law 40, the Turco-Napolitano Law, in 1998. This period is characterised by contradictory processes, whose existence reflects a fundamental ambiguity in the Italian government (made up as it is of often contradictory elements bound together in various pragmatic coalitions) towards issues of migration. Moreover, changes are happening 'on the ground'. It becomes obvious that a proportion of the migrants has definitely settled in Italy. More and more foreign children enter Italian schools, thanks to the growth of family reunification which occurs despite a very restrictive policy. Italy has become *de facto* an immigration country with about 1.5 million foreigners. And yet, in spite of Law 40, the 'emergency' approach continues, both for the settled migrants and for the new arrivals who cannot be stopped. Unfortunately the integration measures proposed by Law 40 (including the award of a permanent residence card to immigrants living in Italy for at least five years) have yet to be implemented. Public opinion polls show that amongst Italians opposition to and stereotypes of immigrants persist, along with a general desire to 'send them home'. In 1998 an exit-poll carried out by the Institute for Research on Population reveals that

55 per cent of Italians cannot see any positive value in immigration, and that the majority considers that a future multi-ethnic society will be exposed to conflicts and unrest (Censis 1999). The Lega collects 600,000 signatures in six weeks for a referendum to abolish the *Legge Turco-Napolitano.*

The ambiguity of the situation of immigrants and immigration in Italy is rooted in two contradictions. First, in spite of the often-announced policies of integration, those immigrants who are in practice settled cannot avail themselves of a long-term residence permit or of stable structures for supporting themselves and their children. The most difficult problem is housing. Immigrants have huge difficulty in accessing decent housing in Italy due to the perverse nature of the housing market – flats are either extremely expensive or, if 'protected' with lower rents, reserved only for people who have been renting them for a long time and who cannot be evicted. Immigrants are thus pushed, against their will, into marginal housing environments. This form of exclusion affects their health, their ability to have a good job, and their general social conditions. The press somehow 'blames' the migrants for occupying squalid accommodation and lowering the tone of certain neighbourhoods.

The second contradiction is that, in spite of an official discourse of closing borders, it is impossible for the Italian authorities to prevent new arrivals. The Balkans are consumed by war, ethnic cleansing and instability; flows of refugees try to enter Italian territory by whatever means available. Trafficking has appeared as a new variable in the distribution of the flows; only a militarised control of the Mediterranean Sea could stop it. Many of the so-called illegal immigrants are *de facto* refugees who would have the right to the status of asylum-seeker, but they do not even consider applying for it given the harsh restriction of the Italian legislation (for instance asylum-seekers cannot work) and the low likelihood of success.

The media discourse on immigration changes over these three migratory periods. On the one side, it follows (or criticises) the government discourse; on the other it reflects, and shapes, public opinion's growing fear and hostility towards the immigrants. In the first phase, the leftist parties defend the notion of the multicultural society (which is quite a vague concept in Italy at the time); the Christian Democrats are fearful of irritating the Catholic Church, which sees the immigrants as the 'new poor' of the world; and the Socialists, including the law-maker Martelli, insist on the fact that Italy is an economically powerful country which needs immigrants. The media, especially television, tend to reflect these various views and interpretations.

Everything changes in the second phase. The mass arrival of the Albanians in March 1991 and the risk of flows from other East European countries pushes the government towards a discourse which begins to articulate fear of invasion and rejection of immigration. Martelli himself begins to use hydraulic metaphors: the Albanian flow has to be stopped (*'bisogna chiudere il rubinetto'* – the tap must be closed off). The expulsion of the second wave of Albanians (around 20,000 of them) in August 1991 is strongly justified by the government as the only possible solution. The media begin to present immigration as a danger, even if some voices in the media are openly critical of the government handling of the Albanian 'crises': in March the Albanians are left for days in the rain at Brindisi, and in the heat of August they are locked in the sports stadium in Bari for several days, thrown food by helicopter and are finally deported, after having received the promise that they would be allowed to stay.

Since the early 1990s, the discourse on immigration in the media, as expressed by the four major newspapers (*La Repubblica, Il Corriere, La Stampa* and even *Il Giornale*), considers that migration, if well managed, can be useful both for the Italian economy (which needs workers to do certain categories of jobs) and for the demographic balance (Italy has an extremely low birth rate now), but that at present, migration is a potential danger because of the high number of undocumented immigrants – what would be called in France the *sans-papiers*. The media generally ask for more control, more rules, and point to the connection between immigration and growing criminality. Of course, there are very different ways of presenting such a connection: the immigrants can be seen more as the victims (of poverty, of organised criminal gangs) rather than the instigators of crime (the view often portrayed in *La Repubblica*); or they can be presented as dangerous characters, as in *Il Giornale*. I will come back to this vexed debate on immigrants and crime a little later on.

The media point of view on migration – useful if well-controlled but otherwise dangerous – seldom considers the structural aspects of the Italian system: its civil society and economy, which can produce favourable conditions for illegal immigration. Hence readers and listeners hear little about the huge informal labour market in Italy; about the long-established system of organised crime in Italy which exploits immigrants and involves them in trafficking;[7] about the corruption of parts of the police; about visa-selling scams at Italian embassies and consulates abroad;[8] or about the *clientelismo* system at the local level which distributes and diverts NGO funds which are supposed to create structures to help immigrants settle and integrate. In other words, the media discourse on immigration rarely touches on those points which would above all question the involvement of the 'Italian system', which is in fact the main cause of the precarious condition of immigrants in Italy. Sometimes, it is true, the media discover an employer who disgracefully exploits immigrants. They denounce the fact, but they do not make a general critique of the Italian economic and social system which produces this type of exploitation. Abdelmalek Sayad (1992) has theorised the 'mirror effect' of migrants, which tends to reflect and show up the contradictions of the receiving society. This is certainly the case in Italy: migrants suffer the extreme consequences of the contradictions of Italian society because they are the most vulnerable section of the population.

If the general position as regards immigration is not very different among the four national newspapers mentioned above, there are marked differences when we examine the reporting of racism and racist acts. *Il Corriere della Sera* and *La Repubblica* are formally anti-racist, although some articles do resort to stereotypes when describing immigrants and they tend to 'explain' racism as a consequence of the high number of immigrants and of the lack of rules. Very different is the stance of *Il Giornale*: many racist acts reported by this newspaper are justified as the logical consequence of the criminality of the immigrants, and the reports constantly resort to racist stereotypes to define migrants, expressing prejudices and accusing immigrants of widespread criminality. To an outsider, the lack of any awareness of politically correct language is stunning.

The party papers obviously reflect the respective political positions. *Liberazione*, the paper of Rifondazione Comunista, can be defined as 'pro-immigration' and 'pro-immigrants', not only in the sense that it fights racism but also for its argument for more open borders in a new frame of international relations (Rifondazione Comunista is quite isolated in this position, the other leftist parties having accepted the Schengen perspective). At the other extreme, the newspapers and magazines of the far-right parties, such as *Il Secolo d'Italia* (ex-fascist party) and *La Padania* (Lega Nord), exploit the fear of 'migrant invasion' and high criminality and are clearly opposed to immigration. These papers use racist expressions which, in another country, would be grounds for a prosecution for racism. In Italy, it seems, everything is permitted. Irene Pivetti, former President of the Italian Parliament, was allowed to get away with saying that the Albanians should be thrown into the sea: she was not prosecuted, she is still a parliamentary deputy, is still invited to speak on television, and the present centre-left government still tries to court her vote.

Migrants and stereotyping

The image of the migrant as defined in the media has also changed over the three phases I have outlined above. Until 1990 the migrant is portrayed as a nomadic character, travelling around the country: it is not yet clear whether he (or she, but it is usually a he) will stay in Italy or not. The migrant has the face of Pap Khouma, the 'elephant seller', author of an autobiographical novel (Khouma 1990), or of the main character of the film *Pummarò*, which appeared on screens in 1991 and which is the subject of Chapter 6 of this volume. The migrant has a black face, is male, and comes from Africa. Pap Khouma and Jerry Masslo, the young South African murdered at Villa Literno south of Rome in 1989 and considered the first martyr of racism in Italy, are from Africa. The programme which Italian TV launches at this time and dedicates to immigration has the title *Nonsolonero* – 'Black and not only' – and the journalist presenting it is a young black woman from Cape Verde.

The image changes in 1991. The migrant is no longer solely African but also originates from a large, ill-defined territory to the east – Eastern Europe and the Balkans. The migrant is an Albanian or a Slav, sometimes even a Slavonic Albanian (*sic!*). The Italian media display a comprehensive ignorance of the complex ethnic relations of the Balkan region. Albanians are not Slavonic, and neither are the gypsies who are often described in the media as 'Slavonic nomads'. If anything the negative stereotyping of these populations is more marked than for the Africans. Albanians and Slavs are presented and thought of as being wild people (the horrors of the wars in the former Yugoslavia are used to confirm this) and pimps (in fact, it is true that some Albanians are involved in trafficking prostitutes). A small number of exceptional cases and events are fixed on and used to stereotype the whole immigrant population from that area. At the bottom of this unsavoury representational hierarchy are the gypsies; they are the group which is most discriminated against, for they suffer from an historic inherited prejudice, onto which is superimposed their additional negative status as migrants. They are uniformly regarded as 'dangerous' and prone to theft and violence.

Migrants' images have varied somewhat according to the three periods of migration, but they have three points in common. These are the 'folklorisation' of the migrants, their subordinate position, and their construction as sources of danger; the last of these three stereotypes has become ever more important in recent years. Let us examine these three consistent images in turn.

The *folklorisation* of migrants appears even in articles that try to present migrants in a positive way. For example, articles on the Santacruzan festival which the Filipino community celebrates in May use phrases which describe it as a colourful meeting of people 'with almond eyes' where beautiful girls dressed in strange costumes parade about among the simple happiness of their community. Similarly, the New Year events which the Chinese immigrants celebrate between January and February are described simplistically, focusing above all on the dragon which ventures forth from Chinatown, brought again by simple people with almond eyes, happy to carry him around the streets. These events are described in purely folkloric terms; hardly ever is any attention paid to their historical, cultural and anthropological dimensions. Often the cultural events organised by the migrant communities are found in the *Cronaca* or local pages of national and regional newspapers, where there is an even stronger tendency to folklorise the events.

Another variant of the tendency towards folklorisation is the discourse of *mystery* and *suspicion*, which sometimes shades into our third category of 'danger', to be discussed shortly. This language is often applied to discussions of the Chinese in Italy, always described as living in Chinatown, a mysterious place where everything raises suspicion. Sometimes the image changes even in the same newspaper. For instance in *Il Corriere* or *La Repubblica*, in the 'Health' or 'Culture' pages, we can find articles on acupuncture which describe the technique as an extremely interesting curative treatment, whilst in the *Cronaca* pages of the same issue can be read examples of the worst folklorisation of the same phenomenon – illegal 'so-called doctors' practising acupuncture in 'secret flats' (Campani and Maddii 1996).

The second image stresses the immigrants' *subordinate position*, in which they are always compared to the poorest and most socially marginal Italians. This corresponds partly to reality, but for the immigrants certain stereotypical aspects of their subordination and marginality are often underlined and generalised. A good example is the use by the media of the derogatory term '*vu cumprà*' (slang for 'do you want to buy?') to refer to immigrant street-sellers and also, on occasions, to all immigrants. It is as if all immigrants in Italy were doing such 'marginal' activities. The many cases of success, of 'good integration', of mixed marriages, of the new generation of Italo-Capeverdeans (there are quite a lot of children of these mixed marriages), and the Italo-Chinese (socialised in Italy) are often ignored.

The third image is the *criminalisation* of migrants. Over the last few years, the connection between migration and criminality has become increasingly stressed by the media, to the extent that it has virtually become a national obsession. Lots of statistics are bandied about, which obscure the complexity of the issue. Moreover one has to ask what the statistics mean, how they were collected etc.[9] It is true that in 1998, 89,457 foreigners were *denunciati*, reported to the police, which represents a much higher proportion than for the Italian population as a whole. But such data do not mean much. In fact, if we take into consideration the fact that 77,290 (86 per cent) of those reported were undocumented migrants, who are always going to be in a vulnerable position with the police, the result is that 'stable migrants' – those in possession of a residence permit etc. – do not have a higher rate of criminality than the Italians (Caritas di Roma 1999: 199).

There are several strands of possible explanation for the phenomenon of migrant criminality. Of course, rarely are the subtleties or multifaceted nature of such explanations expounded in the press or other media, whose main concern is to sensationalise the issue. The first explanation is the thesis of Barbagli (1998) that entry into Italy is too easy compared to the real possibilities of employment and socio-cultural integration, and that this contradiction is the origin of a higher rate of immigrant criminality. A second thesis is that the migrants, because of the general discrimination and victimisation that they suffer, are subjected to a stronger social and police control. In other words, migrants are more likely to be picked up by the police, or reported to the police by the victims or witnesses of crimes. Probably there are elements of truth in both these explanations, but there are other factors too. In a recent study, the social research organisation Censis (1999) pointed out that the condition of being an 'irregular' or undocumented migrant pushes such individuals towards various forms of criminality. Other possible causes of immigrant criminality could be the age structure of the immigrant community (dominated by young males who have the highest incidences of criminal offence in most populations) and the more widespread use of violence in the home country (as a result of the Balkan wars for example). Italian criminals, always looking for new helpers and recruits, could also be seen as a relevant cause; migrants are often used for low-paid jobs (selling drugs etc.) within the hierarchy of Italian organised crime. Once again, I repeat the point that, whilst the issue of immigrant criminality is now beginning to be the subject of serious academic research (see, for example,

Gatti *et al.* 1998), the complexity of the situation is rarely exposed in the media, where the messages merely stress the stereotypes and the 'danger' of immigrants' involvement in crime.

Migrant men and migrant women

Finally I would like to consider the gender variable in the media representation of migrants in Italy. It is important to recognise that the image of migrant women has also changed over the past twenty years; this is particularly true for the last five or six years with the arrival of trafficked women who are forced into street prostitution (Campani 1999b). Although I have not carried out systematic research and content analysis of Italian newspapers and magazines, I have followed quite closely the Italian media's coverage of the topic of migrant women, within the framework of research I have been carrying out for the past three years on trafficked women (Campani *et al.* 1999).[10]

In the early phase of immigration into Italy, the sex ratios of the various migrant groups were extremely unbalanced. Around 90 per cent of the Capeverdeans were women, as were 70 per cent of the Filipinos. On the other side, some 90 per cent of Moroccans and Senegalese were men. The presence of women from specific ethnic groups depended very much on the opportunities to find employment as domestic helpers, especially as live-in maids. So, for this first period, migrant women were represented in the media largely as maids. And because of the nature of this specific activity – caring, helping, based in the home etc. – the image of migrant women (most of whom, incidentally, came from Catholic countries) was reassuring, compared to the media image of men at this stage who were, as we have seen, largely portrayed as black-faced exotic strangers from Africa.

In subsequent years, the image of migrant women changed because of the arrival of two other types: the Islamic woman, arriving through family reunification, and the prostitute, often trafficked into Italy. As in France, the Islamic woman in Italy is at the centre of a lively debate between old-style feminists, women anthropologists and TV pundits. Recently a small march of Islamic women who were protesting because they could not wear the scarf on identity card photographs has provoked a wide-ranging reaction. Still, the presence of Islamic women remains quite limited in Italy, although their numbers are growing.[11]

The image of the migrant prostitute carries a huge emotional charge, reinforced by the processes through which many prostitutes are brought into the country – trafficking, trickery and enslavement. If we look at headlines in newspapers and magazines we find expressions like the following: 'Do you want a slave? Four million lire and she's yours', or 'Raped by ten men, forced onto the street' etc. The high degree of emotiveness surrounding this type of migrant woman is of course also connected to the nature of their work – prostitution, sex, 'entertainment' etc. But the fact that they are foreigners, and often black, adds something else to the emotional overload, not to mention their absolute dependence and subordination, on which the media incessantly insists. Hence, in addition to their low status as migrants and as prostitutes, they are also frequently labelled as slaves and as people taken against their will from their home countries. Whilst I have no wish to ignore the terrible circumstances in which migrant prostitutes are forced to exist in Italy, the media portrayal of them as totally subordinate slaves of their pimps and of criminal organisations does overlook the many cases where women working in the sex and entertainment industries have managed to maintain or regain a degree of independence and control over their own lives (Campani 1999b).

Conclusion

The general overview I have presented in this chapter allows me to make the following brief conclusions. The first is to reiterate my opening remark about the paucity of research on the theme of media and migration in Italy. Second, even a general empirical analysis such as the one I have made indicates strongly that the Italian media are, with a few exceptions, reinforcing stereotypes and prejudices about the migrants living in Italy, and they are not at all helping the Italian population to have a greater knowledge or understanding of the phenomenon of immigration or of the various cultures of the migrants who live and work in Italy. There are various reasons for this sad state of affairs. Italian journalism is not sensitive to the desirability of politically correct language, so that there are a lot of denigrating stereotypes (including those to describe various sections of the native Italian population). Still, behind the particular journalistic style of widespread stereotyping, there are precise and powerful political interests and intentions. Italy has never been a country of immigration and, at the moment, does not want to become one: the doors are closed or half-closed. In this context the campaign to combat illegal immigration and to denigrate undocumented migrants as sources of 'danger' seems to be much more important than a serious commitment to integrate migrants who are stably and legally resident in the country.

NOTES

1 In contrast to the situation in France where the strategy of *Le Monde*, or even of *Libération*, is very much along these lines. I make the French comparison as I lived in France for 17 years.
2 Publication runs of these newspapers are as follows: *Il Corriere* 950,000, *La Repubblica* 850,000, *La Stampa* 500,000 and *Il Giornale* 350,000.
3 In no other West European country could such practices have been tolerated, as the affair of La Cinq in France and Telecinco in Spain shows.
4 Examples of such newspapers are *La Nazione*, printed in Florence (190,000 copies) and read mainly in Tuscany, *Il Messaggero* in Rome, *Il Gazzettino* in Veneto and *Il Piccolo* in Trieste.
5 Even the state television channels have been *lottizzata* – carved up amongst the dominant political interests. Traditionally – and still today – RAI 1 belongs to the

Catholic Christian Democrats (now the *Popolari*), RAI 2 to the opposition parties of the right and RAI 3 to the Democratic Left. This situation is accepted and quite 'normal' in Italy.

6 The Lombard League collected 600,000 signatures in order to organise a referendum to abolish Law 40, the last Immigration Law.

7 Trafficking is often presented as if it were an 'external phenomenon' and not something that had its roots in Italy; where it is sometimes acknowledged as internal, this is limited just to the south, especially the region of Puglia, where immigrants arrive from Albania.

8 The best-known case of this is the illegal sale of visas by Italian Embassy employees in Lagos; the visas were bought by local criminals and used to send Nigerian girls to Italy.

9 The annual dossiers produced by the Caritas di Roma are a useful source of data and debate about the interactions between immigrants and the Italian judicial system. For the most recent accounts see Caritas di Roma (1996: 201–9, 1997: 192–8, 1998: 219–27, 1999: 198–202); also Gatti *et al.* (1998).

10 This research has been for the International Organisation for Migration (IOM) and the Daphne Project of the European Union.

11 I exclude Albanian women from the 'Islamic woman' category because of the long secularisation process in Albania.

References

Andall, J. (1990) 'New migrants, old conflicts: the recent immigration into Italy', *The Italianist* 10: 151–74.

Balbo, L. and Manconi, L. (1992) *I Razzismi Possibili*, Milan: Feltrinelli.

Barbagli, M. (1998) *Immigrazione e Criminalità*, Bologna: Il Mulino.

Campani, G. (1999a) 'La politique migratoire italienne: contrôle des frontières, régularisation et intégration', *Cahiers de l'URMIS*, 4–5 May: 117–18.

—— (1999b) 'Immigrant women in Southern Europe: social exclusion, domestic work and prostitution', in King, R., Lazaridis, G. and Tsardanidis, C. (eds), *Eldorado or Fortress? Migration in Southern Europe*, London: Macmillan.

Campani, G., Carchedi, F. and Mottura, G. (1999) *I Colori della Notte*, Milan: Franco Angeli.

Campani, G. and Maddii, L. (1996) 'I cinesi: immagini, stereotipi, pregiudizi nell'ambiente scolastico e nel contesto sociale', *La Critica Sociologica* 117–18: 4–16.

Caritas di Roma (1996) *Immigrazione Dossier Statistico '96*, Rome: Anterem.

—— (1997) *Immigrazione Dossier Statistico '97*, Rome: Anterem.

—— (1998) *Immigrazione Dossier Statistico '98*, Rome: Anterem.

—— (1999) *Immigrazione Dossier Statistico '99*, Rome: Anterem.

Censis (1999) *I Confini della Società Multietnica*, Rome: Censis.

Cotesta, V. (ed.) (1999) 'Mass media, conflitti etnici e immigrazione: una ricerca sulla comunicazione dei quotidiani nell'Italia degli anni novanta', *Studi Emigrazione* 135: 387–497.

Ferrarotti, F. (1988) *Oltre il Razzismo. Verso una Società Multirazziale e Multiculturale*, Rome: Armando.

Gatti, A., Gonnella, P. and Lovati, A. (1998) 'Stranieri e giustizia penale in Italia', *Studi Emigrazione* 131: 427–50.

Ghirelli, M. (1990a) *Razzismo e Media*, Rome: Il Passaggio.

—— (1990b) 'No al razzismo', *Cooperazione*, September: 2–4.

Khouma, P. (1990) *Io, Venditore di Elefanti*, Milan: Garzanti.

Lapov, Z. (1998) 'Nuovi flussi migratori e nuovi stereotipi sul popolo Rom. Il caso italiano', in Campani, G., Carchedi, F. and Mottura, G. (eds), *Migranti, Rifugiati e Nomadi. Europa dell'Est in Movimento*, Turin: L'Harmattan Italia.

Melchionda, U. (1993) *L'Immigrazione Straniera in Italia. Repertorio Bibliografico*, Rome: Edizioni Lavoro-Iscos.

Sayad, A. (1992) *L'Immigration ou les Paradoxes de l'Altérité*, Brussels: Editions Universitaires.

van Dijk, T. (1994) *Il Discorso Razzista*, Catanzaro: Rubettino.

Zinn, D. L. (1996) 'Adriatic brethren or black sheep? Migration in Italy and the Albanian crisis, 1991', *European Urban and Regional Studies* 3, 3: 241–9.

4

'BLAMING THE VICTIM'

An analysis of press representation of refugees
and asylum-seekers in the United Kingdom in the
1990s

Ronald Kaye

Introduction

How the press deals with refugee and asylum issues is an important factor in
their appearance on the public and political agenda. This chapter examines the
press portrayal of refugees and asylum-seekers in selected broadsheet and
tabloid newspapers in the United Kingdom during the 1990s. The methodolo-
gies adopted combine a content analysis approach, involving quantitative
analysis, with an interpretative/discourse approach, and examine a number of
themes.

The chapter has four sections. The first comprises an outline of developments in British refugee and asylum policy over the last decade, and a survey of
existing research on the press treatment of refugees and asylum-seekers in the
UK. The second section, utilising published and unpublished research by the
author, will explore the theme of the 'genuineness' of refugees, as this issue
emerged in the press between 1990 and 1996 – a period of Conservative
government. The third section will examine a number of other themes which
have emerged in the press discourse on refugees and asylum-seekers, focusing
mainly on two selected periods during 1997–98, the first two years of the new
Labour government. Finally the chapter will draw some conclusions in relation
to the material presented.

The political context

Refugee and asylum issues began to appear on the United Kingdom's public
and political agenda in the context of a large increase in the number of
applications for asylum in the last decade. The number of applications rose from
about 5,000 in 1988 to approximately 46,000 in 1998. By the early 1990s, it
had become clear that the traditional methods of immigration control were

insufficient to limit the flow of new asylum-seekers, and a large backlog of applications for asylum was building up. In response to concerns about the increasing numbers, the British government turned to legislation to stem the inflow, and also to speed up the decision-making process.

Thus in the Asylum and Immigration Appeals Act (1993), the core provisions were: the fingerprinting of applicants; toughened carrier sanctions; the fast tracking of 'manifestly unfounded' applications; and, for the first time, an in-country right of appeal. The Act's fast processing of 'manifestly unfounded' asylum claims led to an unprecedented decline of the UK refugee recognition rate. The rate of refusal jumped from 16 per cent in 1993 to 75 per cent in 1994. The Act also led to an increase in the number of asylum-seekers detained from 300 in 1993 to over 700 in 1994.

However, it soon became noticeable that the changes introduced in the 1993 Act had not produced the desired effect of dramatically reducing the numbers of those seeking asylum. From 1994 onwards, the number of asylum-seekers began to rise again from a low of 22,000 in 1993 to nearly 44,000 in 1995. In addition, the number of cases awaiting decisions actually increased, and the length of time for a decision on asylum also rose. The response of the government was to increase resources and to introduce new legislation and regulations in 1995 and 1996 which would tackle these problems. First, staffing in the Asylum Division of the Immigration and Nationality Department was increased to process the applications, and extra adjudicators were appointed to hear the cases. Further, the government introduced a shortened appeal procedure in March 1995, which was subsequently extended to nearly all asylum appeal applicants under the 1996 Asylum and Immigration Act.

The second major feature of the 1996 Act was the list of 'safe countries' – usually known as the 'white list' – from which asylum applications would not normally be considered, or whose claims would be regarded as 'without foundation' and susceptible to fast-track appeals. The other major feature was the removal of most social welfare benefits from asylum-seekers who applied for asylum in-country. Originally the government attempted to bring in these changes by regulation, rather than by legislation, but after being successfully challenged in the courts, they incorporated these proposals into the new Asylum and Immigration Bill which became law in July 1996.

It became evident very quickly that the new Act did not solve any of the major problems. In particular, the number of asylum-seekers still continued to increase, and the waiting times for decisions on both the initial applications and on appeals rose. Second, the withdrawal of social welfare benefits from those asylum-seekers who were already in the country was in effect rendered invalid by decisions in the courts, which placed the obligations of welfare support for asylum-seekers onto the local authorities.

Following the 1997 election, the new Labour government at first hinted at some possible relaxation in the new asylum legislation.[1] However it was clear, early in the administration, that they were not prepared to reverse the previous government's policies until they had undertaken a review of all asylum procedures.[2] By mid-July 1998, elements of the new policies were gradually being leaked to the press. Finally a White Paper outlining the major changes to the immigration and asylum system was published in late July (Home Office 1998). The general response to the White Paper, including that of most of the press, was mainly positive. Although there was criticism, especially of the new social welfare measures, most of these critics were to be found outside the main political process and the media, mainly in the NGOs and other social welfare bodies.

It therefore came as little surprise that the legislation proposed in the new Immigration and Asylum Bill in early 1999 followed closely the proposals echoed in the White Paper. The key features of the bill affecting asylum-seekers were: a national welfare support system for asylum-seekers while they await a decision on their applications; the creation of a 'one stop' right of appeal for asylum-seekers; and allowing bail hearings from detained asylum-seekers; but on the other hand giving immigration officers new powers to enter and search premises and arrest asylum-seekers, in some cases without a warrant.

Research on refugees, asylum-seekers and the press

There has been relatively little serious analysis of the press treatment of refugees and asylum-seekers. Studies such as those of Tomasi (1993) and Brosius and Eps (1995) can be regarded as either rather general or lacking much specificity for the United Kingdom. Coleman carried out an analysis of the UK press for a short period in 1995. This pioneering work, while of interest, was rather limited and lacked much analytical quality. In addition, it covered a wider focus than refugees and asylum-seekers, and was as much concerned with the broader issues of immigration and race relations (Coleman 1995).

The work of Winstanley-Torode focused more on a very specific period (October 1997) and on a specific group of asylum-seekers, namely the Czech and Slovak Roma. Winstanley-Torode's approach combined both a content and qualitative approach and argued that the coverage of the press was 'largely stereotypical, sensationalist and inflammatory and contained signs of a moral panic' (Winstanley-Torode 1998: 3). However, whilst I would agree with much of Winstanley-Torode's analysis of this episode, it also has to be recognised that this group of asylum-seekers was from a specific background suffering from long-term historical and cultural prejudice in Europe. There are therefore problems in generalising their press treatment to that of the bulk of asylum-seekers who have come to the UK in recent times, particularly in the last decade. Clark (1998), also focusing on the Roma, argued that 'discrimination, politics and various associated factors have led to a situation whereby population figures for one of the most discriminated-against ethnic minority groups are unknown, manipulated and contested' (Clark 1998: 35). Although there were some brief references to the press in this article, the main focus was on general discrimination towards the Roma people and the unsatisfactory population statistics in relation to this discrimination.

Ali and Gibb (1999) used the well-developed method of content analysis, which had been widely used in relation to race by previous authors, in their analysis of the treatment of ethnic minorities. However Ali and Gibb argued that the earlier approaches which depicted ethnic minorities either as 'invisible' or as 'problems' were insufficient. They maintained: 'One must also take into account a more complex and nuanced picture of Britain as a diverse society (which) is now reflected in the ... press' (Ali and Gibb 1999). While accepting this point may be valid in relation to ethnic minorities, there is the tendency on the part of Ali and Gibb, and by many other commentators, to conflate issues of racism and the treatment of ethnic minorities with those relating to asylum-seekers (Kaye 1994). Further, although in part their study dealt with a few of the issues that are central to this chapter, above all the treatment by the press of asylum-seekers and refugees in the UK, the coverage is limited in terms of the period being examined, namely events in 1998.

In the next two major sections of the chapter the press treatment of refugees and asylum-seekers is examined in more detail. The first section describes research by the author using a quantitative approach to analyse the use of terms which reflect questioning of the refugee and asylum-seekers' status. This analysis is presented under a number of subheads. The succeeding main section describes a more qualitative analysis, and considers the emergence of a number of themes that have been prevalent in the press coverage of asylum-seekers and refugees throughout the 1990s.

The representation of refugees and asylum-seekers, 1990–96

This section describes two studies which focused on the questioning of the status of refugees in terms of the UN convention as interpreted by the UK authorities; that is, questioning whether they were genuinely driven from their home country by persecution, or whether they were more economically motivated. This was approached through analysis of the language used by the newspapers in relation to this topic. The terms studied were: 'bogus' and 'phoney' refugees or asylum-seekers; 'economic migrants'; and 'economic refugees'.[3] While they vary in the degree of pejorativeness, they have the same implication, namely that the individuals referred to are not in reality refugees, and that their wish to enter the UK is due to a desire to improve their economic circumstances.

Seven newspapers were selected to span the political spectrum. Four were broadsheets: *The Times,* generally seen as a moderately conservative newspaper; the *Guardian,* noted for its more liberal views; the *Independent,* which claims freedom from political influence or affiliation; and the *Daily Telegraph,* a broadsheet paper of consistent right-wing views, and generally negative in its approach to immigration issues. In addition, three tabloids were surveyed. These were the *Daily Mail*, a middle-market right-wing conservative paper; the *Sun*, which is the highest circulation tabloid newspaper, with traditionally strong right-wing views including negative views about immigration; and the *Daily Mirror*, the second highest circulation tabloid, which has traditionally supported the Labour Party.[4]

Utilising the methodology developed in my earlier published research (Kaye 1998), a newspaper entry was included in the study if it met the following criteria. First, it had to concern the entry of asylum-seekers to the UK. Second, it had to contain one or more of the following expressions:

- phoney or bogus refugee(s) or asylum-seeker(s);
- economic migrant(s) (when referring to refugees or asylum-seekers);
- economic refugee(s).

The analytical questions posed were as follows:

1 What is the overall frequency of the use of each expression?
2 What form do the items take, e.g. editorial, letter, article etc.?
3 In what way is the language itself framed, i.e. to what extent is the writer making use of the language in their own writing, and to what extent are they reflecting or reporting its use by politicians or others? In addition is there any commentary in newspapers about the actual use of the language?
4 How does this use of language reflect the newspaper's political orientation and its tabloid or broadsheet status?

Frequency of use of terms

The frequency of use varied widely between the newspapers. The highest was the *Independent* with 116 selections, the *Guardian* was next with 96, the *Mail* third with 80, and *The Times* fourth with 70 selections. Although the *Telegraph* recorded only 28 selections, the period covered for this paper was only from 1995 onwards; a proportional grossing-up calculation would produce a similar figure to that of *The Times*.

One surprising finding was that, over the period studied, no meaningful analysis was possible for either the *Sun* or *Mirror*, as only five entries were found for the *Sun*, and just one for the *Daily Mirror*. It is possible that the fact that these were manually searched, rather than via a database, led to some data being omitted. However it is unlikely that this would explain such dramatic differences. A more plausible explanation for the *Sun* is that it may have utilised much stronger language and also that it conflated differences in terminology between 'refugees' on the one hand and 'immigrants' on the other. It had been noted in a previous study (Kaye 1994) that the *Sun* frequently referred to refugees as immigrants without any attempt to make distinctions. A consideration of some

Sun headlines during the period September–December 1995 supports the proposition of stronger and conflated terminology. Headlines included: 'Fines for hiring illegal workers'; 'Mad Somalians £183,000, The Samaritans £30,000'; and 'Smash the immigrant smugglers' (Coleman 1995). Therefore a different, more qualitative, approach to studying the portrayal of refugees would have to be taken in the case of newspapers, such as the *Sun,* which trade on strong and sensationalistic language.

In the case of the *Mirror,* a possible explanation, supported by less systematic observation, is that the newspaper ignored refugee and asylum issues. Although traditionally a more left-wing newspaper, the fact that its readership is thought to be generally negative about immigration could lead to it resolving this tension by not reporting these issues in any detail. Further the *Mirror,* when referring to asylum-seekers, often conflated the issue with ethnic relations. Thus in an article on the Asylum Bill the *Mirror* headline read: 'Major spurns Blair plea on race laws: John Major has rejected calls to take race off the election agenda'.[5]

Therefore, given the paucity of the use of terms by the *Sun* and the *Mirror,* the quantitative analysis only covers the *Guardian, Independent, Times, Telegraph* and *Mail.*

Type of item

It could be argued that the significance of some types of newspaper item may be greater than others, in terms both of their relationship to the newspaper's attitude and of their potential influence on the reader. The content of letters is likely to be a less significant indication of the newspaper's approach to a subject (although historically *The Times* may be an exception) than is either the content of an article or report, or an editorial which explicitly states the newspaper's views.

Of the five newspapers analysed, in four there was a broadly similar distribution. For example in the *Independent,* which had the greatest number of selections (116), over 50 per cent were reports, 5 per cent were editorials, 17 per cent were letters, and 30 per cent were articles (numbers rounded to the nearest percentage). However, the pattern of appearance in the *Mail* is different to that of the other newspapers, with a higher frequency found in editorials. There was in addition a stronger pattern of dual appearance in articles or reports and in editorials in the same issue.

Use of different expressions

Overwhelmingly the most widely used expression was 'bogus' or 'phoney'. The greatest user was the *Mail,* which used the expression nearly 90 per cent of the time. The frequency descended to 56 per cent in the *Independent.* Conversely the term 'economic migrants' (as applied to refugees) was much less frequently used and there was a different pattern across the newspapers. The *Independent* used this term 35 per cent of the time, the *Mail* at the other end of the scale only used it in 4 per cent of entries. However, for the purposes of this analysis, the data on the terms 'bogus' and 'phoney', which are judged to have almost identical significance, were aggregated.[6]

I would argue that the terms 'bogus' or 'phoney' could be considered more directly insulting and potentially harmful to the public perception of refugees than other terms which questioned their status. These terms, as we have already noted, together made up the highest proportion of use of all the expressions. While this is evident in all the newspapers, it is the most evident in the *Mail*.

Extent of criticism of use of language

The pattern of the use of the terms is noteworthy, particularly taken in conjunction with the overall frequency of type of item. There are clear differences between the newspapers in the extent to which the use of the expressions is in the context of criticising their application, or reporting criticism of their use by others. The *Guardian, Independent* and *Times* all criticise or report criticism to a significant extent with, for example, around a third of the total use in this context being in the *Guardian* and *Independent*. This would be consistent with either their liberal or 'independent' stance and with the fact that they were critical of government policy on refugees. A typical example of the quotation of criticism was the comment by Claude Moraes, then general secretary of the Joint Council for the Welfare of Immigrants (JCWI), who was quoted by the *Independent*: 'What gets me is that the government has fixed the system so that people in real fear of their lives are classed as bogus'.[7] In contrast, the *Telegraph* and *Mail* rarely criticised or reported criticism of the use of the expressions.

Original usage of language

One key question concerns the relative primacy of the press in setting agendas and framing news about refugees and asylum-seekers. The articles were therefore coded as to whether the author of the article (nearly all were journalists) made direct use of the expressions, or whether the use was in quotation of another person. The question was further posed as to who was the original user of the expression, distinguishing original use by a politician or government official from use by others.

Again there was a clear difference between the newspapers in the extent to which the journalists were using the expressions themselves, or were reporting their use by others. The *Guardian* and *Independent* were partly originating the expressions (43 per cent and 51 per cent respectively), and partly reporting their use by others (49 per cent and 51 per cent respectively), most frequently a UK politician or government official. However in *The Times, Telegraph* and *Mail*, it was more common for the journalist to simply write the expressions rather than refer to their use by others. This was most evident in the *Mail* in which 85 per cent of use was by the writer.

Summary of similarities and differences between newspapers

While some difficulties in interpretation arise from differences in the availability of data for each newspaper, nevertheless some striking patterns do emerge from the above analysis. In some cases the differences could be seen as lying along a broadly 'left-wing/right-wing' dimension (although this is usually an imperfect construct), and in others the *Mail* stands out as quite distinctive from the other newspapers.

For example, all the newspapers made more frequent use of the more pejorative terms 'bogus' and 'phoney', than the possibly less damaging 'economic migrants' or 'economic refugees'. However, the context of use was different. The *Guardian*, *Independent* and *Times* were frequently quoting politicians or government officials when they applied the terms and, in the case of the *Guardian* and *Independent*, were often criticising or reporting criticism of their use. In contrast, in the *Telegraph* and *Mail*, the journalists were largely using the terms themselves rather than quoting others, and made virtually no criticism of their use. The pattern for *The Times* was more varied, with more frequent use by the journalist, but some criticism of use, though somewhat less than the *Guardian* and *Independent*. However, it may also reflect the more careful use of language on the part of broadsheet editors.

The *Mail* was also distinctive as it made more use of the terms in editorials than other newspapers. It could be argued that this is a clearer barometer of the newspaper's attitude to refugees, especially as the *Mail* at times also published a report and then reinforced it in an editorial in the same issue. A typical example of this pattern was to be found in June 1996. The *Mail* reported the decision of the appeal court to overturn the government regulations removing emergency council housing for asylum-seekers. This report was then reinforced in an editorial on the same day headed 'No benefit for bogus refugees', which stated, 'For too long Britain has been regarded as a soft touch by bogus asylum-seekers. That is why the government brought in regulations to deny benefits to all foreigners who claim asylum ... but ... the court of appeal ... ruled that ministers have exceeded their powers.' The editorial concluded, 'The mind boggles ... indeed our guess is that most citizens will be positively outraged that judges can so block the declared will of parliament.'[8]

While most of the newspapers used the terms, the attitudes expressed were quite different, and it could be argued that the impact on the reader's attitude to refugees may also be different. However it is necessary to be cautious in drawing such an assumption. As argued elsewhere (Kaye 1998), the strongest impact may be through the frequent use of these expressions, regardless of context, with the reader becoming socialised to reading them, and coming to assume that the 'genuineness' of refugees is a significant question.

Press discourse on refugees and asylum-seekers, 1997–98

The second study focuses on a number of themes which emerged both from the research described in the preceding section and from preliminary analysis of the data for 1997–98. The analysis used for this study drew mainly on the perspective that the news is 'a frame through which reality is socially constructed' (Tuchman 1978: 2). The selection and presentation of news are seen as all important – indeed some writers talk of 'the manufacturing of news' (Cohen and Young 1973). The analysis draws on newspaper coverage of refugees and asylum-seekers during this period, but more specifically during two shorter periods. The first period, during October 1997, became known in the press as the 'gypsy invasion'. The second period covers a longer time-frame of June–July 1998, but specifically focuses on the press reaction to an Immigration Service Union (ISU) report, which came out in June 1998, and the period leading up to the publication of the White Paper on Asylum in late July (Home Office 1998).

Four themes were considered:

1 the 'genuineness' of asylum-seekers' claims (using a more qualitative approach than in the first study);
2 the social welfare problem;
3 the 'numbers game';
4 racism/xenophobia.

The same seven newspapers that were analysed in the previous section were searched again.[9] The time periods were two weeks in October 1997, and the two months between the beginning of June and the end of July 1998. The newspapers were analysed in terms of references to asylum-seekers and/or refugees either in the headlines or the text. After the references were identified, they were further refined by eliminating those which did not refer to refugees and asylum-seekers in the UK. Six of the newspapers were searched by means of CD ROMs; the *Sun* was only available manually.

The 'gypsy invasion', October 1997

This nearly two-week period became known in the tabloid press as the 'gypsy invasion'.[10] Whilst the broadsheets, whatever their political orientation, attempted to separate news from analysis, and also tended to use language more carefully, the tabloids were more blatant in their approach, both in terms of clear political bias and as regards their journalistic treatment of the material.

Genuineness of asylum-seekers' claims

There was surprisingly wide consensus by most sections of the press, both tabloid and broadsheet, including those normally sympathetic to the plight of asylum-seekers, in portraying the Roma as illegitimate asylum-seekers. The *Mail* ran the headline 'The Dover deluge' (20 October 1997) and the article that followed referred to the 'flood of bogus asylum-seekers swamping Dover'. It also quoted the then Conservative Shadow Home Secretary, Brian Mawhinney, who said, 'the so-called refugees should be sent straight back to France'. Later in the article the paper referred to other asylum-seekers as 'would-be immigrants'. The *Independent*, unusually, led with a fairly provocative headline: 'Gypsies invade Dover hoping for a handout' (20 October 1997). Later during this period, the *Independent* referred to measures taken by the Home Secretary to restrict entry and speed up the procedures in the headline 'New curbs on bogus asylum seekers' (28 October 1997). Although the term bogus was put in inverted commas in the article, the headline did not have this qualification. Only the *Guardian* which, along with the *Independent*, had usually taken a more liberal approach, took a less alarmist approach to the Roma influx – at least in their headlines; for example 'Homeseeker' (20 October 1997). However, even in some of the *Guardian* articles, journalists tended to emphasise negative aspects of the asylum-seekers (see, for example, Bellos 1997). Subsequently the Home Office made clear its opposition to the use of the word 'bogus', preferring to use the word 'abusive', and this term too was reiterated during this whole period – for instance by the *Independent* (28 October 1997).

The social welfare problem

As demonstrated in other research (Kaye 1999), the issue of social welfare payments had already risen high on the political agenda in 1995–96. In anticipation of legislation on asylum-seekers, the Conservative government singled out the attractiveness of UK social welfare benefits as a major factor leading to an influx of asylum-seekers. However by the time the first major Roma influx arrived in September 1997, the issue of welfare support for asylum-seekers had, as already indicated, been put in abeyance by the new Labour government. An inter-departmental body was preparing a White Paper on the whole issue of asylum-seekers. In particular they were given the remit to sort out the 'shambles'.[11]

This was given added emphasis when it was alleged that a TV programme shown in Czechoslovakia, emphasising the generosity of welfare benefits, was a major catalyst in attracting Roma refugees to the UK (see Alec Hargreaves' account of this in Chapter 2). In an article in *The Times* (26 May 1998) published several months after the 'invasion', the paper argued that a Czech documentary in autumn 1997 about Canada prompted more than 600 Roma to set off to North America: several hundred made for Britain after a similar report suggested that they could expect generous social assistance. Except for the *Guardian*, nearly every article or news item in the press stressed the cost of the increased numbers on social welfare and housing benefits. The *Sun*, for example, claimed in a headline (20 October 1997) that it was costing the UK already £20 million, and made it fairly clear to readers that the Roma were here solely because of the benefits.

The *Mail* in particular emphasised this alleged causal relationship in an article whose whole tone emphasised the social welfare motives (20 October 1997). It began, 'We examine why thousands of Czech and Slovak gipsies (*sic*) are now claiming political asylum in Britain.' The article then set out to describe life for the Roma in Czechoslovakia, including the persecution and racism directed towards them. However, it then went on to describe what it called the 'gipsies most lucrative scam [which] involves claiming benefits in both Dover and London'. The article claimed to deny any prejudice but concluded by asking, 'How long before the other million gipsies ... abandon their grinding poverty and head towards Dover?'

Even the *Mirror* which, as I have already noted, tended not to comment on refugee and asylum issues, could not resist the temptation to join in the debate. While the tone of the *Mirror* article was not hostile, it repeated the story that the influx was set off after a TV documentary told of Britain's 'generous' benefits system (21 October 1997). Only an article in the *Guardian* (22 October 1997) put a contrary view, pointing out the unlikelihood of several hundred people uprooting themselves and moving across Europe on the basis of a TV programme.

The 'numbers game'

Colin Clark's (1998) article quotes Paul Gordon's warning that, 'whilst accurate figures may very well help with general fact-finding to inform government policy and bring about social reform, we need to bear in mind the political context within which such data are used [and be aware] of the potential abuse of statistics as well as problems of definition' (Gordon 1996: 30–5; see also Travis 1998). As Clark sharply observes, the use of numbers and the language associated with it become very clear by the reporting in the press, and terms such as 'exodus', 'flood' and 'invasion' become the standard descriptors (Clark 1998: 2).

During this period the press indulged in a kind of game in which each tried to out-bid the other in reporting the numbers of Roma arriving in Dover, thereby emphasising the 'invasion'. Although the actual numbers of Czech and Slovak Roma were approximately 170 in October (excluding dependants),[12] the various newspaper estimates of numbers varied widely. The *Guardian* and *Independent* reported under 200 (21 October 1997), *The Times* 800 (21 October 1997), the *Telegraph* 800 and '3,000 on the way' (21 October 1997), the *Mirror* 800 and 'the final figure could reach 3,000' (21 October 1997), and the *Sun* '3,000 head for England' (20 October 1997). The *Mail* also reflected the confusion and over-exaggeration by using various numbers during this period ranging from 600 to 3,000 and hinting ominously that 'there are a million more where they came from' (20 October 1997).

Racism/xenophobia

As noted above, the portrayal of Roma as 'social welfare spongers' was quite common among some sections of the press, either by direct use of such terms or implicitly. Even more inflammatory were the 'vox pop' interviews with the general public which a number of papers used. Phrases such as 'shoot them all' or 'put 'em on a boat and ship them back' or 'we should dump them in the English channel' and 'they steal – not that I've met any myself' were not uncommon.[13] These comments were part of the overt racist tendencies which a number of the leading figures of the refugee NGOs commented they had not seen for many years. As the *Guardian* observed, 'It would be an interesting exercise to go through this week's papers substituting the word Jew for gypsies. One thing it would do is make clear that the anti-Romany campaign is specifically racist.'[14] This analysis was supported by elements of the ethnic minorities press. For instance, the *Voice* argued: 'All the racism that the national press feels too ashamed to express about Black people, it felt free to aim at the Gypsies' (27 October 1997).

Press comment on the White Paper on Asylum, June–August 1998

The second period analysed starts with comment on issues relating to the Immigration Services Union (ISU) report in early June 1998 and continues through the early leaks on the impending White Paper on Immigration and Asylum to its publication (Home Office 1998) and the initial commentary on the document. As noted earlier, the new Labour government had set up a wide-ranging review of all aspects of the asylum process in the summer of 1997, although this was increasingly delayed because of the comprehensive spending review.

Genuineness of asylum-seekers' claims

The Immigration Services Union is a trade union, with the majority of immigration officers within their ranks, and known to be hostile to a more liberal regime towards immigrants, refugees and asylum-seekers. In June 1998, it published a report to which the press gave wide coverage (Immigration Services Union 1998). The report made it clear that the status and genuineness of asylum-seekers were, in the view of the union, highly suspect. According to John Tincey, a spokesman for the ISU, 'people who arrive can say the magic word 'asylum' and automatically get right of entry. Once in the system they get married, which allows them to stay, or they just disappear.'[15] As *The Times* (7 June 1998) commented, 'The report blamed organised gangs with supplying thousands of fortune-seekers with false documents.' The *Sun* in typical manner seized on the report and repeatedly referred to 'bogus' asylum-seekers (8 June 1998). Likewise the *Mail* used the report to criticise the government's handling of asylum, stating they had 'gone soft on immigration' (8 June 1998). The

Telegraph, in an editorial commenting on the report, also raised the 'genuineness' issue, although recognising that 'bogus asylum seekers are by no means the only illicit migrants reaching Britain' (8 June 1998).

There was little evidence of a counter-challenge to these reports within the press itself, and the Refugee Council was stung into action by issuing its own press release to counter the claims of the ISU. Its chief executive, Nick Hardwick, also wrote to the newspapers to refute the ISU report. On the issue of 'genuineness' the Refugee Council pointed out that the ISU claim that only 6 per cent of seekers are awarded asylum was inaccurate and that, in 1997, 24 per cent were granted refugee status or exceptional leave to remain.[16]

When the White Paper was about to be published, under the title *Fairer, Faster, Firmer* (Home Office 1998), the government, concerned at the reaction of the press, particularly the tabloid press, not only leaked some details early, but ensured that the date of its formal release to the press coincided with the first Labour government reshuffle, on which it was apparently hoped that media attention would be more focused.[17] Thus on the Sunday/Monday before the White Paper was to be formally published, some newspapers took up a number of the themes. References to 'bogus' migrants and asylum-seekers were common (*Mail on Sunday, Sunday Mirror* and *Sunday Times*, 26 July 1998). By 27 July (the date of official publication), most of the details of the White Paper had already been leaked to the press. In a television interview, the Home Secretary stated that he was going to get 'tougher' with asylum-seekers. Utilising the technique of personal anecdote as a justification for the proposals, the Home Secretary stated, 'As a constituency MP, I am seeing a great growth of people abusing the asylum system' (*Times*, 27 July 1998).

Meanwhile, press editorials suggested that the White Paper had in effect announced an 'amnesty' for nearly 30,000 asylum-seekers to allow the backlog to be cleared up more quickly. This the Home Secretary vehemently denied (*Times*, 27 July 1998). The *Independent* commented, 'while the term amnesty may be politically unacceptable to the government, the Home Office comments may still allow for a regulation of the status of pre-1993 cases (10,000 cases) to allow them to stay' (27 July 1998). A number of papers pointed out that an additional 20,000 others, who had made applications between July 1993 and December 1995, and who had established ties in the UK, would be granted leave to remain for at least four years (*Times, Independent, Daily Telegraph*, 28 July 1998). Claude Moraes commented that it was 'an amnesty in all but name' (*Daily Telegraph*, 28 July 1998). As might be expected, the *Mail* and *Telegraph* led with this aspect of the new proposals, portraying it as a concession borne out of necessity to clear the backlog, but raising doubts as to whether the 30,000 asylum-seekers could all be classified as genuine (*Mail*, 26 July 1998; *Telegraph*, 27 July 1998). The *Guardian* referred more positively to a 'limited amnesty' (28 July 1998).

The social welfare problem

The issue of social welfare was one that had been highly sensitive for both the previous Conservative government and also for the new Labour administration. The Labour government was acutely aware that the current welfare support system which had evolved from legal challenges to the previous proposals of the Conservative government – and which in effect made the local authorities responsible for the welfare of asylum-seekers – was unsatisfactory to all parties (Kaye 1999). Thus when the ISU report claimed that the cost of asylum-seekers arriving in the UK would reach over £2 billion in 1998, a figure four times the government's previous estimates,[18] those hostile to asylum-seekers took this as a reliable estimate (*Daily Telegraph*, 8 June 1998). The Home Office responded by claiming that the figures were 'scaremongering' (*Express*, 8 June 1998). When the Home Office Minister stated in Parliament that the cost was actually £500 million, the ISU disputed this, and repeated their own higher figures (*Daily Telegraph*, 12 June 1998).

It was therefore widely anticipated that the cost of social welfare was one of the key issues which the long-awaited White Paper would address. The solution to this problem was to give back to central government the responsibility for the welfare of asylum-seekers. However, from the way that social welfare issues were portrayed by the Home Secretary in Parliament, it was clear that this was to be seen as a 'tough' approach, especially with regard to housing (*Times*, 28 July 1998). This approach won plaudits from the more conservative press; the *Telegraph* (28 July 1998) commented, 'We are happy to congratulate him for apparently toughening his approach to bogus asylum seekers.' However the White Paper proposals were criticised by the refugee NGOs. The Refugee Council referred to the new support arrangements as 'costly, cumbersome and chaotic' (*Guardian*, 28 July 1998). Claude Moraes, of the JCWI, said the package was 'more tough than fair. Asylum seekers need money not vouchers, because it gives them dignity and independence' (*Independent*, 28 July 1998). The strongest criticism was voiced by an editorial in the *Independent* which described the White Paper as 'flawed, fudged and feeble' (28 July 1998).

The 'numbers game'

The ISU report gave rise to a number of factually correct press comments that the numbers of asylum-seekers were increasing (*Daily Telegraph*, 7 June 1998). However, there was dispute over the actual rate of increase, with the ISU reporting a 22 per cent increase, while the Refugee Council argued that they had only increased by 9 per cent. The White Paper then gave further opportunity for most newspapers to comment on the number of asylum-seekers.

As already noted, an 'amnesty' was considered to bring down the backlog that the *Mail* insisted would be 'a blitz to clear approximately 75,000 bogus asylum seekers harbouring in the UK' (*Mail on Sunday*, 26 July 1998). There was also comment on the numbers applying for asylum. The *Mail* (27 July

1998) alleged that numbers in 1998 were running 25 per cent up on the previous year's figures (32,500). Several newspapers, drawing on the figures published in the White Paper, pointed out that, if current trends continued, there would be 50,000 applying for asylum by 2001 (*Times*, 28 July 1998). However some newspapers, notably the *Independent*, treated the numbers in a less provocative manner, and commented generally on the positive benefits of migration (*Independent*, 29 July 1998).

Racism/xenophobia

There were relatively few examples of overt racism/xenophobia during this period. Perhaps this is partially explained by the press's critical reflection on their previous coverage of the Roma 'invasion' in 1997.[19] Thus, when both the ISU report and the White Paper were published in mid-1998, little evidence of overt racism could be observed in the press. The mainly legal-administrative nature of the White Paper and the specific nature of its proposals did not engender much critical comment from those sections of the press which were usually unfavourable towards asylum-seekers and more inclined to voice racist views. Indeed, the Home Secretary's proposals appeared to be more positively viewed by this section of the media than by the more liberal elements. Nevertheless although later events are outside this period of analysis, it should be noted that when there was a renewed influx of Roma into the UK in the autumn of 1998, both the *Mail* and especially the *Telegraph* returned to the attack, with reporting and comment in a very similar tone to that of 1997 (see *Independent*, 19 September 1998; Ali and Gibb 1999: 132).

Conclusions

A decade ago there was relatively little published either in the academic literature or reported in the press about the treatment of refugees and asylum-seekers, as distinct from ethnic minorities (Miles and Kay 1992). Discussions of immigration very rarely referred to refugees, and even then, only as a minor postscript to UK postwar immigration. In the British press there was little understanding of or knowledge about refugees and asylum-seekers, and this also reflected the general ignorance displayed by the major political elites or political parties when discussing their situation. Now there is growing recognition of the 'newsworthiness' of asylum-seekers.

In addition, there is a tendency for television to take its cues from the morning paper headlines, as do the political elites who are increasingly sensitive to the agendas of newspaper coverage. Therefore the idea has gained ground that the media aim to frame the political agenda; that is, they influence not what people think, but what they think about (McCombs and Shaw 1993). However this view is somewhat over-simplified, and this chapter has attempted to show the more complex relationship between political elites and newspapers in setting and framing the refugee agenda.

In terms of the use of language and themes, one of the most recent developments has been the very demotion of the term 'asylum-seeker' itself.[20] It has become apparent that the term is increasingly being used almost as a term of abuse in the media, and that those who are seeking asylum are seen as in effect asking for something to which they are not entitled, whereas the term 'refugee' is still seen as having a legitimate status, and those fleeing from conflict should be offered refuge. It was interesting to observe these terminological distinctions in relation to Kosovans; before the recent Balkan conflict, they were usually referred to as 'asylum-seekers', but with the outbreak of war they became 'refugees' (Greenslade 1999).

To conclude on a much broader point, a decade of reporting and coverage has not significantly improved either the knowledge about or the level of analysis of the plight of refugees and asylum-seekers. Too often, either out of laziness or, more dangerously, as a form of racism/xenophobia, the press mistreats the subject. If these practices persist, the continued scapegoating of some of the most vulnerable victims of modern conflict will be unavoidable.

NOTES

1 See the *Independent*, 29 May 1997.

2 *Migration Newsheet*, September 1997.

3 The frequent use of such language had already been reported in my earlier study on political parties and the refugee agenda (Kaye 1994); in addition, the use of these terms has been widely commented on by others, e.g. Le Lohe (1992) and Young (1998).

4 The long time-frame – covering many thousands of issues of the various newspapers – demanded, where possible, access to newspapers through electronic rather than manual methods. This limited to some extent the availability of data. CD ROMs/ FT databases were available for *The Times, Independent* and *Guardian* for the whole time period, for the *Telegraph* from July 1995, and for the *Daily Mail* from January 1993 (a selective manual search for 1990–93 was also carried out). However it was considered crucial to access a wider range of tabloid newspapers, including those which were not available on either CD ROM or FT database. Therefore searches were commissioned on the *Daily Mirror* and the *Sun* from the FT Business Research Centre, who used their own manual sources to identify articles covering the relevant theme of refugee access to the UK, and to identify and provide copies of any articles that used the key terms. These different methods used to access the data must be taken into account when interpreting the findings from the quantitative analysis, as it is possible that they may have varied in comprehensiveness.

5 *Sunday Mirror*, 19 November 1995.

6 It should also be noted that more than one term was used in some articles.

7 *Independent*, 22 June 1996.

8 See the *Mail*, 26 June 1996.

9 A few examples from other newspapers were also used where it was thought that they added to the analysis.

10 Although I will use the term Roma, which has now been accepted as the most appropriate way to describe the specific group of asylum-seekers who were trying to

claim asylum in October 1997, the more commonly used term, especially by the newspapers, was either gipsy or gypsy, and this remains in quotes from the press.

11 Jack Straw's favourite term to describe the existing arrangements; see the *Mirror*, 13 May 1998.

12 Home Office figures show the numbers of Czech and Slovak nationals applying for asylum for the whole year of 1997 were 240 and 255 respectively, excluding dependants; see Home Office Research and Statistics Directorate, *Asylum Applications Received in the United Kingdom for 1997*, London: The Stationery Office, 14 July 1998.

13 Quotes taken from *The Observer*, 26 October 1997; *Daily Telegraph*, 25 October 1997; *Independent on Sunday*, 26 October 1997.

14 See *Guardian*, 25 October 1997; also, on refugee leaders' comments, *Guardian*, 22 October 1997.

15 Quoted in *Sunday Times*, 7 June 1998.

16 Refugee Council Press Release, 9 June 1998; *The Times*, 21 June 1998.

17 *The Economist*, 1–7 August 1998.

18 As well as social welfare benefits, these figures also included legal aid, education and medical expenses. *Sunday Times*, 7 June 1998.

19 See *Guardian*, 25 October 1997, and the criticisms from the Commission for Racial Equality and the Press Complaints Council quoted in Winstanley-Torode (1998: 39).

20 I am grateful to Tammy Speers, a postgraduate student at the University of Cardiff, for drawing my attention to this change in the use of language, email correspondence, July 1999.

References

Ali, Y. and Gibb, P. (1999) 'Le racisme, le droit d'asile et la presse britannique', *Migrations Société* 11, 62: 123–34.

Bellos, A. (1997) 'Tide of gypsy asylum seekers ebbs', *Guardian*, 20 October.

Brosius, H.-B. and Eps, P. (1995) 'Prototyping through key events: news selection in the case of violence against aliens and asylum seekers in Germany', *European Journal of Communication* 10, 3: 391–412.

Clark, C. (1998) 'Counting backwards: the Roma "numbers game" in Central and Eastern Europe', *Radical Statistics* 69: 35–46.

Cohen, S. and Young, J. (eds) (1973) *The Manufacture of the News: Social Problems, Deviance and the Media*, London: Constable.

Coleman, P. (1995) 'Survey of asylum coverage in the national daily press', *The Runnymede Bulletin* 291: 6–7.

Gordon, P. (1996) 'The racialisation of statistics', in Skellington, R. (ed.), *Race in Britain*, London: Sage Publications/Open University.

Greenslade, R. (1999) 'When is a refugee not a refugee?' *Guardian*, 12 April.

Home Office (1998) *Fairer, Faster, Firmer – A Modern Approach to Immigration and Asylum*, London: The Stationery Office (Cm 4018).

Immigration Services Union (1998) *The Cost of Asylum Applications to the United Kingdom*, Harwich: ISU.

Kaye, R. (1994) 'Defining the agenda: British refugee policy and the role of parties', *Journal of Refugee Studies* 7, 2–3: 144–59.

—— (1998) 'UK media portrayal of asylum seekers', in Koser, K. and Lutz, H. (eds), *The New Migration in Europe: Social Constructions and Social Realities*, Basingstoke: Macmillan.

—— (1999) 'The politics of exclusion: the withdrawal of social welfare benefits from asylum seekers in the UK', *Contemporary Politics* 5, 1: 25–45.

Le Lohe, M. (1992) 'Political issues', *New Community* 18, 3: 469–74.

McCombs, M. and Shaw, D. (1993) 'The evolution of agenda setting research', *Journal of Communication* 43, 2: 58–67.

Miles, R. and Kay, D. (1992) *Refugees or Migrant Workers: European Volunteer Workers in Britain 1946–51*, London: Routledge.

Tomasi, S. (1993) 'Today's refugees and the media', *Migration World* 20, 5: 21–3.

Travis, A. (1998) 'Playing the numbers game', *Guardian*, 12 May.

Tuchman, G. (1978) *Making News: A Study in the Social Construction of Reality*, New York: The Free Press.

Winstanley-Torode, N. (1998) 'The gypsy invasion', unpublished MA dissertation in Human Rights, University of London.

Young, C. (1998) 'Political representations of geography and place in the introduction of the UK Asylum and Immigration Act (1996)', in Nicholson, F. and Twomey, P. (eds), *Current Issues of UK Asylum Law and Policy*, Aldershot: Ashgate.

5

PROTECTION OR HOSPITALITY

The young man and the illegal immigrant in
La Promesse

Mireille Rosello

Introduction

Before *La Promesse* was presented at Cannes, Jean-Pierre and Luc Dardennes, two Belgian directors who primarily specialised in non-fiction films, had failed to gain the recognition they deserve (Burdeau 1996; Derobert 1996). And yet, when the film was hailed by critics and by international audiences in 1996, the two directors were hardly beginners: their fiction films have inherited a sensitivity developed during the first phase of their career when they concentrated on a type of social cinema exemplified in their own documentaries[1] and in the work produced by their companies (Les Films du Fleuve and Dérives Productions). The quality of their cinematographic studies of blue-collar workers and of the urban underclass (especially around Seraing, a suburb of Liège) was largely ignored by the public although it was recognised, in 1997, by the 'European Documentary Award' for 'the excellence of their work, their social and human concern, and its research oriented spirit' (Dorzée 1999). Louis Honorez, commenting on the 'Palme d'or' awarded to their latest film *Rosetta* (1999), notes that 'many foreign journalists thought that *Rosetta* was only their second film after *La Promesse*' (Honorez 1999).

If *La Promesse* changed the course of the directors' career, it might be because the story of Igor, a young teenager (Jérémie Rénier) whose father is involved in the trafficking of immigrants, resonated powerfully in a European cultural echo chamber where the status of the foreigner has become a crucial issue. Francophone films of the last decade have reflected a general European interest in and concern for the 'stranger' whose presence in our cosmopolitan cities often represents the return of the colonial repressed. In France, the emergence of so-called 'banlieue films' and 'Beur' cinema, made both by children of immigrants[2] and by European directors,[3] has presented the public with a vision of life in suburbs where *métissage*, or rather ethnic and cultural cohabitation, is the norm rather than the exception (Bosséno 1992; Rosello 1998a: 65–82; Sherzer 1996; Tarr 1993).

With a few exceptions however,[4] French cinema has focused on what is commonly interpreted as 'the second generation' and it may take a while before directors choose to reflect on the most recent evolution of migration patterns: since '*l'affaire des sans-papiers de Saint-Bernard*' in 1996 (Rosello 1998b), it is clear that the figure of the undocumented immigrant (or *clandestins* as the administration and the media insisted on calling them) has become one of the most visible political icons. That *La Promesse* was released at the same time as the 'Saint-Bernard' crisis could be a good indication that the next generation of immigration films will concentrate on the issues raised by illegality and social precariousness rather than on the delicate and often problematic process of integration.

It should also be noted that *La Promesse* is exceptional in its decision to confront the issue of human trade. In the Dardennes' film, the hiring of undocumented labour is not a vague collective practice that takes place away from the camera and that journalists or politicians self-righteously condemn on the national news: Roger is one of the protagonists scrutinised by the film and his sordid activity is pictured down to the most gruesome practical details. The spectator, who is used to vague governmental promises about penalising anonymous people who encourage illegal immigrants by providing them with jobs, gets a completely different picture in *La Promesse* because the film refuses to treat the 'illegal immigrant' as a separable entity. This story is based on the premise that the 'illegal immigrant' should not be treated apart from the figure of the 'illegal employer' and it studies the evolution of one such tragic couple: Igor (Roger's son) and Assita, who have no choice but to become inseparable. *La Promesse* can thus be viewed as the exploration of how the relationship between the host and the guest, the native and the immigrant, must be reinvented if neither protagonist wants to see their humanity destroyed by pre-existing roles (the exploiter and the exploited, the cynical host and the victimised guest).

Interpreting *La Promesse*

At the beginning of the film, we discover that Igor's father, Roger (Oliver Gourmet), employs a few illegal immigrants and makes them work on the construction of his own future house. The episode that explains the title occurs towards the beginning of the film, when the workers are interrupted by the arrival of work inspectors who are obviously looking for irregularities. Alerted by his father, Igor warns all the men who are on the premises that day and they all run away. The migrants are well aware that the law penalises the illegal employer, but they are even more conscious of the fact that they, on the other hand, risk nothing less than deportation. But as he tries to jump from the scaffolding, one of the African immigrants, Hamidou, falls off the ladder and lies on the ground, severely wounded. In the few minutes that it takes Roger to get rid of the inspectors and to come back, Igor tries to help Hamidou, who makes him promise that he will take care of his wife, Assita (Assita Ouedraogo) and his baby son, who have just recently arrived in Belgium and who live in one of the squalid rented houses managed by Roger. That promise is the narrative engine of the film and the tragic crucible where hospitality will have to be redefined and reinvented by the characters.

For when Roger discovers how badly wounded Hamidou is, he adamantly refuses to take him to hospital for fear of legal complications. And in spite of his obvious reservations and long hesitations, Igor finally obeys his father when he orders him to help him hide the wounded man and, later, to bury his body under freshly mixed cement. It is not absolutely clear to me whether the African worker is really dead at that stage, and the rest of the film will continue to insist that something, in Hamidou, refuses to die.

There is no doubt that the episode is one of the most spectacular junctures of this uncompromising story but rather than concentrating on that specific moment, and rather than analysing the ways in which the directors have chosen to tell the visual story of a murder, I would like to explore the long-term consequences of Roger and Igor's act on the relationship between Assita, the immigrant, and Igor, the native host. After Hamidou's disappearance, Igor keeps his promise and takes care of his wife and son but, until the very end of the film, he does not tell her the truth. Assita will continue to believe that her husband has temporarily disappeared, and that he may have decided to go away of his own free will (gambling debts are conveniently suggested by Roger). Her ignorance puts her at a disadvantage and maintains an imbalance between her and Igor who, although doing everything he can to help her, will refuse, until the very last minutes of the film, to share the guilty secret that links him to his father like a perverse umbilical cord.

Remarkably, the film suggests that this belated revelation cannot constitute a narrative closure but it functions like a beginning, an open door: here, the end, in the form of a confession, is an inaugural gesture that allows both characters to enter the realm of shared hospitality between equals. The scene during which Igor finally tells the truth to Assita is crucial both from a dramatic and from a cinematographic perspective in that it defies the visual and narrative conventions that usually govern the topos of revelation and confession. For example, we could reasonably expect the sequence to be structured like a *face-à-face*, a confrontation where the two characters symbolise, respectively, the universe of home, legitimacy and power and that of homelessness, illegality and powerless-ness. This could be the moment when the two worlds slowly created by the film (Africa versus Europe, black versus white, man versus woman, employer versus employee, in a word, same versus other) are finally brought together: the two entities may be irreconcilable, but at least they are acknowledging each other's reality.

The directors, however, have opted out of that possibility and choose an unexpected way of filming this final dialogue. The last scene is not a conclusive discovery that puts an end to a long game of hide-and-seek but a strange ballet where one character is always positioned behind, and not facing, the other. Until that moment, the logic of the film has led us to believe that the secret of Hamidou's death would continue to function as the spring that keeps the plot moving: both characters are set in motion by this structuring absence that keeps them in a perpetual forward movement, a reverse migration away from the murderous father and employee. The destination of this trip is explained as a quest for safety and the desire for Assita to find a place where she can take care of her son without being threatened by Roger. After a few discussions with Igor and the rare characters who agree to help her along the way, it becomes clear that she has some relatives in Italy: this provides her with a new destination, her extended family weaving a tight network of solidarity across hostile national borders that are emotionally and politically irrelevant to her. Inverting a traditional and culturally meaningful axis of migration between Italy and Belgium,[5] Assita, who comes from a third country, would have to cross borders as an invisible pawn on the international chess board.

Hamidou's disappearance is thus the cause of new migrations. Ever since Igor and Assita have met, their relationship is based on a shared experience of forced exile. They travel together, they are constantly going somewhere else, sometimes turning in circles around the original place of the murder. At first, they have to run away from the father, Igor practically kidnapping Assita, who does not know that Roger is plotting to take her to Germany to sell her as a prostitute. After this initial flight, they stay together, hiding in the city except for a few incursions into institutional buildings where Assita's status has to be negotiated: they both go to the police station because Assita insists on reporting that her husband has gone missing, they must go to hospital when the baby becomes sick, they also consult an African traditional healer before returning to Igor's employer's flat where they will stay until being discovered by the father, whose threatening presence triggers another flight.

Apparently, the two characters stay together, but the film makes the point that they are not fellow travellers: they are separated by a narrative abyss. Igor knows that Hamidou is dead, whereas Assita wants to know what has happened to her husband. The film links their travelling to a metaphorical movement toward or away from the truth: Assita seeks to reach a coherent narrative that would explain Hamidou's absence whereas Igor is metaphorically running away from the telling. In other words, the film manages to suggest that two characters who seem to be travelling together are, in reality (and until the very last scene of the film), moving in opposite directions; or perhaps that their frantic and continual movements are compensated by the stubborn immobility of the plot in another domain – literally and figuratively, these two people are going nowhere because the only element that would create change remains unsaid, silence accumulating as a growing tension between them. Assita wants to know, Igor knows, but she does not know that he knows. And to complicate the issue, Igor's position forces him to reconcile two completely incompatible imperatives: his promise (Assita is under his protection) and the necessity to lie to her due to his own role as accomplice in Hamidou's murder, but also out of a sense of loyalty that prevents him from reporting his own father to the police.

I suggest that this split in Igor's consciousness has thought-provoking consequences for the spectator because it affects the European character rather than the immigrant: traditionally, the type of uncertain allegiance caused by 'double consciousness', 'creolisation' and 'hybridity' is expected to be the immigrants' province because they are supposed to bear the burden of integration (Bhabha 1994; Gilroy 1993; Glissant 1989). Linguistically, culturally and emotionally, the stranger is perceived as living in an ambiguous space that is described either as a 'neither here nor there' or sometimes, euphorically, as a 'both here and there'. Here, the impossibility to choose one side and the effects of 'double consciousness' rest squarely with the European character who is entirely responsible for the immigrant's situation. Assita's loyalty to her son and to her absent father is unproblematic and her relationship to her environment is tactical and practical: survival for herself and her infant.

Igor's contradictory desires are symbolised by his ambiguous attitude towards the truth: he wants to tell and at the same time he wants not to tell. He is terrified that Assita will discover the truth but at the same time, he would like her to find out. Both characters are tragically lonely but Igor is even more isolated than Assita because he alone carries the weight of the secret: during the whole film, he is seen carrying Assita's bag. The typical attribute of the immigrant is displaced onto him, as if the film wanted to suggest the impossibility of being immune from the fate of those whom the heroes treated as 'they' before Hamidou's death.

Their wandering through Liège is punctuated by key moments when Assita gets closer to the truth, to Igor's intense fear and dismay. Her desire to know, however, is thwarted, not only by Igor's silence but by the fact that her search produces a multiplicity of fragmented and complex narratives that she cannot correctly decipher. The tragically simple and brutal story ('Hamidou is dead') is withheld, its elements being replaced by sometimes accurate but incomplete versions provided by well-meaning friends or foes ('Hamidou has disappeared', 'he may or may not come back', 'he ran away from gambling debts', 'he is in Germany'). Each time, Igor witnesses the emergence of a story, placing the spectators (who share his knowledge) in the uncomfortable position of having to ask themselves if they would have done the same thing, who they would have protected, who they would have sided with. The situation brings home a dilemma that is supposedly reserved for the other, the stranger.

The entrails of a chicken sacrificed in Igor's presence by a seer thus reveal that Hamidou 'has not gone away and that he is not very far'. Technically, the chicken is right: Hamidou never decided to leave and he is buried on the premises. But only the spectator, now an accomplice of Igor's silence, knows that non-departure and proximity signify the confirmation of the worst rather than a glimmer of hope. The film does not blame Assita for relying on traditionally despised methods of truth-seeking but it shows that, like any narrative, the chicken's prediction is interpretable and over-determined by the context and by the characters' desire.

Even Assita's will to know is coloured by her own situation. In one of the worst episodes of the film, when two racists urinate on Assita and brutalise her, attacking her when she is at her most vulnerable because she fears for her sick child's life, the issue of the truth comes up once more: overwhelmed and distraught, Assita now begs Igor to tell her, not the truth, but the truth that she wants to hear. She wants him to say that Hamidou is not dead. At that moment, faced with a desperate plea, Igor deliberately chooses to continue to carry the burden of the secret. Their moment of complicity and solidarity is dependent on Igor's willingness to lie. And yet, when he least needs to speak, when the end of the film seems to promise the possibility of a definitive burial of the truth, he will decide against that closure.

It is true that the film as a whole constantly proposes and withdraws the hypothesis that a buried body can be hidden forever. Burying and the disappearance of the corpse is a structuring reference from the very beginning of the story, even before Hamidou's death. Chicago-based critic Jonathan Rosenbaum notices that the very first scene already establishes a parallel between crime and burial (Rosenbaum 1997). When we are first introduced to the young hero, the scenario hastens to suggest that Igor is not only a thief but a definitely unglamorous, cowardly and cynical character. At the petrol station where he works, he is asked to check the engine of an old woman's car and takes advantage of a few seconds inside the vehicle to steal her wallet on the passenger's seat. And not only does he remain totally unfazed when she discovers its absence but he recommends that she quickly goes back where she just came from because 'there are so many unscrupulous people around'. Already, the film is challenging us to be on his side, asking whether we think it is funny to be placed in that position of shared knowledge. Only Igor and the spectator can appreciate the irony, since no one else will ever find out. The episode makes us accessories to the crime and also suggests that burying evidence might just work: once the victim has disappeared, Igor empties the wallet and digs a hole where he disposes of the incriminating object.

Similarly, when Hamidou falls off the scaffolding, Roger covers him with a dark tarpaulin that he pulls over his face as if to start erasing his identity. And on top of this already shapeless form, he places a door, a door separated from its frame, that opens on nothing any more, but ironically reminds us of other metaphorical doors that could have been opened to let in the immigrant and his wife. Here, the host does not open doors but closes them back on the immigrant, or rather transforms doors into the cover of a non-coffin where Hamidou will remain lying, half-dead, half-alive, so that the murder can go unpunished. And when the body is finally covered with cement, Hamidou becomes a fragment of the house that Roger is building, as if the immigrant had literally become a piece of cheap raw material imported from developing countries. Both invisible, impossible to find and impossible to forget, his body is removed from normal human communication and finds itself locked in some sort of hellish non-place that Assita's and the seer's fragmented stories half-guess without being able to fully explain. Hamidou cannot be integrated but he cannot be deported either. Or rather the specific form of 'integration' that he undergoes is a monstrous form of absorption. Like the administrative aberrations created by the Pasqua Laws before 1997, he is beyond the opposition between '*expulsable*' and '*régularisable*'. Murdered, then buried without proper funeral rites, without even a grave, he becomes the symbol of the repressed about which psychoanalysis has taught us that it can only lead to future traumas and incomprehensible narrative renditions.

After repeated allusions to the possibility of hiding the *corpus delicti*, the film was thus preparing us for a final departure that would seal Hamidou's fate: in the hospital where she must take her sick baby, Assita has met a nurse, a fellow-African, who is willing to let her borrow her identification papers so that she can cross over to Italy. In one of the rare vaguely amusing scenes where Igor makes fun of the Europeans' inability to identify African faces, he makes her wear her new friend's multi-coloured headscarf and shows the identity card to a passer-by. Predictably, the man mistakes Assita for the person whose photograph is affixed to the official paper. Assita's invisibility thus works both ways: it deprives her of her right to be protected by the police (who cannot look for an illegal immigrant who 'does not exist') but also allows her to move through barriers controlled by human beings who interpret passports with a biased sense of recognition. Having established that Assita is read as an interchangeable immigrant, the film makes us expect that she will leave Belgium, go to Italy, and that her getting on the train will coincide with the end of their shared adventure.

But this forward movement is suddenly stopped: unexpectedly, Igor suddenly reverses the direction of the trip that he has carefully organised. After helping Assita with her fake papers and her new identity, after selling his father's ring to buy her ticket, after taking her to the train station and accompanying her almost all the way to the platform, he abruptly stops and the logic of the film turns around. The story as a whole seems to move backwards, as if we were in a montage room, or as if an interactive narrative was suddenly offering us the possibility of another direction, of another migration whose destination will remain untold.

This last scene is shot in a strange and hybrid space that is conventionally not associated with revelations and important conversations: Igor's confession will take place in the stairway leading to the platform. From a filmic point of view, the platform is almost a cliché or at least an intertextual reference to a number of departure and arrival scenes.[6] It represents the last horizontal space before one character is separated from the other by the train departure; it is a sort of in-between stage, designed to accommodate last declarations, promises and goodbyes. But if the platform represents a last chance to stage a meaningful conversation, it is not the case for the flight of stairs that sometimes leads to it:

by definition, stairs connote passage, movement, no-one stops there, which makes it all the more remarkable for Igor to choose this interstitial space to shatter the precarious equilibrium that he has managed to maintain around the fiction of Hamidou's willing departure.

Before we can see the two characters on this flight of stairs, for almost a minute three long silent shots follow Assita and Igor, the camera slowly getting closer and closer to the protagonists. In the first shot, they are walking together, or rather one in front of the other, without saying a word. The camera follows them as they cross the frame from right to left. In the next shot, that direction is reversed: we now see them moving inside the frame from left to right, which gives us the impression that they are retracing the steps as if to announce that the ultimate destination and meaning of the trip is about to be turned around. When they reach the train station and proceed through a long and dark corridor, the camera lets them move away from its gaze and we see their backs as they walk together. The last shot catches up with them with a close-up of their faces as they are about to disappear at the end of the hallway. They still have not exchanged a word but this shot, which begins with their two faces captured at the same level, right next to each other, will be the time of Igor's confession and revelation. And the first word uttered by Igor coincides with the moment when the camera separates them: for several long and monotonous seconds, we have been watching the characters' parallel progression but when Assita climbs the first few steps, the camera moves away from Igor, eliminating him from the frame. From the spectator's point of view, the screen is now completely filled by Assita's back. Her head, covered with a multi-coloured scarf and her baby boy with his red bonnet add striking touches of colour to an otherwise sombre image.

When Igor abruptly says: 'Hamidou is dead', Assita stops climbing the steps and remains immobile. Around her everything becomes still, as if the film was paralysed. Only the camera retains a tiny margin of latitude, panning slowly away from the woman's face to Igor's and back again. Although we normally understand what happens 'behind people's backs' as betrayals and unforgivable acts of cowardice, although we could interpret Assita's turned back as a symptom of vulnerability and distress, I would suggest that this scene reinterprets the characters' position as the sign of a fragile return to a form of communication that remains tainted with a pathological form of silence.

As if all the resources of normal dialogue had been exhausted, Igor's confession resonates in a bleak silence. There is no reply. The camera can do nothing but register the silence and the only other possible form of communication between Igor and the woman who can no longer function as the ostracised foreigner. Dialogue is now reduced to subtle body language, intense looks, a code that we can decipher or feel comfortable with only because we have become familiar with the two characters' background. When Igor finishes his confession (and the camera does not seem too sure of when the end has come, insisting, as it does, on the teenager's downcast eyes), Assita does not move for a few seconds and her first gesture is not to turn around but to remove the headscarf that added a bit of colour to the picture, that had earlier seemed to suggest that ordinary racism could be humorously reappropriated against racists. The disguise was supposed to make her resemble the documented immigrant who was willing to let her borrow her identity card and give her the freedom to travel. By removing the mask that lets her pass for another African woman, she deliberately chooses to reclaim her own identity. She is now Assita, an illegal immigrant from Burkina Faso, whom the police are bound to stop on the border. But giving up on that ruse is also the first real act of freedom that Assita can perform: she can make her own decision about her identity only because Igor has recognised her, has acknowledged her as a real interlocutor. He not only gives her the freedom to choose but, as his father's accomplice, he also places his own destiny in her hands.

From that moment on, Assita entirely recaptures her power of decision. And when she finally turns around, the two characters look at each other as equals. Their relationship is almost indescribable but it is also unique. Nothing is said, as if words were ruled out, as if no one trusted them anymore. And during the same long shot, when Assita turns around without a word and starts walking back from where they came, Igor does not ask any questions. Neither the hero nor the spectator knows where Assita is going, what she intends to do, nor why she refuses to leave for Italy, but Igor does not try to understand or to dissuade her. After a short moment of hesitation during which the frame separates them one last time, he runs after her, catches up with her, and starts walking alongside, as if the silent look they have exchanged had established a new protocol. It is not clear that she accepts him, that she has forgiven him, nor does she express any affection or sympathy; but they walk together in the same direction as if they could not do anything else, as if his place was now beside her no matter what happens. The camera is happy to let the African woman, her baby and the young man who carries her bag disappear under the credits at the end of the corridor: it does not seem to know whether the corridor in question opens on to some kind of future for the two immigrants and their companion.

Conclusion

I would like to conclude on the meaningfulness of this new form of complicity that definitively excludes the father. I would suggest that Igor's decision radically modifies the relationship between Assita and himself because it inaugurates a new era in which they are equal partners in a game where each can now be host and guest. Rather than portraying the immigrant as the eternal guest of a powerful native host, *La Promesse* reaches a point at which the imbalance is corrected. And, remarkably, the gender of each character adds a powerful comment on the problematic intersection between gender and hospitality. The relationship between Igor and Assita has never been stable but has always rested on a hypothesis that Igor's confession renders obsolete – that

Assita was under the protection of men, of her husband, of Igor, and even of Roger who pretends to take her under his wing when Hamidou goes missing. His way of 'protecting' Assita is certainly a cynical form of exploitation that throws hypocrisy into the bargain: he stages a fake rape to pretend to rescue her from her attacker, only to insist that she cannot take care of herself. 'What would have happened if I had not arrived?' he asks Assita. She very correctly interprets his show of protection as a disinvitation. Answering his rhetorical question with a real one she replies: 'Are you throwing me out?' – a formulation that makes it obvious that she understands what Roger's hospitality really means. Igor's efforts to help her, on the other hand, are a genuine attempt not only at defending her interests but at identifying what such interests might be before presuming that he knows better than she does. But until the moment when he finally tells her the truth, Assita functions as an entity that is exchanged rather than as a guest greeted by the host. In her introduction to the special issue of *Communications* devoted to hospitality, Anne Gotman notes that there is a radical difference between welcoming and protecting. When a woman finds herself in the position of the potential guest, she is often perceived as a non-dangerous stranger because she is assumed to be weaker or harmless. As a consequence, she often finds that she is offered degraded forms of hospitality (Gotman 1997: 11). I would argue that in *La Promesse*, at least until the very last scene, Roger and Igor as well as Hamidou share this definition. Igor takes care of Assita because of the promise he made to a dying man: ultimately, his responsibility is to the husband. That husband's goal was to protect his wife but he could not survive. As for Roger, he was cynically hiding behind the cliché that women need protection to refuse her his hospitality.

The whole film demonstrates that the characters would be more than happy to treat her as merchandise that is exchanged, the most commonplace ploy used by communities to exclude women from the type of contract that links the host and the guest. In that model, women can be neither hosts nor guests, they can help the host be a better host by following his orders to make the guest more comfortable. Sometimes, they are even imagined as a gift presented to the host.[7] The most traditional myths portray women not as agents who can offer or receive hospitality but as an element of the system that allows the guest and the host to establish an harmonious relationship. In extreme cases, the woman becomes a form of currency, the hostage that the host will sacrifice so that the sacred laws of hospitality can be respected: I am thinking of the Biblical story of Lot protecting his angels from the neighbours who want to molest them and offering 'his' women in exchange.

Throughout the film, it is as a woman that Assita is rejected by the other characters who invoke her vulnerability and would-be powerlessness. When Roger barges into the room where his foreman is attacking Assita, the camera lets us witness money passing from one man to the other, sealing the pact between them. And when even that attempt fails because Assita refuses to be intimidated into leaving, he goes further down the same logical road: after pretending to 'protect' the woman, he now blatantly tries to sell her. He is seen negotiating her price with her would-be pimp. After killing the legitimate protector, Roger usurps the role and his cynicism highlights the invisible link between protection and possession.

When Igor takes control of the situation, his role consists, at first, of dealing with the situation on an emergency basis. He steals the father's van and takes his place behind the wheel to prevent the transaction between Roger and the pimp. But theoretically, at that point, his function is not fundamentally different from his father's: he protects her by displacing her body, by preventing her from being exchanged. But only when he tells her the truth does he truly give her back her freedom by treating her like an agent with whom he can share a dangerous story, that is by offering much more than his protection. If there is a true moment of hospitality in this film, it is probably the moment when Igor shares his story like elsewhere people share a meal, or bread, or salt. His revelation thus turns Assita into an etymological companion who now has as much power over him as he did over her. Her identity as an illegal immigrant is not negated by this rearrangement of roles but the implications of her status are profoundly redefined.

NOTES

1 *Le chant du rossignol, Lorsque le bateau de Monsieur Léon descendit la Meuse pour la première fois, Pour que la guerre s'achève, les murs devraient s'écrouler, Jean Jouvet.* See also their 1992 *Je pense à vous*, a portrait of steelworkers in Seraing.

2 Malik Chibane's *Hexagone, Douce France*, or Karim Dridri's *Bye Bye*.

3 Mathieu Kassovitz's *La Haine*, Jean-Claude Richet's *Etats des lieux*, *Ma 6T va craquer*.

4 Merzak Allouache's *Salut cousin!* focuses on two Algerian cousins, Mok and Alilo. Mok, who thinks of himself as 'French', will eventually be deported to a country that he does not know, while his cousin, who originally planned to spend only a few days in Paris, stays on as an illegal immigrant when his business venture fails.

5 Belgium was an important destination for Italian migrants in the early postwar period. For an interesting documentary history on this immigration, which was especially focused on recruiting labour for the Belgian coal mines, see Franciosi (1997).

6 *Salut cousin!* is framed by two sequences filmed on a platform: the first scene shows us the feet of two cousins, Alilo having just arrived from Algiers and being greeted by his host, Mok. At the end of the film, Alilo tries to go back to Algiers, and is waiting on the platform with his suitcase. As in *La Promesse*, the movement of the migration is about to be inverted but the decision is precisely made on the platform where the characters have plenty of time, while waiting for the train, to make a last-minute decision, while the camera has much latitude to explore the symbolic potential of Alilo's suitcase. Unlike Assita's bag, it will stay on the platform, abandoned by its owner, and will eventually be destroyed by the police, who fear that it contains a bomb.

7 Such models abound in literature and are variously justified depending on the context. Sometimes the gift of the native woman to the newly arrived foreigner is ultimately understood as a civilised gesture, as a well-understood attempt to increase the community's birth rate (in Diderot's *Supplément au voyage de Bougainville*).

References

Bhabha, H. (1994) *The Location of Culture*, London and New York: Routledge.

Bosséno, C. (1992) 'Immigrant cinema, national cinema: the case of Beur film', in Dyer, R. and Vincendeau, G. (eds), *Popular European Cinema*, London and New York: Routledge.

Burdeau, E. (1996) 'L'offensive des Dardennes', *Cahiers du Cinéma* 506: 40–7.

Derobert, E. (1996) '*La Promesse*: la flèche Wallonne', *Positif* 428: 37–8.

Dorzée, H. (1999) 'Cinéma du réel et les frères du fleuve', *Le Soir*, 16 May: 12.

Franciosi, M. L. (1997) ... *Per un Sacco di Carbone*, Brussels: Associazione Cristiane Lavoratori Internazionali.

Gilroy, P. (1993) *The Black Atlantic: Modernity and Double Consciousness*, London: Verso.

Glissant, E. (1989) *Caribbean Discourse: Selected Essays*, Charlottesville: University Press of Virginia.

Gotman, A. (1997) 'La question de l'hospitalité aujourd'hui', *Communications* 65: 5–18.

Honorez, L. (1999) 'Ces disciples de Stork et de la fleur maigre', *Le Soir*, 15 May: 11.

Rosello, M. (1998a) *Declining the Stereotype: Ethnicity and Representation in French Cultures*, Dartmouth: University Press of New England.

—— (1998b) 'Representing illegal immigrants in France: from *clandestins* to *l'affaire des sans-papiers de Saint-Bernard*', *Journal of European Studies* 28: 137–51.

Rosenbaum, J. (1997) '*Buried Blues, La Promesse*', *Chicago Reader*, 22 August: 7.

Sherzer, D. (ed.) (1996) *Cinema, Colonialism, Postcolonialism*, Austin: Texas University Press.

Tarr, C. (1993) 'Questions of identity in Beur cinema: from *Tea in the Harem* to *Cheb*', *Screen* 34: 320–42.

6

AFRICAN IMMIGRATION
ON FILM

Pummarò and the limits of vicarious
representation

David Forgacs

In the 1990 Italian film *Pummarò* Thywill A. K. Amenya plays a young
Ghanaian man, Kwaku Toré, who has left home to meet up with his elder
brother, Giobbe (Job) Kwala Toré. The latter has been working as a tomato
picker north of Naples and has been given the nickname Pummarò (the word
for tomato in some dialects of southern Italy; also the name of a brand of
peeled and sieved tomatoes). He went to Italy ahead of Kwaku, who has since
qualified in Ghana as a doctor, to raise money to enable him to go on to
Canada to specialise so that he can then return home to practise, thereby
fulfilling a promise they made to their grandfather when they were children. All
this detailed story information is given in voice-over before the film's opening
credits in the form of a taped letter, made by Kwala for Kwaku, which the latter
listens to on his cassette player as he heads towards Naples as a stowaway on a
cargo ship. Still in the pre-credits sequence we see Kwala in the tomato field, in
line with other black men and a white co-worker whom they call 'professore'
(Franco Interlenghi), waiting to be paid. When the boss, a camorra[1] man, Don
Palombo (Gerardo Scala), tries to pay him less per crate than the others, Kwala
seizes his pistol and steals his truck. Before he leaves he gets the professor to
capture him on a Polaroid as he poses standing on the front bumper. This is the
last time we see Kwala before the end of the film.

The rest of the story traces Kwaku's itinerary through Italy as he tries to find
his brother, on the run both from the police and the camorra. On arriving in
the town where Kwala/Pummarò had been living, Kwaku stays at a hostel run
by the Catholic voluntary organisation Caritas, but when the other men in the
dormitory learn that he is Kwala Toré's brother they shun him. The professor
explains about the stolen truck and helps Kwaku get work shovelling manure to
raise the 500,000 lire he needs for a forged residence permit. Don Palombo
finds out that the professor has been helping Pummarò's brother and his men
smash his arm with a brick. The professor tells Kwaku to leave to save both their
lives. Kwaku travels to an area on the edge of Rome where he has been told he

will find Kwala. When he arrives, a young Kenyan woman, Nanou (Jacqueline Williams), who is working as a prostitute, explains that Kwala lived with her there for a while but has since left for Verona. She has subsequently discovered that she is pregnant by him. When Nanou's pimp starts to beat her up in the street for running off the police arrive; she and Kwaku get away and they stay the night in a disused railway carriage, used as a shelter by some immigrants as well as by white drug users. A young Finnish woman there goes into labour and Kwaku helps deliver her baby. Kwaku leaves and Nanou begs him to find his brother.

In Verona Kwaku meets another Ghanaian, Isidoro, who puts him up in his apartment and gets him a job in a foundry. At the centre for foreign workers run by the local council he meets Eleonora (Pamela Villoresi), a white teacher. After a party at the social centre, where Kwaku plays the drums, they begin a sexual relationship and spend a month of nights together. The father of Eleonora's young daughter, of whom he has custody, finds out and threatens to cut off her access. Isidoro, a respectable type who maintains his two school-age daughters, also gets angry with Kwaku for going with a white woman. This is followed by a scene where Kwaku, taunted by Eleonora's racist neighbour, gets into a fight outside a bar and is knocked to the ground. At first Eleonora stands by Kwaku, but when they are later buzzed by a gang of teenagers on motorcycles who shout abuse at her she becomes distraught and she too tells Kwaku to leave. He heads north again, towards Frankfurt, where his brother is working as a bouncer in a hotel nightclub. At the border control he is detained for not having an entry visa and the German police, who telex the hotel to verify that Kwala is there, learn that he has been stabbed to death by two drunk marines. Kwaku is driven to Frankfurt, where Nanou, who has also been contacted by the police, identifies Kwala's body in the hospital mortuary. Kwaku receives a compensation cheque from the hotel management and he and Nanou leave the hospital together. The last shot is of them walking through a crowd celebrating Christmas.

Pummarò was made partly with funding from the Italian television channel Raidue (RAI 2), which since the late 1960s has had a remit for supporting cultural films and which in the 1980s hosted the first black affairs programme on Italian television, *Nonsolonero* ('Black and not only'). The film represented the first attempt in Italy to deal, in a subject made for general cinema release, with the situation of migrants from Africa who had been arriving during the 1980s, in particular from the Maghreb, sub-Saharan and west-central Africa, with the largest influx after 1986, on the tide of the country's second postwar economic boom. It effectively documented the presence of criminal organisations and petty mediators in the informal low-wage economy (the professor takes a cut from the black workers for finding them shelter or getting them forged documents), the role of white pimps and gangs in the control of black prostitution, poor housing and the ubiquitous threat of violence in areas of black settlement, as well as the racial intolerance prevalent throughout Italy, particularly in the wealthy northern cities where the Lega Nord was then attracting votes through its opposition to the alleged threat posed by the unrestricted immigration of *extracomunitari*.[2]

The film was made, too, at a time when the 'immigration problem' had suddenly become very visible in Italy. In 1989 Jerry Masslo, a black South African, was killed in the tomato fields outside Villa Literno, a town in the province of Caserta, north of Naples, which was one of the poles of attraction of the seasonal labour of African immigrants (Villa Literno was used as the location for the street scenes and the interior of the Caritas hostel in the opening section of the film). That a refugee from apartheid should have been murdered in a democratic European country which had officially proclaimed parity of employment status between immigrant and non-immigrant workers (this principle had been established by Law 943 of 1986, the first major piece of postwar legislation on immigration in Italy) was not only highly embarrassing for the Italian authorities; it also served to alert public opinion to the plight of the immigrant workers and to galvanise trade unions, political parties and other associations into action on their behalf. The killing of Jerry Masslo was initially reported in the media as racially motivated, and although this may have been incorrect (at the trial of his killers they were found to be not very competent petty crooks who had been carrying out a string of armed robberies on poor labourers in the Caserta area), it did not alter the fact that, as a group, black migrant workers were particularly vulnerable to intimidation and violence (Pugliese 1996: 940). On 7 October 1989 around 100,000 people converged on Rome from all over Italy to take part in the country's first ever demonstration against racism. At the head of the march were the friends of Jerry Masslo, and one of the placards read 'Jerry Masslo ce l'ha insegnato, lavoro e diritti per ogni immigrato' ('Jerry Masslo has taught us: work and rights for every immigrant'). The delegation from Milan held up a banner saying 'Milano come Pretoria' ('Milan like Pretoria'), alluding to the arrest, imprisonment and alleged beating by the Milan police of the Senegalese political activist Pap Khouma (see Della Rovere 1989). In 1990 the Interior Minister, Claudio Martelli, rushed through Parliament what was to be the second major piece of immigration legislation, the law which took his name and which eventually regularised the legal status of 240,000 immigrants.

Although the circumstances seemed propitious, then, for a positive reception for the film, *Pummarò* had difficulty getting commercial distribution. Its director, Michele Placido, complained subsequently that the distributors pulled it after a brief theatrical first run in 1990; thereafter it was screened only at a few political festivals and in some independent and parish cinemas. It was packaged for video rental and then sell-through in 1991. It has also had one showing in a late-night slot on British television, on BBC2 on 1 February 1997. It is ironic indeed that a film which was intended to raise popular consciousness in Italy about the condition of black migrants ended up being seen only by a relatively small audience, many of whom would have belonged to an already politically aware minority, and it is hard not to feel sorry on these grounds for Placido, whose first directed feature this was, and for his co-scriptwriters Sandro Petraglia and Stefano Rulli. Petraglia and Rulli had been members in the 1970s of the radical left organisation Lotta Continua and films about social problems had always been their stock-in-trade. Their credits included a 1975 documentary about the condition of the mentally ill and mentally handicapped in long-stay institutions, *Matti da slegare*,[3] directed by Silvano Agosti and Marco Bellocchio, which was also effectively boycotted by distributors; a fictional film about a transsexual in a juvenile reform centre, *Mery per sempre/Forever Mary*, directed by Marco Risi, 1988; and the highly successful television drama about the mafia, *La piovra (The Octopus)*, the first series of which was broadcast in 1984. (Placido had starred as an actor both in *Mery per sempre* and in *La piovra*, in which he played police commissioner Cattani.)

However, it is also necessary to recognise certain intrinsic limitations in *Pummarò*. Ostensibly a film showing the experience of a black African migrant from his point of view, it was in reality a text addressed by a white production team to a white audience using black actors to perform white-scripted roles. A black audience already knew about these problems and did not need to be told about them. Although black people recited the lines, the film 'spoke' through and on behalf of them; it was not spoken (written, researched, filmed, produced) by them. Even the African-sounding music which recurs on the soundtrack was written by two white musicians, Lucio Dalla and Mauro Malavasi, and the end credits thank as consultants a number of white experts on immigration: Massimo Ghirelli, Silvestro Montanaro and Giuseppina Scala.[4] At best the film allowed a partial identification with black immigrants on the part of the white viewer. At worst it reproduced, in ways I shall indicate, some of the very racist categorisations which on a conscious level it sought to repudiate. In this way the film raises important questions about the limits of this type of vicarious representation of black people's experience by white people.

Focalisation and spectatorship

The film is a fusion of two basic story types: the odyssey, in which the wandering protagonist discovers new things and faces new trials in each place he visits; and the thwarted pursuit, in which each time the protagonist nearly catches up with the person he is trying to reach (Kwala/Pummarò), he arrives just too late. Although both these story types make Kwaku central, the story is not really told, in a technical sense, from his point of view. To be sure, there are a number of 'subjective' or 'point-of-view' shots which follow immediately on from shots of Kwaku looking, and by convention the audience interprets these as shots of what he sees: for instance the shots of streets, buildings and people each time he arrives in a new place. These shots are carefully chosen to show us the raw reality of contemporary Italy as the ingénu Kwaku observes it: poor Italians throwing slops out of the windows of shanties; police stopping black immigrants in the street; intravenous drug users sprawled on the floor of a disused train carriage. However, Kwaku does not give a voice-over narration (the only piece of voice-over in the film is Kwala's tape at the beginning) and Kwaku himself appears in every sequence and in most shots of the film, so he is in fact a filmed character rather than a narrator, and an object of the viewer's gaze rather than just a neutral pair of eyes through which the viewer sees events.

We might adopt here Gérard Genette's terms (Genette 1980), devised to describe texts of narrative fiction, and say that Kwaku is an example of a 'focaliser' rather than a narrator – in other words a character within the story frame or diegesis who 'sees' or experiences events rather than the person who tells the story (who may be situated either inside or outside the story frame). However we need to be clear about what these terms mean respectively in the case of a verbal text and a film. Genette's concepts do not map exactly onto feature film narratives, most of which do not contain either a story-telling voice (except where there is voice-over narration) or an extra-diegetic realm outside the story frame equivalent to those of literary narration and most of which do not show things directly from the point of view of a single character (literary narratives, of course, do not 'show' things at all in a literal sense). What films, including this one, commonly do contain is a central focalising character who is *looked at as he or she looks*: the viewer both sees the focalising character and sees him or her seeing. This means that such characters are both objects of contemplation for the viewer and for other characters in the film and objects of empathetic projection with whom the viewer may identify and who, when they look, ideally draw the viewer's gaze away from them to something outside them.

The notion of 'identification' itself is also quite complicated in this case: it could be described as a form of 'cross-race identification' by an implied white viewer with a black focaliser, similar in some ways to the cross-gender identification by an implied male viewer with a female focaliser which has been astutely analysed by Carol J. Clover in her work on the slasher horror genre (Clover 1992). In both cases the identification is internally conflictual, if not self-contradictory, because of the tension between empathy with and desire for the character and because of the asymmetries of power and privilege between looker and looked-at. As a focalising black character, Kwaku may be looked at by the white viewer in two contrasting ways: with a look of vicarious identification, whereby the white viewer is drawn to merge in fantasy with him and empathise with his plight, as if he were undergoing it in the viewer's place; and with a distancing or alienating look by which Kwaku is held at bay by the camera, made an object of contemplation and eroticised as a body. The vicarious identification produced by the first type of look allows the white viewer to occupy a space outside his or her normal viewing position and enables him/her to see racism from a defamiliarised, critical vantage point, much the same as that opened up by classic defamiliarising texts such as *Les Lettres persanes* and *Huckleberry Finn*. The fact that Kwaku is polite, mild-mannered, soft-spoken and has a higher level of formal education than most of the white people in the film helps the white viewer to empathise and see the world as if from his position. Yet the fact that he is repeatedly photographed so as to draw attention to his physical beauty and muscular physique invites a look of erotic contemplation which in some ways negates the first look. The viewer, that is to say, now looks at him, no longer with him.

Since the two looks cannot be held simultaneously – the first involves an identification with the character as subject, the second a distancing from him as object – the relationship between them is highly unstable and volatile. As subject, as a pair of eyes looking out, it is as if Kwaku were without colour, and the implied looking with him is therefore consistent with liberal, egalitarian versions of anti-racism which ask one to look beyond the surface, the skin; in effect, to deny the skin, to say 'don't look at these bodies as bodies', or 'look beyond them to the person within'. However, as object, as body to be observed by the camera, Kwaku's physical difference is made manifest, as it must be, in order either that the camera can celebrate it erotically or show how it serves as a focus for the racist violence of some white people. The only way this second look can be accommodated back into an anti-racist discourse is to adopt a different version of anti-racism, one which says 'look at these bodies, take pleasure in the sight of them, but not in a racist way'. Yet the makers of the film were clearly uncomfortable with this second form of anti-racism, presumably because of its precariousness, its risk of slipping back into racism.

Pummarò, moreover, does not just offer the viewer the possibility of these two different kinds of look. It positively polarises them and enables the white spectator to switch between them in a self-conscious way, though exactly what the intentions of the film's makers were in this respect is not clear. Thus, there are various devices which produce a distancing or objectifying look – one, that is, which positions the black person as an object of spectatorial fascination. The use of posed photographs is one of these. The still photograph of a person within a motion picture constitutes a form of second-order objectification because by stripping away their speech and movement it exposes them to contemplation as 'pure' body. An example of how this works is the rapid sequence of shots of Brigitte Bardot (not in fact stills, although she strikes static modelling poses) in the garden of Prokosch's rented villa in Godard's *Le Mépris* (1963). Within the diegesis the shots show the character, Camille, as she is seen by the desiring suitor Prokosch (Jack Palance); but simultaneously they are shots of the actress and model Bardot 'as herself' offered up to the gaze of the film's viewers. So too Kwala/Pummarò photographed on the truck is captured at a moment of conscious physical display, posing flamboyantly in white singlet, hand on hip, pistol tucked behind his belt. He is seen by the professor, through the viewfinder of his Polaroid, and by the others present at the scene, but he is simultaneously seen by the mainly white audience as a black actor posing for the film camera. In a later scene, the black co-workers pose to be photographed with the professor. At other points in the film there are shots of Kwaku and the other immigrants working, accompanied by music; although these are motion shots they too are somewhat like still photographs in that their status in the film is as interludes of pure spectacle between the stretches of narrative and they too concentrate on the physique of the workers.

The most extreme example of this kind of objectifying look comes in the scene of the party in Verona where Kwaku starts playing a pair of hand-drums to demonstrate to Eleonora how they can be used to communicate in 'his culture' and then gets up to play the large drums on the stage. Isidoro joins in, then the whole band, and the slightly drunk Eleonora gets visibly excited and aroused as she watches Kwaku play. In the next scene he walks her home; they stop outside the balcony of 'Juliet's house', where he surprises and impresses her by reciting from memory in English an extract from Romeo's speech, and then jokes, rather ponderously, 'Just what did Juliet's parents have against Romeo? Was he black by any chance?' After that they end up in bed in a scene of tender lovemaking to soft music. The whole sequence is assembled out of a series of racial stereotypes (educated black man reverts to the primitive, excites white woman, proves to be also amazingly cultured, so she takes him to bed) and it is hard to believe it is not intended to be ironic. But it is equally hard to imagine just why such stereotypes, and such a rehearsal of racist motifs, and then an ironisation of them, would have been written into a film which elsewhere wears its liberal anti-racist heart so clearly on its sleeve. The most plausible explanation, I think, is that the sequence is intended to celebrate African cultural difference, in other words to promote a positive multicultural vision, and to show the possibility of mixed-race relationships, before allowing them to be exposed to attack by the racists in the film: Eleonora's neighbour, her family, the boys on the bikes. But the gauche way in which this is handled shows how coy and uncomfortable the film actually is with its moments of celebration of racial otherness.

Alternative narrative strategies

It is tempting, perhaps, to excuse the weaknesses and awkwardness of *Pummarò* on the grounds that it was an *early* attempt to deal with the problems surrounding black immigration in Italy, and that it was made at a time before immigrants themselves had started to gain access to the means of mass cultural production and to channels of distribution for their products, to speak up for themselves. This situation started to change in the early 1990s, most notably with the rise of black rap bands in Italy, as elsewhere in Europe. However, this excuse does not stand up to close scrutiny. At the most obvious level, that of the film's narrative strategy, we might make a comparison with Colin MacInnes's London-based novel of 1957, *City of Spades*. This too was an early white-authored text about black immigration which, like *Pummarò*, assumed the standpoint and language of a newly arrived immigrant, Johnny Fortune from Nigeria – or at any rate it assumed them for part of the time, since the text in fact alternates between Johnny's narrative and that of a young white welfare officer, Montgomery Pew, assigned to liaise with the Afro-Caribbean community. Both Johnny's narrative and the other representations of black people's speech in the book are produced by a form of ventriloquism in which the white writer impersonates African and Caribbean English, projects himself into black characters, appropriates their slang, invents snatches of calypso, and so on, in much the same way as Placido, Rulli, Petraglia, Dalla and Malavasi impersonate African voices, music and songs in *Pummarò*. Black immigration on a relatively large scale was a new enough phenomenon in both cases to exert a seductive cultural fascination on white authors, and this included a powerful erotic attraction towards black males and the way 'they' talk, move, dance, dress. In MacInnes's case the erotic attraction is overt; in *Pummarò* it is driven down into the film's unconscious: repressed from its impeccably anti-racist storyline, it returns in the ambivalent structure of looking which the film offers the spectator.

It is true that in both cases – Britain in the 1950s, Italy in the 1980s – black immigration was a new enough phenomenon for it to be considered acceptable, even 'progressive', for white people to speak on behalf of black people, particularly when the white author's assumption of a black person's perspective was used as a defamiliarising strategy to give the white audience a critical distance on their own culture. Yet there is an important difference between the two works. MacInnes's book is irreverently humorous in an anarchic, multidirectional way – its satirical targets include the British colonial mentality, BBC liberals, the West Indians' contempt for the Africans – whereas Placido's film is irremediably serious and sombre, and its only humour is unintentional, as when Eleonora makes big eyes at the drumming Kwaku. Nevertheless, it is these moments of unintentional humour that reveal the film's latent pull of desire towards the exoticised racial other and they are therefore the most symptomatic instances of its ideological contradictoriness.

We might also invoke a number of other texts, made around the same time as *Pummarò*, which embody alternatives to its style of vicarious representation. These include written memoirs, testimonies or fictionalised representations produced by immigrants themselves, sometimes with the assistance of an Italian writer as mediator.[5] Tahar Ben Jelloun's collection of stories *Dove lo Stato non c'è* (*Where the State is Absent*) was published in 1991 and it includes a text entitled 'Villa Literno' reconstructing the killing of Jerry Masslo (Ben Jelloun 1991). Salah Methnani's *Immigrato* (*Immigrant*), co-written with Mario Fortunato, has a structure similar to *Pummarò*: it recounts in a series of chapters, each set in a different city, the Tunisian author's journey northward through Italy (Fortunato and Methnani 1990). In film, a striking counter-example to *Pummarò* is provided by *Vu cumprà no tiene sentido* ('*Vu cumprà* is meaningless'), a forty-minute documentary, shot in the same year as Placido's film, 1989, in San Giuliano Terme and Pisa, by an international crew of film school students based in Latin America, including a black camera operator, Issoufu Tapsoba from Burkina Faso. The film, which is available on videocassette from the Archivio Audiovisivo del Movimento Operaio e Democratico in Rome, has, in the first place, the advantage of authenticity in its documentation of white attitudes. It opens, for example, with a series of extracts from interviews with the tourist stallholders in Pisa's Piazza dei Miracoli expressing their attitudes towards the itinerant black vendors on 'their' pitch: 'an invasion of barbarians'; 'they claim rights here which if they asked for them back home they'd get a kick up the backside', and so on. Second, it also has some revealing interviews with black immigrants, some of them taken from archive film (including an interview with Jerry Masslo taped for *Nonsolonero* before he was killed, in which he discusses racist attitudes in Italy, and talks about black and white people having the same bodies apart from their skin colour), others recorded direct by the film-makers, such as an interview with Mass Thiam, president of the Senegalese community organisation in Pisa. This film certainly uses various rhetorical devices to reinforce its points, including for example a long travelling shot from the white vendors inside Piazza dei Miracoli to outside the wall, where the itinerant black vendors have been banished and where they lay out their carpets covered with goods. At just the moment that the camera passes beyond the wall African music is cut in on the soundtrack, so that both the camera movement and the editing make explicit the inside/outside division. Nevertheless at no point does this film, or these other accounts of immigrant experience, get drawn into the contradiction of *Pummarò*, that of switching from the vicarious look with the black subject to the objectifying or eroticised look at him. The contradiction, in other words, is not inherent in the material being treated. It comes from the type of treatment adopted, the narrative strategy of the film and the relations of power and knowledge between the film-makers and the people they are representing.

A final contemporary counter-example can be used to illustrate this point. Claire Denis's feature film *Chocolat* (1988) does not attempt to get inside the experience of an African in Europe. Instead, Denis reverses the migratory journey and tells the story of a white woman, appropriately named France, who grew up in colonial Cameroon in the early 1950s, returning there in the 1980s as an adult intending to revisit the house where she lived as a child. Rather than disavow or repress inter-racial desire, Denis's film draws it explicitly to the surface – the film in fact offers in some ways the eroticised colonial fantasy of the exotic familiar from the movies set in Africa made, both in Hollywood and in Europe, in the 1930s and 1940s – but it does so in such a way that the spectator can acknowledge the powerful sway of the fantasy and begin to understand it. This is established in the opening long shot, as the title credits roll, of a black man and a young boy frolicking in the waves at the seashore to music by Abdullah Ibrahim. The shot is ultimately reversed to reveal that the two are being watched by a white woman – the adult France (Mireille Perrier) – and, through her, by Denis's camera and thence an implied audience of white spectators. France's journey of return to the scene of her childhood provides a narrative frame for a prolonged flashback, constituting most of the film, in which the young France (played by Cécile Ducasse) serves as the partial focaliser of the action. Here too the body of a black man, the house-servant Protée (Isaach de Bankolé), who has among his duties that of looking after the young France, is explicitly spectacularised and eroticised but the device of subjective narration and focalisation from France's memory means that the audience is conscious that he is implicitly 'framed' from a white perspective. This framing might appear to be complicated by the fact that France does not actually witness or directly focalise all the scenes with Protée (indeed at various points in the film when the camera displays Protée's body most prominently to the audience, the young France is absent from the scene, or is in the shot but is not looking at Protée, so these scenes cannot strictly belong to the older France's memory), but in fact the effect of this 'flawed' focalisation is to transfer France's gaze, so to speak, to that of the generic white viewer. Stuart Hall (1992: 51) remarked shrewdly about *Chocolat* shortly after its release that it 'may be the only kind of film European film-makers should be making about Africa just now. It may be time for Europeans to confront what colonisation has done to *them* rather than instantly taking on the white man's burden, once again, of speaking for the "other".'

A symptom of the ideological difference between the respective projects of *Pummarò* and *Chocolat* is the handling in each case of the white man who 'crosses over' and joins the black workers: the professor in *Pummarò*, the young ex-seminarist Luc (Jean-Claude Adelin) in *Chocolat*. Kwaku asks the professor why he likes to be with them and he says: 'Because I feel I am one of you. I like everything you do. I like the way you cook, the way you eat, the way you sing, dance, play, and I also learn new things.' He also alludes to an unhappy childhood spent in orphanages that he would rather forget. However, the film also shows him running a scam by which he takes a cut from his black friends for getting them work or fixing them up with forged papers. The implication is that his background of social marginality, together with his education, gives him an openness to the immigrants' culture and a political solidarity with them, but this does not stop him playing a double game and being also a petty shark who preys on the immigrants. This double game exposes him to risk and he ends up victimised, attacked by the bigger sharks, the camorra, so that on balance the audience will feel sympathy for him. Luc in *Chocolat* is also playing a double game, albeit of a different kind and in a different situation, that of colonial domination. He wants to have it both ways: to 'go native' and remind his fellow-whites they are straddling a power-keg of incipient anti-colonial rebellion, while being able to retreat whenever he chooses to the privileges of the colonial elite. Yet his particular way of playing across the boundaries makes him merely contemptible in the moral economy of the film. When he taunts and insults Protée for having internalised too well the rules of colonial submission he has learned from the priests, Protée reacts by throwing him off the balcony, in effect redrawing for Luc the boundary he himself refuses to observe. In much the same way, Protée had earlier refused the sexual advance of the white mistress of the house, France's mother Aimée (Giulia Boschi), with whom Luc had had no difficulty having an affair, since for Protée to accept her offer without altering his formal status as servant would merely continue his subjugation by other means. And indeed this is confirmed when, angered and humiliated by Protée's refusal and by his having caused Luc to leave, Aimée punishes him by banishing him from his privileged job as house-servant and France's minder to a menial job in the garage.

Chocolat is not, of course, a film about immigration, and *Pummarò* is; one is set in contemporary Europe, the other in colonial Africa. But this does not make them any the less comparable with one another, for they are both films by white directors and they are both trying to deal, in contemporary Europe, with the politics of racial difference, which rests upon the collective memory of imperialism and colonial exploitation. Italy, as much as France, had a brutal colonial past. The critical fault-line in the treatment of racial difference, as I have argued, is that of inter-racial desire. Whereas the Italian film tries to paper over this fault-line with disavowal and liberal good intentions, the French film makes the desire explicit and thereby confronts head-on the complex inter-twinings of sexuality, inequality and power.

NOTES

1 The camorra is, broadly speaking, the Neapolitan equivalent of the Sicilian mafia, in other words a criminal fraternity much involved in racketeering and the exercise of power.

2 The literal meaning of *extracomunitari* is people from outside the European Community; in practice the term is used to refer to poor immigrants from Africa, Asia etc., and not those who come from rich countries such as Switzerland, the United States or Japan.

3 This title, 'Mad People to Untie', is a word-play on the common expression '*matto da legare*' – 'so crazy he should be tied up'.

4 Ghirelli subsequently published the well-known *Immigrati brava gente* (Ghirelli 1993).

5 For a broad overview of this literary genre in Italy see Di Maio (2001).

References

Ben Jelloun, T. (1991) *Dove lo Stato non c'è. Racconti italiani*, Turin: Einaudi.

Clover, C. J. (1992) *Men, Women and Chainsaws: Gender in the Modern Horror Film*, Princeton NJ: Princeton University Press.

Della Rovere, R. (1989) 'Roma capitale di tutti i colori', *Corriere della Sera*, 8 October: 7.

Di Maio, A. (2001) 'Immigration and national literature: Italian voices from Africa and the diaspora', in King, R. (ed.), *The Mediterranean Passage: Migration and New Cultural Encounters in Southern Europe*, Liverpool: Liverpool University Press.

Fortunato, M. and Methnani, S. (1990) *Immigrato*, Rome: Theoria.

Genette, G. (1980) *Narrative Discourse*, Ithaca NY: Cornell University Press.

Ghirelli, M. (1993) *Immigrati brava gente*, Milan: Sperling and Kupfer.

Hall, S. (1992) 'European cinema on the edge of a nervous breakdown', in Petrie, D. (ed.), *Screening Europe: Image and Identity in Contemporary European Cinema*, London: BFI Publishing.

Pugliese, E. (1996) 'L'immigrazione', in *Storia dell'Italia Repubblicana Vol. III, L'Italia nella crisi mondiale. L'ultimo ventennio, I, Economia e società*, Turin: Einaudi.

7

'ITALY IS BEAUTIFUL'

The role of Italian television in Albanian migration to Italy

Nicola Mai

Introduction

Between 7 and 10 March 1991, some 25,700 Albanians crossed the Otranto Channel between Albania and Italy; in August 1991 another 20,000 arrived. At the end of 1997, 83,807 Albanian immigrants were legally present in Italy (Caritas di Roma 1998: 79), although it is estimated that the actual figure, including so-called irregular immigrants, may be as high as 150,000 people (UNDP 1998: 36).

The first explanations for the reasons behind this rather dramatic wave of migration highlighted the key role that Italian television had played in attracting Albanians to Italy. Driven by economic necessity to be sure, but lured by images of success provided by the imaginary world of television, Albanians had flocked to the country that fuelled their hopes and desires. However, interviews with Albanians carried out on both shores immediately after their migratory attempts provided accounts of disillusionment with television's fairy tale promises, starting with the brutality they encountered on arrival at the hands of the Italian police (see Barjaba *et al.* 1996: 32–5; Vehbiu and Devole 1996: 29–30).

If it is uncontroversial that the Italian media, and especially television, have played a major role in the Albanian migratory experience, the precise nature of this agency remains relatively unexplored. My concern here is to suggest the ways in which Italian television has helped to construct and shape the 'migratory project' itself. By 'migratory project' I am referring not so much to actual geographical displacement but to the wider discursive processes by means of which Albanians have come to perceive, describe and situate themselves with respect to their wider social and cultural environment – whether this be Albania or Italy.

More specifically my analysis, based on a year and a half of fieldwork in 1998–9, will draw on the migratory project as it was described to me in interviews with Albanian young people, aged between 15 and 30 years, living in the cities of Tirana and Durrës. This is not a random choice: Tirana and nearby

95

Durrës are Albania's capital and major port respectively – an area which is now the most urbanised and the most exposed to foreign cultures. My decision to interview young people was partly the consequence of my fieldwork placement – I was working for a development programme, funded by the Italian government, aimed at establishing a network of youth centres in Albania's major cities – and partly dictated by the fact that Albania is one of the youngest countries in Europe. Forty-two per cent of the total population is under 19 years of age and the average age is 24 years (UNICEF 1998: 14–15). It is mainly younger people between the ages of 15 and 45 who have been and are being involved in migratory dynamics; these age groups account for 94.6 per cent of the total number of migrants (Gjonça 2000). Moreover, according to a survey of Albanian urban youth carried out in 1995, more than three-quarters of those interviewed declared that they would like to go abroad to study or work if they had the possibility (Trifirò 1995: 168–70). Finally, although only about 44 per cent of the population is urban (UNICEF 1998: 16), it was urban youth, particularly from Tirana and Durrës, who most vehemently opposed Enver Hoxha's 40-year-long Communist regime and who were the main actors in the overturning of his statue on 20 February 1991.

Here it should also be recalled that because of the geographical proximity between the two countries – just 150 kilometres separate Puglia, Italy's south-eastern extremity, from Albania's coastline – Italian television could be seen in Albania since the early 1960s. I will argue that Italian television also played an important role in fomenting this oppositional stance, though not by overt political exhortation, but by engaging the needs and aspirations of young people in a manner that ultimately led them to conclude that only through the overturning of the Communist regime could their full identities be expressed. In this respect, I regard the formation of 'ethnic' identity as a process whereby social groups – in my case, urban Albanian youth – have constructed themselves through selective appropriation and rejection of the socio-cultural contexts in which they find themselves, and this primarily in their capacity as 'consumers rather than creators of their conditions of culture' (Miller 1995: 4). Insofar as their cultural landscape has been heavily occupied by Italian television, it is my argument that this imaginary world has managed to articulate for these young people a crucial aspect of their identity that could not find expression in their local socio-cultural context (Miller 1992: 117).

A note on Albanian culture and history

Because of its historical condition of marginality and isolation and its recent Communist past, Albania never actually extricated itself completely from values and traditions which are typical of a pre-modern society. These stem from an agro-pastoral mode of production and a related model of social relations and power which is structured rigidly around a central and authoritarian male figure. Albanian traditional values have in fact been historically consistent with the life cycle of the extended patriarchal family, characterised by the supremacy of the adult male subject who exercises moral authority over all other members of the family, and by the absolute submission of women to men. Moreover, because for most of its history Albanian society was an aggregation of many extended family networks where power was exerted exclusively by a central leading figure, social relations have always tended to be conflictual, personalistic and manipulative.

Although the most extreme implications of these values and traditions were challenged and partially changed by the Communist regime and have historically been more typical of the northern part of the country, their main traces still shape the most meaningful features of contemporary Albanian culture, which is characterised by the overwhelming centrality of the institution of the family, the prevalence of authoritarian and personalistic modes of understanding and management of power, and a marked predominance of the masculine over the feminine in all aspects of society. The Communist ideology of Enver Hoxha, the man who ruled Albania virtually undisputed for more than forty years, can be seen to share and continue some of the very features of Albanian traditional culture that it initially wanted to dismantle. In fact, Hoxha's particular brand of communism ended up by exacerbating even further Albania's condition of cultural marginality and isolation, as well as the rigid and pervasive social control by a central authority, this time the state, over all aspects of everyday life. By demanding obedience and submission, values deeply entrenched within Albanian traditional structures, by gradually gaining control of every function of the state, and by imposing himself as the father-figure of the family-nation, Hoxha also represented an important element of continuity within the historical development of Albanian culture and society. Thus, while the regime undoubtedly promoted female equality and emancipation, fostered urbanisation, industrialisation and universal education, and fought family feuds, because it imposed these reforms exclusively from above, without the active participation of civil society, it adopted the very patriarchal and authoritarian values, models and behaviours that were being ostensibly challenged and overturned.

More specifically, there are three main features of Albanian communism which have important implications for the migratory projects of young Albanians and for the nature of Albania's transition to democracy:

- the lack of contact with the outside world;
- the systematic stigmatisation of popular pleasures in everyday life;
- the subversive meaning which consumption acquired in the Enverist state.

As far as the lack of contact with the outside world is concerned, it would suffice to say that bureaucratic, social and border controls were very efficient in preventing Albanians from leaving their own country for forty-five years.[1] The diffusion of a very efficient system of social surveillance through the establishment of a capillary network of informers at every level, and in both public and private life, made it extremely dangerous for any Albanian to transgress the regime's many rules and prescriptions. All this assisted the official propaganda's claims that Albania was the only country in the world where the Communist utopia of universal material improvement and emancipation was actually being thoroughly realised, free from any compromise with the Western capitalist world of exploitation and moral depravation. Keeping this in mind it is all the more interesting, then, that one repeated form of transgression was the (unauthorised) viewing of Italian television, which started on a mass scale in the late 1970s.

Before turning to this phenomenon, it is important to underline that Albanian traditional culture has been shaped historically by the difficulties and hardships of an economic context characterised by the extreme scarcity of goods and by extreme competition for resources. It should therefore come as no surprise that, in an environment in which cultural and social life have been tightly harnessed to the survival and reproduction of the extended family network, very little room has been left for the ephemeral or the pleasurable. Songs and stories which are expressive of Albanian traditional culture refer to the individual conceived exclusively as part of a family (or network of families) and in relation to its attendant needs and priorities: marriage, defence of honour, funerals, labour, procurement of food and the reproduction of the new generations. To this cultural heritage one should add the fact that under the Communist regime of Enver Hoxha the prioritisation of the aesthetic dimension was equated with an anti-Communist and subversive act, a betrayal of the working class, and a confirmation of the bourgeois contempt for popular culture.[2] This combination of isolationism and the stigmatisation of pleasure which has characterised Albanian culture throughout its historical development, and more specifically in its recent Communist past is, in my view, a key factor in understanding the role played by Italian media in the process of transformation from totalitarianism to democracy, and ultimately in the stimulation of the migratory flow to Italy.

Finally, it is important to understand how in Albania, as in other Socialist regimes, consumption came to acquire a central role in the emergence of a political opposition and how this has influenced the nature of the Albanian understanding of both capitalism and democracy. According to the anthropologist Katherine Verdery, by insisting that under socialism the material standard of living would improve, socialism aroused desire without focalising it, and kept it alive by deprivation. Because the improvement of the material living conditions had been an essential measure of the advancement of the Soviet Socialist system, this desire was constituted as a right. Within Socialist countries, the combination of the dynamics of arousal and simultaneous frustration of the desire to consume led people to build their social identities specifically *through consuming*. Acquiring foreign consumption goods became a strategy of constituting a selfhood against a regime, its set of rules, its laws and values (quoted in Humphrey 1995: 55–6).

Moreover in Albania, like in many other states which have experienced a Socialist totalitarian regime, the social construction of the individual occurred through an oscillation between a public, hyper-moralised identity based on an ideal model of the Communist citizen, and an alternative private space of consumption and pleasure (Kharkhordin 1995: 214–17). The schizophrenic oscillation between a public space of pretension and heroism and a private space of leisure and mundanity has very important implications for how capitalism and democracy came to be perceived under, and immediately after, communism in Albania, and for the role of foreign media in the phase of transformation from communism to democracy. In fact in Albania, a political alternative to totalitarianism was constructed within a private dimension of leisure and desire that was purposely and reactively disengaged and non-moralised.

As a consequence of all of these dynamics, Albanians have come to associate freedom and democracy with a higher level of material wealth, specifically with the possibility of purchasing Western commodities and also, especially in the immediate post-Communist years, with the possibility of transgressing any rule whose observance was identified with the Communist past. These perceptions have been reinforced by foreign television to the extent that it proffers a utopian and amoral world of unrestricted fulfilment of the consumerist imagination, with little room for a public, ethical and collective dimension. Another significant aspect which seems to be lacking in the Albanian cultural construction of capitalism and democracy is awareness of the key role played by labour and production, set aside from consumption. Beyond this association of the Western world with a situation in which consumer goods, entertainment and pleasure can be attained with little work or sacrifice, one can easily read the projection into the West and into capitalist democracy of the Communist utopia of a world free of material hardship and of the burdens of inequality, discrimination and exploitation – the historical promise Enver Hoxha had failed to keep. Such a projection had an important function both in the creation of the illusionary expectations embedded within the migratory projects of young Albanians and in the negative perception of their migratory experience afterwards.

This reductive and disempowering understanding of democracy and capitalism mainly in terms of a higher level of material wealth coexists with another striking aspect of contemporary Albanian culture: its heterogeneity and fragmentation. The presence of conflicting and contradictory systems of power, values, gender roles, expectations and models of personhood, generates confusion and unrest at every level of the society. Within contemporary Albanian society there is a profound crisis of the individual in relation to his/her social function and available models of identification. The omnipresence of the collective as the founding dimension of the self and of society, imposed and managed by the apparatuses of the Communist state, has given way to a reactive process of individualisation which lacks any shared system of knowledge and understanding (see Fuga 1998: 151). Thus, Albania seems to be displaying a 'reaction-formation' to the obsessive collectivist mentality which characterised Enverist times; the main symptom of this reaction process is the anarchic privatisation of all public life – from politics through to any form of civic behaviour.[3] Enver Hoxha's monument in Skanderbeg Square in Tirana, which was first replaced by a fairground attraction and then, at the end of January 1999, reclaimed by the state as a site for a national monument, is a fitting symbol of the state of confusion in which Albania's post-Communist identity finds itself. The pedestal stands statue-less, as if Albanians are still unsure as to who or what incarnates legitimate state power.

The advent of Italian television

The history of Italian television viewing in Albania is a very adventurous and political one. Albanians began watching Italian television in the early 1960s when the RAI 1 VHF signal could reach most of the coastal region of the country during the summer and in good weather. Even if watching Italian television became increasingly popular among Albanians, it was strictly forbidden until 1985, the year in which Enver Hoxha died, and was punishable by a seven-year jail sentence. Still, the great majority of Albanians secretly tuned into Italian television and radio every night.[4] While the Communist regime tried to crack down on this 'anti-Communist activity', a flow of Italian films, game-shows, advertisements and news beamed into people's homes up to seven hours a day.

When asked what they particularly liked about Italian television in Communist times, most of the young Albanians I interviewed replied that they were fascinated primarily by the beauty and colours, and that they preferred entertainment programmes – shows, films and even advertising itself – to information or documentaries. What Albanian viewers found in Italian television was a cultural landscape of beauty and pleasure that contrasted with the cultural monotone offered by both Albanian television and society. Even if Albania prided itself on its high cultural fare – opera, theatre, classical music – these paled in comparison to the glitter, glamour, wealth and sheer audaciousness on display in Italian popular television. 'Italy is beautiful!' was by far the most common answer to my question 'what do you think about when you think about Italy?' (this question was asked in a general sense both to young people who were thinking of going to Italy and to those who had been there and returned). Looking back at the television images, the contrast between the coercive dark and uniformly grey cultural landscape offered by Albanian television, and the triumph of beauty, colours and wealth offered by Italian television must have been stark indeed.[5]

When, in the 1970s, the Italian Saturday night shows beamed into Albania, with their world of colours, dances and songs, their display of physical beauty, their disproportionate prizes, Albanian people must have thought these programmes came from another planet. (About twenty years later, Italians thought the same about the first Albanians who landed on the shores of Puglia, immediately after the fall of the Communist state.) The appeal of Italian programmes must be understood in terms of their radical difference from cultural products available in Albania and of their potential function to make *tangible* an aspect of life that the local culture was lacking and had not been able to provide. What Albanian people appreciated most in Italian television, I would contend, was a cultural landscape of pleasure and beauty which both responded to and surpassed their most audacious fantasy. And if images of Italian culture and society more generally seemed to conform to this pleasurable aesthetic, this has been reinforced by the programming strategy of both public (RAI 1, RAI 2 and RAI 3) and private (Berlusconi's Canale 5, Rete 4 and Italia 1) national networks, which give far more space to entertainment than to information. Even more than their European counterparts, Italian television networks are characterised by the spectacularisation of physical (especially female) beauty, by a strong emphasis on fun and pleasure, and by the continuous celebration of the satisfactions which are allegedly for the taking in Italy's consumer capitalism. Viewed through the prism of Albania's deprivations, Italian television appeared to offer mediated access to radically different ways of being and having.

The cultural construction of Italy in Albania

Nowadays satellite dishes and aerials of every possible shape and dimension are a pervasive and distinguishing presence in the Albanian urban and rural landscape. Indeed, it is as if their receptive concavity enacts the people's revenge on the convexity of the fortifications which symbolised Albania's acute isolation – notably the 600,000 mushroom-shaped bunkers which still dot the landscape and which Enver Hoxha had erected to assuage his paranoid fears of foreign occupation. In Albania's cultural landscape today, it is the artefacts of Italian popular culture which are now pervasive: clothes shops proudly advertise Italian fashion, local and national radio and television networks consistently broadcast Italian music, you can order Italian food in the majority of restaurants and young children use Italian in street play.[6] Italian television is also an integral part of the Albanian television system. Films of every nationality dubbed into Italian, Italian films, entertainment and news are available not only on the many Italian public and private television networks reaching most of the Albanian territory, but are consistently taped and re-broadcast on local television networks. It is very common to watch on Albanian private television (Koha TV, Nesër TV, Alba TV, Teuta TV, TV Arbëria among many others) films taped from Italian networks and then transmitted with Albanian subtitles and with the logo of the Albanian channel superimposed over the Italian one (still clearly detectable in the background).

This process of selective cultural appropriation is now a very common feature of global television viewing, and of 'media effects' analysis. However I would argue that aspects of Italian culture have been appropriated and incorporated into Albanian culture in a distinctive manner – one that reflects the complexities and ambivalences shaping the relationship between the two countries in the last few decades. On the one hand, the consumption of Italian television has produced the association of Italy with the West,[7] a galaxy of images and symbols hierarchically ordered according to the economic and material prosperity they connote. In terms of levels of perceived prosperity, Italy by no means heads the list, but ranks behind America, Canada, Australia, the Scandinavian countries, the UK, Germany and France; only Greece is considered less developed than Italy in this repertoire. On the other hand, because of the constant presence of 'subversive' Italian television within everyday family life, Italy was the imagined space onto which Albanians first projected their hopes and desires; Italy enjoyed the status of the country most likely to provide an 'answer' to local needs, to offer a refuge from the growing disappointment and disillusionment with Albania's own dim prospects. In the process of this idealised projection, Italy has been configured as not only culturally closer to Albania than other Western nations, but as a more advanced version of local culture. A common 'Mediterranean identity', structured around the primacy and centrality of the family in both societies, is often invoked to explain this feeling of affinity. At the same time, this idealisation of Italy is increasingly on the wane, especially amongst contemporary young people whose dreams of escape are now tempered by the actual experience of migration to Italy of their older compatriots, and by information made available by returning migrants and by the Italian and Albanian media. For a growing number, as we shall soon see, the experience of migration to Italy is now marked not so much by longing but by bitter disillusion.

Between places: the condition of contemporary Albanian youth

As far as young people are concerned, then, if the aspects of Italian television which seem to have the most appeal are those which evoke a hedonistic lifestyle free from the most conservative aspects of Albanian culture, I would suggest that this is not merely the familiar expression of youthful opposition to traditionalism, but an articulation of the emergence of a new social subject in Albania, namely migratory youth. This is a subjectivity which imagines different ways of being, different realities, different lives – whether physical displacement is actually carried out or not. From this perspective, migration can be understood as a condition of subjective displacement, as a disembedding of subjectivity from the social and cultural sites which have previously anchored it, and the reconfiguring of new identities in relation to new perceived priorities, possibilities and necessities. Migration is a 'potential state of being' which any subject may pass through during his/her lifetime, whether it is followed by physical displacement or not (Pœrregaard 1997: 41). It is this migratory subject which Italian television both appealed to, and helped to construct.[8]

Italian television has provided Albanian young people with models of personhood, of identification, of social behaviour, of interaction, that they immediately preferred to those at work within their immediate environment. With only a fleeting experience – if any – of the Enverist regime, and accustomed to watching 5–6 hours of Italian television daily during their childhood and adolescence, Albanian young people are feeling increasingly disembedded from the cultural, social and economic context that surrounds them. In this concern what separates them from their parents nowadays is not merely a generational gap, but an epochal one. Whereas most parents tend to conform to patriarchal values and to accept the renunciation of pleasure which underpinned Albanian communism, Albanian young people want to have fun, to live free sexual lives, to study and to work, to go on holiday and travel – just like their peers elsewhere in Europe. But those raised expectations are thwarted at every turn. Albania suffers from widespread unemployment, and even one of the most active sectors – the construction industry – is mainly funded by the remittances of migrants working abroad (UNICEF 1998: 19). Although the commercial and services sector is expanding, particularly within and around the main conurbations and with the help of foreign aid and investment, this is still not sufficient to absorb the number of young Albanians seeking work. For many, bars and video game halls are all that is on offer – though even these distractions are not available to young women, who are still kept on a tight leash by wary parents. Public space is perceived as threatening and dangerous and while this is no doubt a reflection of enduring patriarchal values, there is also a real basis for this perception in the legacy of the economic scandal that rocked Albania in 1997, when a network of private pyramid-selling financial schemes, unofficially endorsed by the state, collapsed and bankrupted at least 70 per cent of Albanian families (UNICEF 1998: 24). For a time, Albania foundered on the verge of civil war and local and national criminal organisations stepped in as the country's power-brokers. In the wake of this chaotic breakdown of any semblance of law and order, many Albanian towns responded by shutting down at sunset. Metaphorically speaking, often the only colour in the streets at night is that reflected by private television sets constantly flickering from behind closed doors.[9]

This being the situation, it is not surprising that, in comparing their lives to those of their peers as they are portrayed on foreign television programmes, Albanian young people may feel at the margin of the so-called global culture in relation to which they seem to have developed a sort of inferiority complex.[10] Everything that connotes quality, beauty, prestige and glamour is necessarily foreign to Albanian young people; everything that is Albanian denotes backwardness, unfashionableness and shoddiness.[11] Albanian young people seem left with nothing more than a purely affective and emotional attachment to their country, which they often describe as 'the country of my family', rather than their own.[12] This is especially and increasingly true of younger generations.

When in interviews I asked Albanian young people who had migrated which expectations were not met in their first encounters with Italy, invariably the answer was that they had expected life to be easier, they had not expected to work so much for so little money or with so few prospects. Many people thought that the consumer goods that they had seen advertised and promoted through Italian television could be attained at a lesser cost, through less hardship, work and sacrifice. They did not expect to struggle so much to find a decent job, nor to work more than 10 hours a day for salaries inferior to those of their Italian colleagues.[13] In fact, a good proportion of youth who migrated into Italy in the early 1990s had university or high school diplomas and expected their qualifications to be automatically acknowledged. Many people who had studied to become actors, painters, teachers, engineers, surgeons or architects found themselves, whether in the short or longer term, in occupations avoided by Italians: working night shifts, washing cars, waiting on tables, in construction or other manual occupations. This common tale of disillusion has helped to shatter the idealised image of Italy as a landscape of material wealth and freedom. This is compounded by the widespread diffidence at best and racism at worst with which many Italians 'welcomed' Albania's migrants. Italy's attitude to these migrants changed very rapidly within the first eight months of 1991 (Zinn 1996). If the first Albanians arriving in Italy immediately after the collapse of the Communist regime in March 1991 were greeted by local and national media as 'deserving' refugees, by the end of August of the same year these same people were treated as illegal 'economic migrants' and sent back to Albania, after a period of detention in provisionally arranged camps. Those who remained had to endure media coverage that in large measure contributed to – indeed was responsible for – the pervasive stigmatisation and criminalisation of Albanian migrants.[14]

The new generation of Albanian youth are benefiting from the experience of the many friends and relatives who have returned from Italy and from the information they convey about the actual possibilities available in Italy and about the social discrimination and stigmatisation migrants are likely to encounter there. Having said this, it is also true that the illusionary dynamic of projection and idealisation that brought young Albanians to Italy in 1991 appears to be substantially unchanged when it comes to the migratory destinations that are replacing Italy in the popular imagination: like the US, Canada or Australia – countries they have come to know once again nearly exclusively through television programmes and in which they are increasingly imagining their futures.

Conclusion

In order to give an account of the role of Italian mass media in the process of political and cultural transformation in Albania, and ultimately in the migratory flow from Albania to Italy, it is important to be reminded of Arjun Appadurai's definition of knowledge as primarily a local process, which constructs a knowing subject and its knowable environment (Appadurai 1995: 206). It is also necessary to underline how material products are culturally embedded. They 'represent culture, not because they are merely there as the environment in which we operate, but because they are an integral part of that project of objectification by which we create our selves as an industrial society: our identities, our social affiliations, our lived everyday practices' (Miller 1987: 215). Cultural products in turn are very complex 'social forms of construction and distribution of knowledge' that 'acquire especially intense, new and striking qualities when the spatial, cognitive, or institutional distances between production, distribution, and consumption are great' (Appadurai 1986: 41, 48). This is particularly true if we consider the reception of cultural constructs from the West in the rest of the world, particularly in post-Socialist states like Albania, where consumption of Western products acquired a politically subversive function. With reference to migratory flows from post-Communist countries, a rigid distinction between the two contrasting concepts of the 'political refugee' (or 'asylum-seeker') and the 'economic migrant' should be challenged, because the desire to improve material living conditions through migration emerged in connection to the attempt to find a political alternative to a despised regime through the challenging of its material environment.

If it is true that different local cultures can borrow elements from other cultures in ways which best fulfil locally emerging social needs and appeal to the imagination (Howell 1995: 179), then Italian television programmes have conveyed and were identified with models of personhood and of social interaction, which better corresponded to local social and cultural needs than the Albanian ones: hence the appeal of Italian television and the ensuing migratory flow. These associative dynamics have stimulated the desire to migrate in order to be able to experience those aspects of the self, and those networks of social relationships which could not be experienced by staying in Albania, but whose very possibility of existence was made available by Italian television.

Albanian people, then, because of the state of isolation they were kept in by the Communist regime, were exposed to capitalist modernity via Italian television viewing, which provided them with a reductive landscape of consumerist satisfaction, celebration and beauty. If we consider consumption as it is presented within capitalist late modernity, it is in fact apparent that it creates an imaginary space of viewership and participation in which individual choice and freedom exist at the level of consumption (Lee 1993: 165–78). Returning to the relation between media and migration, the most politically relevant aspect of the process of appropriation of cultural constructs from Italian television with reference to the migration of young Albanians is their association with an imaginary and inclusionary space of viewership, participation and universal entitlement that is linked primarily to the sphere of consumption and recreation and in relation to which the desire to migrate has emerged.

105

The role of Italian media in the process of construction of the migratory project of young Albanians can be seen as two-fold. On the one hand by having provided alternative models of subjectivity and social relationships, Italian media stimulated social change and have been deeply involved in the gradual emergence of youth as a new social and political subject on the Albanian social, cultural and economic scene. On the other hand, such media have offered Albanian young people a very simplified, partial and illusionary account of Italian society. This imperfect 'understanding' privileged dramatically the utopian inclusionary discourses related mainly to the spheres of consumption, recreation and leisure, and underplayed the existence of a very efficient and complex system of social practices which limited, regulated and too often prevented people (especially immigrants) from the universal and full enjoyment of citizenship. These unexpected restricting and discriminating practices have greeted Albanians only immediately after they had reached the other side of the Adriatic Sea and are nowadays at the root of both a growing disillusionment about the actual possibilities offered to a young Albanian migrant in Italy, and of a process of re-projection of the same idealised reading of the capitalist utopia towards more distant and unknown places.

NOTES

1 Until 1991, it was literally impossible for any Albanian citizen to leave the country. Every mile of the border was patrolled day and night. Even internal migration was very limited and people were strictly forbidden from coming in contact, without official permission, with the very few foreigners who visited the country. Until 1985, the year of Enver Hoxha's death, post and telephones were very carefully checked and Albanians were forbidden to watch foreign television. Little foreign literature was available and the press was state-run and controlled. The road network was never rationalised in order to make it more difficult for Hoxha's perceived enemies of the state to occupy the country in case of invasion – thus, it still takes more than 18 hours to drive the 350 km that separate the northern and southern extremities of the country (see Vickers 1995: 185–209).
2 In Communist times, Albanian women and men were forced to wear grey and standardised clothes. Jewellery, make-up, 'non-popular' (i.e. folkloristic) music – in short anything which could be seen as not strictly functional to the priorities and directives promulgated by the directors of the national cultural and political appara-tuses – was banned. Again, see Vickers (1995: 193–209). In both rural and urban areas, concrete and brick-built houses seldom had decorated façades – this because, according to official policies and propaganda, houses need only to be comfortable inside; external decoration would have betrayed popular values and would surely have aroused in foreign nations the desire to occupy the country (see Hall 1994: 153–5).
3 The labyrinth of kiosks which has replaced the Youth Park and partially occupied the pavements of the main boulevards and squares in central Tirana is a very telling testimony of how a public space of relaxation and leisure has been fragmented and replaced by privatised and unregulated spaces of consumption, by a chaotic assembly of clothes shops, record shops, bars and restaurants whose cultural universe of reference is evident from their names: Bar Amerika, Pizzeria Santa Lucia, Bar Soros, Bar Marlboro, Bar West, Bar Lady Diana, etc. In Berat, the hall in which the Provi-sional Government of Albania was first created on 20 October 1944, a small building

positioned right in the centre of the town, once an important national monument, has been transformed into a 'Tele Bingo', where many unemployed young men spend their days betting, smoking and drinking.

4 As Albanian television sets could only receive VHF waves, other foreign public and private television networks broadcasting in UHF waves (Yugoslavian and Italian in central and northern Albania, Greek and Italian in the south of the country) could only be seen with the help of a special aerial, which would be kept indoors during the day and stretched out in the open at night, and of a *canoçe* (tin, in Albanian), an electronic device made secretly and illegally out of a couple of transistors, a condenser and a tin. One had to be very careful not to talk about Italian television or to sing an Italian song openly. During my interviews, many Albanian young people told of having been punished severely by their school teachers when caught singing an Italian television advertisement jingle or whistling an Italian song. A group of young friends from Tirana told me how, in order to call one another and arrange meetings from window to window, they used to whistle as a secret common code call the opening tune of the Italian RAI 1 evening news programme.

5 In fact, there is a perception amongst young people that there is also a sinister side to the appreciation of Italian media. Enida, 26, from Tirana, offered the blunt judgement that so overwhelming was the power of those images, that you could say that 'the Italian media raped Albanian young people'; Neritan, 28, also from Tirana, mused that during Enver's regime, 'Albanians used to masturbate with Italian television.'

6 Not only do most Albanian young people under the age of 30 speak Italian fluently, but they also swear mainly in Italian. When I asked for an explanation, I was told that, in Albanian, insults would sound too offensive. This is not only a testimony about how swearing is not socially admissible in Albania, but also an example of the function Italian culture came to have for Albanian young people, that of a complement for most of the areas in which Albanian culture was seen as lacking, namely beauty, entertainment, consumption and sexuality.

7 Italian television has been an open window on the world as a whole and not Italy alone; the fact that very often Albanians' favourite programmes have been American, British or German dubbed in Italian played a major role in the association of Italy with the West. This association can be traced in the frequent juxtaposition of the Italian, American and Albanian flags at petrol stations, on new houses under construction, and not least on the ultra-modern and highly symbolic Coca Cola plant on the Tirana–Durrës motorway. Street kids selling key rings and cigarettes have often tried to get my attention by shouting 'Hey, Italian, American, do you want a packet?'

8 Though not Italian television alone. Helti, 23, from Durrës, who is dreaming of going to London and trying his luck with his rock group, reported how the main source of information about life in the UK had been MTV, available for years on the Macedonian public television network. Music videos gave him the idea of the UK as a place where 'you can be what you want, young people can wear strange clothes, have long hair, they are free'.

9 Albanian young people particularly complain about the level of criminality, the conservativism of traditional culture, and the lack of entertainment facilities and opportunities. The combination of these factors increasingly confines them and does not allow them to lead a less inhibited life with peers of both sexes.

10 Neritan, 28, from Tirana, told me that the Egyptian alien portrayed in the American blockbuster 'Stargate' spoke Albanian. Whether this is true or not really does not matter; what is significant is the role most Albanian young people feel they are playing on the global scene, which is the cultural space that really matters for them.

11 Denis, 18, leading member of 'The Extreme Boys', a boy band based at the Youth Centre of Durrës, informed me that most of his friends had emigrated to Italy and

often phoned him to report how much fun it was, 'you know, full of girls, music, discos … '. Renalda, 23, from Tirana, told me that 'Mali i Robit', a luxury tourist resort for foreign entrepreneurs and rich Albanians on the Golem Beach between Durrës and Kavaje, was a wonderful place, as 'it doesn't even seem like Albania!'.

12 In December 1998 at the AKSI Youth Centre in Berat and at the Durrës Youth Centre I organised two debates about young people's identity in the period of post-Communist transformation, which saw the participation of approximately forty girls and boys between the ages of 18 and 23. Although many of them spent half of the time professing and swearing their love for their homeland, silence, embarrassment and hesitation were the most telling responses to the questions 'Why do you like Albania? For which particular aspect?' Albanian young people do unquestionably love their country, but this love is of a very difficult and tormented kind. Most of the girls and boys I interviewed agreed on the conclusion that Albania was indeed a wonderful and unique place, but definitely not a place for young people.

13 Gerti, 24, from Durrës, who escaped to Italy hidden in a lorry, could not believe that he would have to go through a three-month probation period for specialised training before even being allowed to use an automatic lathe. Eventually he found employment as a skilled worker in a machine shop, for a salary which was two-thirds that of his Italian co-workers.

14 For a comprehensive analysis of the way Italian media have portrayed Albanian migrants see Vehbiu and Devole (1996). The degree of interiorisation of this stereotype is evident from a comment by Gentian, 23, from Durrës, who confided that 'when I was in Italy I was very careful not to mix with the Albanians'. To my amazed request for clarification – 'Do you mean with the other Albanians that were in your town?' – he replied: 'you know what I mean, the Albanians, the criminals'.

References

Appadurai, A. (1986) 'Introduction: commodities and the politics of value', in Appadurai, A. (ed.), *The Social Life of Things*, Cambridge: Cambridge University Press.

—— (1995) 'The production of locality', in Fardon, R. (ed.), *Counterworks: Managing the Diversity of Knowledge*, London: Routledge.

Barjaba, K., Lapassade, G. and Perrone, L. (1996) *Naufragi Albanesi*, Rome: Sensibili alle Foglie.

Caritas di Roma (1998) *Immigrazione Dossier Statistico '98*, Rome: Anterem.

Fuga, A. (1998) *L'Albanie entre la Pensée Totalitaire et la Raison Fragmentaire*, Paris: L'Harmattan.

Gjonça, A. (2000) 'Demographische Trends', in *Albanien: die weite Welt und das Dorf*, Vienna–Cologne–Graz: Boehlau Verlag.

Hall, D. (1994) *Albania and the Albanians*, London: Pinter Reference.

Howell, S. (1995) 'Whose knowledge and whose power? A new perspective on cultural diffusion', in Fardon, R. (ed.), *Counterworks: Managing the Diversity of Knowledge*, London: Routledge.

Humphrey, C. (1995) 'A culture of disillusionment', in Miller, D. (ed.), *Worlds Apart: Modernity through the Prism of the Local*, London: Routledge.

Kharkhordin, O. (1995) 'The Soviet individual: genealogy of a dissimulating animal', in Featherstone, M., Lash, S. and Robertson, R. (eds), *Global Modernities*, London: Sage.

Lee, B. (1993) 'Going public', *Public Culture* 5, 2: 165–78.

Miller, D. (1987) *Material Culture and Mass Consumption*, Oxford: Blackwell.

—— (1992) 'The young and the restless in Trinidad: a case of the global and the local in mass consumption', in Silverstone, R. and Hirsch, E. (eds), *Consuming Technologies: Media and Information in Domestic Spaces*, London: Routledge.

—— (1995) 'Anthropology, modernity and consumption', in Miller, D. (ed.), *Worlds Apart: Modernity through the Prism of the Local*, London: Routledge.

Pœrregaard, K. (1997) 'Imagining a place in the Andes', in Fog Olwig, K. and Hastrup, K. (eds), *Siting Culture*, London: Routledge.

Trifirò, A. (1995) 'Albania and its youth during transition: dreams, hopes, fears', in Caka, N. (ed.), *Passage to the West*, Tirana: Dora d'Istria.

UNDP (1998) *Albanian Human Development Report 1998*, Tirana: UNDP.

UNICEF (1998) *Situation Analysis 1998: Children's and Women's Rights in Albania*, Tirana: UNICEF.

Vehbiu, A. and Devole, R. (1996) *La Scoperta dell'Albania. Gli Albanesi secondo i Mass-Media*, Milan: Paoline.

Vickers, M. (1995) *The Albanians: A Modern History*, London: I.B. Tauris.

Zinn, D. L. (1996) 'Adriatic brethren or black sheep? Migration in Italy and the Albanian crisis', *European Urban and Regional Studies* 3, 3: 241–9.

8

FOLLOWING THE SENEGALESE MIGRATORY PATH THROUGH MEDIA REPRESENTATION

Bruno Riccio

Introduction

This chapter focuses on the experiences and representations of Senegalese transmigrants, tracing their migration path from Senegal to one of their principal destinations in the 1990s – Italy. I should stress at the outset that the material presented in this chapter can be regarded as an offshoot from a wider research project on Senegalese migration to Italy.[1] This research explored the interplay of two social phenomena: the representations and the institutional practices in the receiving society on the one hand; and on the other, the experiences and strategies adopted by immigrants, who rely on material and symbolic resources drawn through transnational networks. Although this broad research agenda did not have a central media focus, during my fieldwork in Senegal and in Italy I came across media representation many times and in different settings. It is not difficult to draw out these media representations and reactions into a narrative which follows the Senegalese migratory path into and out of Italy and Senegal. In particular I want to focus on the Senegalese reception of and response to Western media self-representation and (mis)representation of the 'other', using material gathered from interviews and episodes of participant observation. My analysis encourages me to suggest a cautious attitude towards what seem to me to be two over-polarised positions with regard to the impact of global and local media on cultural identity, namely

- the 'hypodermic' conception of media representation and Western imperialism, which pictures consumers as cultural addicts unable in any way to resist their influence;
- at the other extreme, the over-celebration of the capacity of the receiver to articulate and disarticulate images and media representations, producing 'hybrid' and 'creolised' counter-cultures.[2]

The chapter is structured as follows. I begin with some background information on Senegalese immigration to Italy. Then I start my 'travel' from Senegal, considering the way migrants are portrayed by the Senegalese media and the ways in which they react to European visual media. Next I will consider the receiving context at the local level (the tourist coast of Rimini in the late 1990s), where media produce a scapegoating construct which conflates the phenomenon of migration with the problem of irregular trade, thereby reinforcing the more general criminalisation of immigrants which has become increasingly dominant in the national media discourse (Dal Lago 1996). I will then look at the ways in which the Senegalese deal with racist representations and at their reliance on a broader critique of the receiving society. I will conclude by suggesting that the different examples I describe illustrate the need to consider historical context and personal experiences in order to make sense of how people articulate media messages.

Senegalese migration to Italy

Senegalese migration to Italy started in the early 1980s with flows arriving from France in the first instance. During the postwar labour migrations into Europe, France had attracted a significant number of immigrants from francophone West Africa, and the Senegalese had become established as one of several West African immigrant nationalities in France in the decades before Italy emerged as a major country of immigration in the 1980s. Later in that decade, Senegalese migrated direct to Italy, their main destinations being Rome and the islands of Sicily and Sardinia (Scidà 1993; Treossi 1995). By 1997 there were around 32,000 Senegalese immigrants legally resident in Italy (i.e. with a *permesso di soggiorno* or 'permit to stay'). They are mainly men who migrate as individuals, following the paths shaped by migratory chains which have quickly evolved over the past 10–15 years. The Senegalese are also highly spatially mobile within Italy, a characteristic which reflects their dominant economic activity, street-vending. The number of women has recently been growing (to 1,640 in 1997), largely through family reunions. However the female percentage (5 per cent) is lower than for any other major immigrant community in Italy (Caritas di Roma 1998; ISMU 1997). The reasons for this will emerge later.

The most significant 'moment' for Senegalese migration to, and within, Italy was 1989–90, during the months leading up to the amnesty for illegal immigrants offered by the Martelli Law. The internal move from the south to the north of Italy is partly explained by the much better opportunities in the north for regular employment – a necessary qualification for regularisation under the Martelli amnesty. Hence more settled Senegalese groups are emerging in several northern towns where industrial employment is available.[3] However there are also seasonal migrations like that towards Emilia-Romagna; these migrations are not generally aimed at industrial employment but mainly at the tourist coast which in the summer is a profitable arena for street-selling and hawking tourist goods along the beach.

According to the detailed research on Senegalese migrants in Italy carried out by Ottavia Schmidt di Friedberg (1994), most of the immigrants belong to the Wolof ethnic group and to the Mouride brotherhood. They come mainly from the north-western regions of Senegal – Baol, Djambour and Cayor. The Mouride order was founded in the 1880s by Amadou Bamba who 'drew followers from many levels of society, mostly artisans, traders and slaves, who more than other members of the community had something to gain from the Mouride doctrine of hard work as the way of salvation' (Ebin 1996: 96). The brotherhood today has its capital at Touba, the site of Amadou Bamba's revelation, where the Mourides have constructed the largest mosque in sub-Saharan Africa. The highest office in the brotherhood is held by the Khalifa-General who is the eldest surviving son of Amadou Bamba. More important from the point of view of interpreting Senegalese migration, many studies have shown how the brotherhood's vertical and horizontal ties provide an organisational structure which can be reproduced in transnational networks, and how a strong sense of identity is preserved in the trading diaspora (Carter 1997; Ebin 1996; Schmidt di Friedberg 1994).

Senegalese emigrate mainly for economic reasons, and in particular in response to a crisis in the traditional agricultural structure of their region. A clear historical sequence of migratory types can be observed: first rural–urban migration within Senegal, second international migration within the West African region, thirdly emigration to Europe (mainly France), fourthly internal European migration (France to Italy), and finally direct emigration from Senegal to Italy (Campus *et al.* 1992; Perrone 1995; Scidà 1993). Some studies also underline the 'pull effects' of Italy: established migration paths, the previous representation of Italy as an accessible goal (also reinforced by media), and opportunities for seasonal jobs (cf. Marchetti 1994 on Milan). Important roles in furthering Senegalese migration are played by access to transnational networks and by the distinctive culture of emigration as a 'training' experience for manhood and maturity (Carter 1997; Ebin 1996; Schmidt di Friedberg 1994; Zinn 1994).

Senegalese media self-representation

I now start my migration journey which forms the organisational backbone of the remainder of the chapter. When I was doing my fieldwork in Senegal I was able to observe a system of media representation which celebrated migrants (known as *modou modou*) as the new national heroes.[4] A famous Senegalese journalist once described them to me in the following terms: 'They come from the countryside with their chariots and they travel to different places like New York or Hong Kong speaking different languages, and yet they do not lose even a small piece of their identity.'

The *modou modou* fits the general image of all Senegalese migrants, but is more specifically applied to those from Diourbel, Kebemer, Louga and Touba, towns in north-west Senegal. According to one of my informants, whom I shall call Talla, if we want to picture an 'ideal type' we might think of an illiterate who knows trading well, who is very good at saving and who invests in glamorous things when he is back home: big weddings, big houses. All this pushes others to take their chance on the migratory path as well. Many think, like Talla, though this is not an uncontested claim, that 'without *modou modou*, Senegal would be on its knees. Remittances are the real source of wealth of the country.'

Thus migrants are contemporary heroes in Senegal. This is why such characters are celebrated within the most widespread cultural sphere in the country: music. When I was conducting fieldwork in Senegal the latest record of Youssou N'Dour could be heard constantly on radio and television. Like other famous musicians (Ismael Lo, Ouza), he sings about migrants and peddlers as symbols of contemporary society, pointing to their solidarity and their efforts at coping with being far from home and their families. Yet one may encounter critical opinions too: according to another of my informants, 'They do not work in Italy like when they are in Senegal. The returnee has only money when he comes back, but nothing else, because he did not live abroad as he would have done in Senegal.'

This example shows us that much media interest is focused on national self-representation, but also that the messages are received critically by some, who compare the media representation to actual experience. Furthermore, the discourse on the migrant entails many different dichotomies which are also reproduced in Senegalese films and novels: for instance between saving and investing on the one hand, and wasting and spending on the other; or between preserving Senegalese cultural identity or behaving like an uprooted *toubab* (Westerner) forsaking family ties and obligations. The word *toubab* means 'European' and was the term used in Senegal originally to denote white French people; now, however, it has acquired a broader typological meaning, becoming a synonym for thinking and acting like a Westerner. This 'Western' behaviour – putting money first, forsaking God, solidarity, tolerance, moderation, hospitality and dignity (the main Senegalese values) – becomes the whole negative symbol which summarises all the faults condemned in Senegalese popular culture's view of the West.

Senegalese 'reception' of European films

This last reaction, critical of the behaviour of the Western *toubab*, is key to the 'reception' of European films, where one witnesses a strong sense of identity expressed by explicit differentiation. My evidence here comes from two vignettes of participant observation when I was able to witness Senegalese critical reaction to European films.

Once, I spent an evening watching TV with a Senegalese informant's family in a suburb of Kaolack, a post-colonial town which once flourished thanks to the groundnut economy, but which today is decayed and reliant on trade, and internal as well as international migration. We watched a German police movie called *Inspector Derrik* (also well known to Italian television audiences). The inspector was dealing with a tricky case: an upper-class doctor was being betrayed by his wife who had taken a younger and opportunistic lover. The husband was genuinely in love with his wife and responded in a very selfless way: he did not care too much about the love affair but was very concerned that she was being exploited by the lover for her money. His wife left him anyway. The husband's attitude produced hilarity among the audience, who could not believe he was taking the betrayal in such a controlled and laid-back way. But they became outraged as the story developed further. As the wife drove back in tears from the lover who had rejected her, showing he was really only interested in her money, she was killed in a car accident. The husband blamed the lover for her death and organised a highly complex plot which fulfilled his own intention: he got the ex-lover to kill him after driving him mad through constant harassment. He died smiling, assured that his former rival would be sent to jail.

The audience's silence was palpable proof of their disturbed reaction to what they had just seen. Eventually Mansour, the older brother-in-law of my informant, felt that I needed some explanation, so he told me very concisely: 'Betrayal and suicide are sins. I do not understand *toubabs* sometimes – it seems that the money and freedom given to women go to their heads, they have no faith and are unable to hold the family together any more.' As for myself, apart from having to digest one of the most complicated episodes of *Derrik* I have ever seen, plus the fact that I did so in a very unusual setting, I could only answer with an elusive 'Maybe'. Paraphrasing Abu Lughod (1997), I would suggest that by his explanation, the brother-in-law was distancing himself in moral language from what he perceived as a cultural difference between 'us' (the Senegalese) and 'them' (the Westerner, European, *toubab*). His comments posited this difference in quite an assertive way; money, materialism and the shattering of families being common Senegalese criticisms of Western society.

My second example occurred when I was leaving Senegal. I was flying with Aire Afrique, the company most often chosen by migrants because, although their timing is unreliable, they are much less strict about weight limits. I was the only white person on the plane that day. Everyone else was quite tired due to fasting for Ramadan and many passengers were praying or saying 'saving sentences' before take-off. Many were also reading the Koran or the *quasaids* – poems by the Mouride founder Amadou Bamba. Suddenly the screen started showing a film, *Secrets and Lies* by Mike Leigh. Described by one reviewer as 'an acutely accurate portrait of familial tensions' (Cannon 1997), the film had recently been awarded a prize at the Cannes Film Festival. Some of the passengers could follow the movie thanks to the dubbing on the headphones.

The story is about a young black woman who knew she was adopted but, after her adoptive mother's death, discovers through Social Services that her real mother was white. The forbidding barriers shaped by secrets and lies happily disappear at the end, but throughout the film heavy existential description mixes with rich humour. I laughed several times, but quickly realised I was the only one to do so; embarrassed, I kept quiet afterwards. Around me, passengers were shaking their heads in disapproval of the film. It was clear that Mike Leigh's anti-romantic vision of Britain was not to their liking.

These two examples show a critical reading by Senegalese viewers of European self-representations conveyed by the global media. They show, too, how such a critical filter is also connected to a sort of 'ethno-occidentalism' which pictures the white Westerner as the agent which shatters family unity. Drawing the term from Carrier (1992), by ethno-occidentalism I mean an 'essentialist rendering of the West by members of an alien society' that stresses 'the importance of money and purchase (as distinct from sharing)' as the way that Westerners transact with each other and secure their subsistence (Carrier 1992: 198). We will see later how such a critical perspective is also embedded within an Afro-muslim critique of European society and how this can be a support when dealing with Italian racist misrepresentations.

Italian racist misrepresentations

My journey with the Senegalese migrants now moves to Italy, and specifically to the coast of Emilia-Romagna, where I carried out the longest phase of my field research. According to the most recent data published by Caritas di Roma (1998), there were 93,908 foreigners with a *permesso di soggiorno* living in Emilia-Romagna in 1997, of which 4,587, nearly 5 per cent, were Senegalese. This percentage is higher than any other Italian region except Sardinia. Tourism provides an obvious linkage to an explanation of the concentrations of Senegalese in both Sardinia (a major Italian tourist region) and Emilia-Romagna (where the Rimini coastal strip has long been a favoured destination for North European and Italian holiday-makers). In the case of the Rimini tourist coast, the arrival of numerous Senegalese street-sellers could be observed during the late 1980s. Rimini's economic structure is based almost entirely on tourism and the street-hawking and beach-selling activities of the Senegalese came to be perceived as a threat to the wealth of the town's established merchants and shopkeepers (Riccio 1999). This confrontation partially explains why, although Rimini was one of the first towns in the region to do something for immigrants, so little has been done in the field of immigrants' reception since that first attempt. Although I also carried out fieldwork amongst the Senegalese in Ravenna, the coastal province to the north of Rimini, where a more broadly-based economic structure (agriculture, industry, tourism and trade) offered a less conflictual context for public policies on immigrant reception and settlement, I will dwell more on the Rimini case in this section of the chapter since it provides an extreme caricature of Italian media constructs of immigrants and immigration.

Indeed, when in Italy, the Senegalese have to face a system of media representation which shapes and constructs the imagery of the immigrant for wider national consumption. Newspapers and television increasingly present immigration as a 'social problem' (Grillo 1985), with obvious negative effects on public opinion. While it is thought 'natural' to allow free movement of people and workers amongst wealthy countries, it is considered dangerous to facilitate immigration from countries with some or all of the following characteristics: low per capita incomes, high birth rates, and Islamic religion. A discourse of the 'naturalisation of difference' is spreading in relation to people originating in the poorer countries of the South who, 'for their own good', are requested to 'remain where they naturally belong' (Miles and Thränhardt 1995: 7). This is what has often been termed the 'new racism' (see also Cole 1997). A recent article in the weekly newspaper *L'Espresso* included an interview with Umberto Bossi, the leader of the separatist Northern League, which displayed exactly this kind of ideological 'cultural fundamentalism' (Stolke 1995):

> If there exists a concept which is extraneous to the Lega, it's racism. ...
> Like all *leghisti* worthy of that name, I am incapable of racial hatred.
> For me all men are equal, and have the same dignity. The blackest of
> the black have the same rights as my neighbour. But in their own
> country.[5]

From this statement it is very easy to move towards exclusionary practices and discourses screaming 'go back home'. What is clearly absent is a real debate on the legitimisation of practices of exclusion in everyday life through this new racist discourse (Dal Lago 1996; Palidda 1996). In fact, Italy's contribution to the building of the 'Fortress Europe' imagery still emphasises the paradox that Campani already pointed out in 1993. She asked: 'Is it possible, on the one hand, to promote integration, and, on the other, to increase the controls and the expulsions, promoting the idea that all people coming from the South and East constitute a potential danger?' (Campani 1993: 528).

The difficulties of resolving this discursive paradox are compounded by the great regional diversity of the immigrant experience in Italy, with different ethnic groups doing different types of work and having different experiences of social and economic integration (or exclusion) in different parts of the country (King and Andall 1999). Hence more needs to be said about the specific local context of the Senegalese in Rimini. Here, too, opinions and perspectives about Senegalese immigrants are somewhat ambivalent. Compared to several other immigrant groups in Italy (Moroccans, Tunisians, Albanians), the Senegalese are looked upon favourably. On the other hand there are some stereotypes of Senegalese which worsen with the conflict over 'irregular' trading activities, particularly as viewed from the perspective of shopkeepers and their commercial interests. This conflict between street-peddlers and shopkeepers is played out at the local level and Andall (1990) has described some of the earliest manifestations of this battle in Florence. For Rimini I have demonstrated in a separate paper how the dominant discourse on immigration has become confused with the conflict over irregular trade, with the result that a slippage of categories has occurred so the immigrant is too easily regarded as someone who is 'irregular', criminal, dangerous (Riccio 1999).

Let us observe how, in the summer of 1996, the discourse on irregular trade slowly got confused with the discourse on immigration in the local press. Three distinctive types of social actors shape the receiving context with regard to the immigrant:

- shopkeepers and their organisations, Confcommercio and Confesercenti;
- volunteer associations and trade unions;
- a local government that finds itself uncomfortably positioned between the first two.

These three collective actors also display different attitudes toward the issue of irregular trade. Trade unions and voluntary groups think that irregular trade must be counteracted by offering incentives for other employment, and by regularising the sale of 'ethnic' craft goods, which are not in competition with the local shopkeepers. The trader associations focus on the issue of 'unfair competition' and advocate repressive solutions such as patrols and police control. Local government again expresses an ambivalent position.

The debate carried on almost every day in the local press with headlines like 'No to the hunting of blacks' (*Corriere di Rimini*, 6 July 1996) or 'It's war with the irregular street-peddlers' (*Corriere di Rimini*, 11 July 1996). The confusion and overlapping of terms such as *abusivi* (irregular traders), *extracomunitario* (strictly speaking, any citizen of a non-EU country, but in practice applied to 'Third World' immigrants), *nero* (black), *vu cumprà* (a derogatory term for street-sellers), *irregolari* or *clandestini* (undocumented immigrants) led to a conflated image of the Senegalese as irregular traders, undocumented immigrants, poor, victimised and weak, but also as criminal and violent. This collective image was reified in both the accusers' and defenders' positions, although with different emphases. The overlapping of the discourse on irregular trade with the one on immigration peaked at the end of July. A regional newspaper (*Il Resto del Carlino*, 27 July 1996) provided the reader with a dossier entitled '*Extracomunitari*, the polemic of the summer'. This was the culminating moment in which the complex phenomenon of immigration was reduced to the problem of irregular trade. The month of August was marked by an escalation of violent conflict and riots on the beaches involving irregular sellers, patrols and tourists (who usually acted in defence of the peddlers). In the local and regional press, one witnessed the growth of the language of war (cf. Gilroy 1987) with bellicose metaphors such as 'the army of *vu cumprà'* (*Il Resto del Carlino*, 22 August 1996). The rumour of a big criminal organisation acting on behalf of the peddlers became more and more prevalent, despite this being dismissed by careful academic research (Catanzaro *et al.* 1996).

During the following summer, 1997, the combined discourse on immigrants and criminality became even clearer.[6] In the Rimini area an escalation of crimes – five rapes and the arrest of some drug-dealers – produced headlines declaring an 'emergency of immigration'. Note here the slippage from criminality to immigration.[7] Both in the local press and in the national public arena the phenomena of irregular trade, criminality and migration became conflated into a single issue.[8] Here is just a small, but striking, example of how the 'atavistic' caricature of the 'immigrant rapist of our women' was presented during this period (August 1997). *Il Giornale*, a prominent right-wing newspaper, published a drawing representing a young white woman held tight by a large black man, and facing another man wearing a fez and threatening her. Another powerful image that circulated for a week in many newspapers was a photograph of a naked Moroccan being searched by the police. Both these representations accompanied articles about the criminal events happening along the Romagna coast, not all of which involved immigrants. On both occasions the symbolic link between otherness, crime and atavistic sexuality was clear. The day after *Il Giornale* published the above-mentioned drawing, another newspaper (*Il Manifesto*) reprinted it, juxtaposing a poster of the fascist regime portraying a black man raping a white woman (Figure 8.1).[9] The similarities are striking. Although imagery from Italy's colonial past is not widely spread nor thought to be very meaningful, there do exist hidden continuities (Carter 1997). These have yet to be analysed: instead what Vanessa Maher (1996) has called a 'collective amnesia' has prevailed, preventing a critical post-colonial debate and reflection on the political correctness of constructs and representation in the Italian context.

The images described above construct immigrants as simultaneously threatening and excluded from the moral community. Furthermore, in the photograph of the naked Moroccan, the immigrant is seen from the back and we do not see his face or his expression: he is reduced to a simple body without identity. Instead he is represented as the threatening alien body searched by the agents of police and the guarantors of law and order. Hence demonisation and de-personification seemed to be the key mediatic strategies evident in the construction of immigrants in the hot Italian summer of 1997.

The Senegalese response

Although the Senegalese in Italy mainly watch their own videotapes (of music, speeches of *marabouts*, Senegalese movies etc.), and their consumption of local and national media is largely limited to sport, I would like next to show how they themselves receive and react to the flows of racist imagery and

118

Figure 8.1   Italian racist cartoons. The main cartoon
was originally published in *Il Giornale* in
August 1997; the inset juxtaposes a cartoon
from the fascist period.

Source: *Il Manifesto*, 13 August 1997

representation discussed above. One strategy is what I would call 'adjusting their image'. Matar, for instance, considers himself a specialist in jazz and rap music and acts the character of the African–American – the stereotype that Italians know from TV. He is a caricature out of a blaxploitation movie approaching you with the classic sentence: 'How ya doin' man?' After a month in Italy, Ousmane too learned that Italians were more accustomed to the African–American they see on television: when playing basketball during a break from work he noticed that people were suddenly looking at him differently. The black street-peddler is a despised image construct, whereas the black basketball player is an idol for young whites as well as blacks.[10]

More often, though, the Senegalese immigrants stick with their own self-image and identity and are proud of this strategy to counter the racism they have the misfortune to encounter. Racism and racist misrepresentation are often explained as stemming from ignorance. This view implicitly gives the chance of good faith to Italians, and also allows an empowering self-positioning for Senegalese migrants. Such a discursive strategy and its linkage with media representation are clear in the following remarks by Mamadou, one of my key informants in Rimini:

> The person who has been abroad will always be better than the one who stayed at home all the time. ... The Italian is not informed, he does not travel, and TV gives bad information about Africa, always with bad images. When they show bad things they always show Africa. All the diseases seem to come from Africa. Italians think that, being black, I am a wild person who lives with animals ... and then you discover that you have experienced much more than them and travelled more than them.

The anthropologist Dorothy Zinn also encountered such discursive strategies amongst her Senegalese informants in Bari, in southern Italy. She argues: 'by positioning themselves as more knowledgeable, more worldly than the Italians, the Senegalese provide an interesting reversal of the racist image that they are "primitives" among the more developed' (Zinn 1994: 62). Furthermore, this perspective also stresses the importance given to travel and migration as sources of knowledge and training (Ebin 1996). The empowering self (as migrant) image was present on many occasions in the life-histories I gathered during my fieldwork. Mamadou's statement can be taken as a précis of many other accounts: 'one does not emigrate only to look for jobs. To emigrate is also to know new things, to broaden one's horizons in such a way [so that] one can bring back home what he has discovered and learned.' Therefore a critical reading of the sedentarist, ignorant and racist receiving society is connected to a self-empowering explanation of the Senegalese presence in Italy.

Mamadou's views and Zinn's analysis constitute a shared interpretation which is impressively widespread amongst other studies on the Senegalese in

Italy (Carter 1997; Chiani 1991). It can also develop into a more complex socio-cultural critique of Italian society as a whole: in Mamadou's words, 'this society has lost a lot of its values'. When I asked Mamadou to tell me more about this loss of values, he talked to me for half an hour without a pause. Here are some key passages:

> Italians do not give importance to their parents; when these become old the children want to forget their responsibility, putting them into an old persons' home. This is the worst thing that can happen to a family. In Senegal it would never happen. ... Here, the children have lost their sense of the family too. The two parents go to work and the mother is not there to care for the children any more. Children spend their time in the kindergarten and get back home very late, they feel alone. ... Another thing is that here there is less faith. Faith helps people to think about life. Here people are too materialistic. We need to recognise that the life and the wealth are inside. We need to be clean inside.

Thus far, we have seen that the family is the pillar of Senegalese society in Senegal and remains the key touchstone for Senegalese organisation abroad. However, the social changes of the last few decades have also had their impact. 'We talk to our fathers as we never would have dared before', commented a friend of an informant when discussing young people's more open (but perhaps also more rude) approach to their parents (cf. Diop 1985). Paternal authority is under attack, divorce rates are rising, and young people migrate more frequently now without parental permission (Diop 1993: 18). Despite the beginnings of a breakdown in inter-generational communication, the family remains 'the most durable socio-political institution' in Senegal (Cruise O'Brien 1996: 70). Indeed it is perhaps precisely because of this critical transitional period in Senegal, and people's attendant fears and uncertainties about it, that the critique of the dismantling of the Western family, which I also noted when discussing *Secrets and Lies* and *Inspector Derrik*, seems so severe and is constantly reasserted.

The last point of Mamadou's interview, about the materialism of Western life-styles, is another constant theme running through my conversations with Senegalese in Rimini. Although once again one can detect a degree of ambivalence towards Western materialism, a kind of love–hate relationship (cf. Perrone 1995), fear of the temptations offered by the material world is a common refrain. One day Ismael said to me, referring to a programme on the new season's fashions which we were watching on TV whilst waiting for the football match to start, 'what I am afraid of is to be captured by the material [i.e. materialism]'. The danger of the temptations provided by the Italian environment is also a concern for Omar who recognises that 'it is difficult to be a good Muslim in Italy'. This is why it is so important to go back to Senegal to see the family or that the *marabout* (religious leader) comes to visit and give his blessing.[11]

The major issue of *jom*, moral dignity, is ubiquitous; it clashes with Western temptations, is tested in the public sphere and can be a source of critique of co-nationals as well as of Italians. When discussing the experiences of Senegalese in Marseilles, Ebin wrote: 'Senegalese living abroad tend to stick together, creating a place of warmth against an outside world that is pointedly unfriendly' (Ebin 1996: 101). Such mistrust is not shared by all Senegalese, however. For instance, Paul, whom I interviewed in Ravenna, criticises the tendency toward isolation in the behaviour of the Senegalese abroad. He thinks that the Senegalese should not be ashamed of their culture: 'The other Senegalese seem to be afraid, I don't know why. When they see the *toubab*, it is in their head that the white person will trick the black.' However, it is this mistrust that convinces the Senegalese even more that they should return. In the words of another interviewee, Abdou, 'Senegal is our country and we would not exchange it for any other. Here (in Italy) I would always lack something, I will always miss Senegal. Even if I had many friends here, I would always want to go back.'

Conclusion

Several insights into the impact of media representation on cultural identity may be gained from this 'journey' with the Senegalese migrants. The Senegalese philosopher Diagne (1993), confronting what anthropologists would call a 'primordialist' fear of loss of authenticity (cf. Eriksen 1993), has explained how the Senegalese have historically already undertaken both processes of 'deterritorialisation' (based on Islamisation and the impact of colonialism), and processes of 'reterritorialisation' (referring especially to the Mouride brotherhoods which negotiated between Islam and the cultural norms of the homelands). I argue that this historical trajectory has provided the Senegalese with a 'metaculture of difference' (Hannerz 1997) able to respond critically to global cultural flows coming from the West. The Senegalese case shows that the effects of media on what Appadurai (1996) calls 'the work of the imagination' and 'self-fabrication' are worth tracing to particular historical configurations in specific places, as Abu Lughod (1997) also tells us. Furthermore the specific historical trajectory presented here for the Senegalese shaped not only local circumstances affecting the reception of the media but also a 'translocal' configuration through which a powerful shared identity is preserved throughout spatially dispersed trading diasporas (Werbner 1997). And, as we have seen, this shared identity can even be strengthened by the confrontation with racist media representations – for instance by the process of scapegoating that the newspapers can construct, or by the demonising representation of immigration through its association with illegal activities and with crime.

The ideology that is presented by Senegalese cultural identity both at home and abroad is partially affected by 'ethno-occidentalism' (Carrier 1992). This is not to say that the essentialisation made by 'Western representation of the rest' (Hall 1992) is similar; the historically constructed inequality and asymmetry (in media production too) are beyond question. Yet, disenfranchised people too can be proud of themselves and relate to the other by relying on essentialisation as well. I would take an equal distance between the two polarised positions mentioned in the introduction: the vision of media consumers as cultural dupes on the one hand, and on the other the celebration of the consumer who is always able to rearticulate global messages by producing hybrid culture. In sum, I believe that both the influence of media representation from above as well as the reception of it from below are phenomena understood only by contextualisation (not only in a spatial sense). Even the degree of 'hybridity' or 'creolisation' needs to be contextualised. By providing different individual examples of reactions towards racism and the receiving society, I have been able to show that there are different 'cosmopolitanisms' amongst migrant Senegalese, some more open to negotiation with external cultural flows and others (the majority) more inward in their everyday strategy and occidentalist in their representation of Westerners.[12] I therefore argue that this dialectic between closure and openness – also in the reception of media representation – emerges from the specific historical trajectory of the north-western regions of Senegal and of the Senegalese trading diaspora, and furthermore that it varies also according to the specific individual stories and experiences.

NOTES

1 This research constitutes my D.Phil. in Anthropology at the University of Sussex, funded by an EU Marie Curie pre-doctoral fellowship, and supervised by Professor Ralph Grillo. I also want to thank Russell King and Nancy Wood for their useful comments on an earlier draft of this chapter. The chapter draws on 'multi-sited' ethnographic research done over the course of eighteen months (Marcus 1995), starting with fieldwork in the two coastal provinces of Ravenna and Rimini in the region of Emilia-Romagna (Spring 1996) and then following Senegalese informants returning to Senegal in two further phases (Winter 1996–97, September 1997), separated by another spell of fieldwork in Rimini in Summer 1997. In Rimini and Ravenna I undertook fieldwork through participant observation in Senegalese accommodation and following migrants' paths in public places (at markets, on the beach, at cultural events, in trade union meetings, etc.); I also distributed a short questionnaire amongst attendants at various training courses. The main core of my research, on which I draw in this chapter, consists of sixty long interviews with key informants amongst the migrant community and within relevant institutional settings. From these I have selected meaningful professional and life histories which allow a deeper analysis of experiences, trajectories, expectations and representations, both in Italy and in Senegal (Benmayor and Skotnes 1994).

2 See Bhabha (1994) for the latter view. The 'hypodermic' analogy comes from Morley and Robins' (1995) critique of the 'cultural dupes' approach.

3 See for example Pozzoni's (1997) study of the Senegalese in Lecco.

4 The interviews I carried out in Senegal dealt mainly with informants' opinions on emigrants and of Senegal as a sending context for emigration. Together with some focus-group discussions, these interviews helped me to study collective discourses on

the phenomenon of emigration. All the interviewees and informants mentioned in the text are given pseudonyms.

5 *L'Espresso*, 29 October 1998, p. 87.

6 And has become even more overt in the years since then.

7 It is true that those arrested included Albanians, Moroccans and (wrongly, as it turned out) Senegalese, but Swiss and Belgians were also involved.

8 This symbolic process shows many similar aspects to the criminalisation of young blacks in Britain described by Gilroy (1987).

9 Thanks to *Il Manifesto* for permission to reproduce this cartoon.

10 See Carter (1997) on the 'immigrant construct' and blackness; also Gilroy (1993).

11 On the visit of *marabouts* to the Senegalese residential camp outside Rimini see Riccio (1999).

12 This latter critique, borrowed from an anti-colonialist stance, is, however, tempered by a universalist stance which is also embedded in Mouride ideology: Bamba spoke for all people.

References

Abu Lughod, J. (1997) 'The interpretation of culture(s) after television', *Representations* 59: 109–34.

Andall, J. (1990) 'New migrants, old conflicts: the recent immigration to Italy', *The Italianist* 10: 151–74.

Appadurai, A. (1996) *Modernity at Large: Cultural Dimensions of Globalization*, Minneapolis: University of Minnesota Press.

Benmayor, R. and Skotnes, A. (eds) (1994) *Migration and Identity*, Oxford: Oxford University Press.

Bhabha, H. K. (1994) *The Location of Culture*, London: Routledge.

Campani, G. (1993) 'Immigration and racism in Southern Europe: the Italian case', *Ethnic and Racial Studies* 16, 3: 507–35.

Campus, A., Mottura, G. and Perrone, L. (1992) 'I Senegalesi', in Mottura, G. (ed.), *L'Arcipelago Immigrazione*, Rome: Ediesse.

Cannon, D. (1997) 'Review: *Secrets and Lies* 1996', *Movie Reviews UK*, online version.

Caritas di Roma (1998) *Immigrazione Dossier Statistico '98*, Rome: Anterem.

Carrier, J.G. (1992) 'Occidentalism: the world turned upside-down', *American Ethnologist* 19, 2: 195–212.

Carter, D. M. (1997) *States of Grace: Senegalese in Italy and the New European Immigration*, Minneapolis: University of Minnesota Press.

Catanzaro, R., Nelken, D. and Belotti, V. (1996) 'Un posto per vendere: i commercianti ambulanti irregolari sulla riviera emiliano-romagnola', *Sociologia del Lavoro* 64: 85–120.

Chiani, V. (1991) 'Caratteristiche della immigrazione extracomunitaria nelle provincie di Forlì e Ravenna', in Minardi, E. and Cifello, S. (eds), *Economie Locali e Immigrati Extracomunitari in Emilia-Romagna*, Milan: Franco Angeli.

Cole, J. (1997) *The New Racism in Europe. A Sicilian Ethnography*, Cambridge: Cambridge University Press.

Cruise O'Brien, D. B. (1996) 'A lost generation? Youth identity and state decay in West Africa', in Werbner, R. and Ranger, T. (eds), *Postcolonial Identities in Africa*, London: Zed Books.

Dal Lago, A. (1996) 'Dentro/Fuori, scenari dell'esclusione', *Aut Aut* 275: 3–8.

Diagne, S. B. (1993) 'The future of tradition', in Diop, M. C. (ed.), *Senegal: Essays in Statecraft*, Dakar: CODESRIA.

Diop, A. B. (1985) *La famille Wolof*, Paris: Karthala.

Diop, M. C. (1993) 'Introduction: from 'socialism' to 'liberalism': the many phases of state legitimacy', in Diop, M. C. (ed.), *Senegal: Essays in Statecraft*, Dakar: CODESRIA.

Ebin, V. (1996) 'Making room versus creating space: the construction of spatial categories by itinerant Mouride traders', in Metcalf, B. D. (ed.), *Making Muslim Space in North America and Europe*, Berkeley: University of California Press.

Eriksen, T. H. (1993) *Ethnicity and Nationalism: Anthropological Perspectives*, London: Pluto Press.

Gilroy, P. (1987) *There Ain't No Black in the Union Jack: The Cultural Politics of Race and Nation*, London: Hutchinson.

—— (1993) *The Black Atlantic: Modernity and Double Consciousness*, London: Verso.

Grillo, R. D. (1985) *Ideologies and Institutions in Urban France*, Cambridge: Cambridge University Press.

Hall, S. (1992) 'The West and the rest: discourse and power', in Hall, S. and Gieben, B. (eds), *Formations of Modernity*, London: Open University Press.

Hannerz, U. (1997) *Transnational Connections*, London: Routledge.

ISMU (1997) *Terzo Rapporto sulle Migrazioni*, Milan: Franco Angeli.

King, R. and Andall, J. (1999) 'The geography and economic sociology of recent immigration to Italy', *Modern Italy* 4, 2: 135–58.

Maher, V. (1996) 'Immigration and social identities', in Forgacs, D. and Lumley, R. (eds), *Italian Cultural Studies. An Introduction*, Oxford: Oxford University Press.

Marchetti, A. (1994) 'La nuova immigrazione a Milano: il caso senegalese', in IRER (ed.), *Tra Due Rive: La Nuova Immigrazione a Milano*, Milan: Franco Angeli.

Marcus, G. (1995) 'Ethnography in/of the world system: the emergence of multi-sited ethnography', *Annual Review of Anthropology* 24: 95–117.

Miles, R. and Thränhardt, D. (eds) (1995) *Migration and European Integration: The Dynamics of Inclusion and Exclusion*, London: Pinter.

Morley, D. and Robins, K. (1995) *Spaces of Identity: Global Media, Electronic Landscapes and Cultural Boundaries*, London: Routledge.

Palidda, S. (1996) 'Verso il "fascismo democratico"? Note su emigrazione, immigrazione e società dominanti', *Aut Aut* 275: 143–68.

Perrone, L. (1995) *Porte Chiuse*, Naples: Liguori.

Pozzoni, B. (1997) 'New immigrants in Italy: the case of the Senegalese in Lecco', University of Sussex, *Research Papers in Geography* 31.

Riccio, B. (1999) 'Senegalese street-sellers, racism and the discourse on "irregular trade" in Rimini', *Modern Italy* 4, 2: 225–40.

Schmidt di Friedberg, O. (1994) *Islam, Solidarietà e Lavoro: I Muridi Senegalesi in Italia*, Turin: Edizioni della Fondazione Giovanni Agnelli.

Scidà, G. (1993) 'Senegalesi e Mauriziani a Catania: due risposte divergenti alla sfida dell'integrazione sociale', *La Ricerca Sociale* 47–8: 173–200.

Stolke, V. (1995) 'New boundaries, new rhetorics of exclusion in Europe', *Current Anthropology* 36, 1: 1–24.

Treossi, A. (1995) 'Senegalesi a Faenza', in Landuzzi, C., Tarozzi, A. and Treossi, A. (eds), *Tra luoghi e generazioni. Migrazioni africane in Italia e in Francia*, Turin: L'Harmattan Italia.

Werbner, P. (1997) 'Introduction: the dialectics of cultural hybridity', in Werbner, P. and Modood, T. (eds), *Debating Cultural Hybridity*, London: Zed Books.

Zinn, D. L. (1994) 'The Senegalese immigrants in Bari: what happens when the Africans peer back', in Benmayor, R. and Skotnes, A. (eds), *Migration and Identity*, Oxford: Oxford University Press.

9

COMMUNICATION, POLITICS AND RELIGION IN AN ISLAMIC COMMUNITY

Christine Ogan

Introduction

The gathering of an estimated 40,000 European Turks in Amsterdam's Ajax Stadium on 20 June 1998, televised to Turks in Turkey and all over Europe, was a major achievement for the Islamic political group known as Milli Görüş. But it was not extraordinary in combining religion, politics and a mass medium in a single event. For centuries, some claim even in its birth, Islam has been bound up with politics. And Islamic communities have used communication media to spread their message for almost as long.

This chapter is about a particular Islamic group – the Turks who live in Europe and who are involved with an Islamic political organisation that seeks to re-establish a more 'Islamically-oriented state in Turkey' and to maintain an Islamic perspective in every aspect of Turkish people's lives in Europe (Dasetto and Nonneman 1996: 212). Composed of people who came as guestworkers to Europe in the 1960s, and including their families and others who arrived later from Turkey, Milli Görüş has gained considerable strength. In Turkey political groups who seek to institute *Shari-ah* (Islamic law) to replace the secular state are forbidden to carry out such activities in the open, therefore Europe offers a more hospitable environment for such a movement. Its centre is in Germany, but large groups also exist in France, Belgium and the Netherlands (Amiraux 1997).

To understand the nature of the relationship between religion, politics and communication for the Milli Görüş, it is necessary to first provide some historical background. Then the discussion will centre on research conducted in the summers of 1997 and 1998 in Amsterdam, based on interviews with members and leaders in Milli Görüş and attendance at the June 1998 day-long rally.

Historical context: politics

Though the relationship between Islam, politics and communication could apply to all Islamic societies, this discussion will be primarily limited to the Turks. There are two reasons for this. The first is that the Milli Görüş organisation only has Turkish members. But the more important reason is that Turkey has been a secular society for the last 75 years. Despite numerous laws and acts of censorship to contain radical Islamic groups that have sought to return Turkey to an Islamic state, such attempts persist. Examining the history of the relationship between religion, politics and communication in Islam may help us understand why groups like Milli Görüş can become so powerful.

The foremost scholar of the literature describing Islam's political history is Bernard Lewis, who wrote in *Islam and the West* that the word religion for Muslims always had a greater meaning than it did for Christians.[1] 'The Islamic term is *din*, originally Arabic but adopted in all the many languages of Islam [including Turkish]. The cognate word in other Semitic languages, notably Hebrew and Aramaic, means law' (1993: 3). Lewis elaborates on that by noting that Islam has come to be the counterpart of both Christianity and Christendom – and even more. He likens it somewhat to Byzantium, but says the comparison is only approximate.

> It is a political identity and allegiance, transcending all others. Always in the ideal, and for a while even in reality, the world of Islam was one polity ruled by one sovereign, the caliph, and even after the decline of the central caliphal power and the emergence of strong regional or dynastic or national powers, such as were beginning to appear in Europe in the Middle Ages, ... this ideal of a single Islamic polity, transcending both country and nation, still has considerable appeal for Muslims, as recent events have demonstrated.
>
> (1993: 4–5)

A second characteristic of Islam that separates it from Christianity is the lack of a priesthood, meaning that nobody intervenes between Allah and human beings. There is also no established church that has organisational autonomy. This has historically led to a blurring of boundaries between religion and the larger social system. According to Toprak, this is the source of the justification for Islamic law: 'since the direction of history is divinely ordained, it follows that the entire range of interpersonal and institutional relationships in society are also under sacred control' (Toprak 1981: 23).

Lewis accepts that it is theologically true that Islam has no priesthood, but that under the Ottoman Empire, it was not sociologically and politically true. 'Here for the first time in Islamic history is created an institutional structure – a graded hierarchy of professional men of religion, with recognized functions and powers, worthy of comparison with the Christian priesthoods or those of the ancient Empires' (Lewis 1961: 16). Only in the Ottoman state, he claims, did the religious institution carry out its role as guardian of faith and law.

The direct political connection for Islam begins with Mohammed, who was as much a political leader as a prophet. 'Islam started out as a protest movement against the economic and political supremacy of the Meccan society' (Toprak 1981: 22). Those who opposed Mohammed in Mecca were not so much bothered by Islam's religious tenets, but rather with its perceived threat to the economic interests and the oligarchic structure of local society. Mohammed fought against those interests and his success was as much political as it was religious (Toprak 1981: 23). The Turks came to Islam by conversion, not coercion, however. Lewis calls it a frontier religion, as they encountered it on the frontiers of the Caliphate.

> In Central Asia, one of the two most important frontiers, the Turks, converted for the most part by wandering missionaries and mystics, joined in the struggle against their cousins who were still heathen, and as the military classes of the Caliphate came to be more and more exclusively Turkish, began to play a predominant part in it.
>
> (Lewis 1961: 11)

Lewis believes that it is this frontier nature of Turkish Islam that has set it apart from the way it has developed in other countries. The Turkish frontiersmen were taught by dervishes, wandering mystics and others who preached a different kind of Islam than that taught in the cosmopolitan centres in Iraq or Egypt. And Islam so completely came to be accepted by the Turks that very little trace of pre-Islamic Turkish society remains in the culture (Lewis 1961). An Islamic form of life was spread in the Turkish countryside from the beginning. Though eventually the term 'Ottoman' would come to define citizenship, the majority of Ottoman subjects – particularly those who lived in the countryside – would identify themselves more frequently with Islam (Toprak 1981: 27). And this would persist into the twentieth century and be carried to Europe with the guestworkers who grew up in central Anatolia and the Black Sea region of Turkey.

Toprak identifies several periods of Turkish history and assigns a different role to Islam in each period. Following the period of the Ottoman Empire, which spanned more than four centuries, there was the period of transition from empire to nation state. Toprak notes that Islam served as a source of national unity against the invading Western armies. After the establishment of the Republic in 1923 under Ataturk's one-party rule, the protest against the government used religion as its organising principle (Toprak 1981: 123–4).

When the Ottoman Empire collapsed, the nation that was snatched from its would-be colonisers owed its existence to Mustafa Kemal Ataturk. Ataturk literally created the Republic – socially, politically, militarily – to conform to his own image of a modern Western nation. But to accomplish this transformation, he needed to require conformity by all the country's citizens. Never before had a people been asked to make so many radical changes in behaviour and attitude in such a short time. Many of those behaviours were bound up in Islamic traditions. Ataturk proclaimed that Turks would wear hats instead of fezzes, women would be unveiled and allowed to vote and participate equally in society, all citizens would add surnames to their given names, cease certain religious practices, adopt a new alphabet for their language, and embrace a new legal code based on a European philosophy. He also abolished the Caliphate, the Ministry of Religious Affairs, and religious schools and courts. All this occurred in the space of ten years. Though Ataturk was certainly not the first to introduce these Western ideas to Turkish society, as president of the Republic and head of the only party in the country, he was the man responsible for enacting and enforcing them. Though Ataturk first used Islam to define the state – in fact one-fifth of the members of the First National Assembly were religious leaders (Lewis 1993: 31) – many Turks believed he meant to rid the country of Islam entirely.[2]

Today's Milli Görüş, among other Turkish Islamic groups, has at its heart a fundamental opposition to Ataturk's secularisation of the Turkish state. Since it is illegal to promote the overthrow of the secular state and to advocate the institution of *Shari-ah*, most people who espouse this position do not state it openly. But the major goal of one of the political parties that was precursor to the Fazilet Partisi (Virtue Party – Milli Görüş' current party affiliation in Turkey), the Milli Nizam Partisi (National Order Party), was to 'revive the moral qualities and the spiritual excellence dormant in the Turkish character so that Turkish society can regain peace, order and social justice' (Toprak 1981: 98, citing a party document). The party opposed both capitalist and socialist systems, decrying them as imperialist in character and enslaving of others to their own culture and economic interests. The Milli Hareket Partisi, successor to the MNP, pressed its religious agenda as part of the coalition government with the left-of-centre leader, Bulent Ecevit. The MHP leader, Necmettin Erbakan, succeeded in getting 'government assistance for the building of mosques, "moral" instruction in primary and secondary schools and the accelerated training of imams' (Jansen 1979: 141). Jansen noted that, as a result of Erbakan's pressure on the Ecevit government, in 1977 Turkey had 89 teacher training schools as compared with 244 schools for imams and 50 more in the planning stage. At this point in modern Turkey, Islamic influences in the political arena were beginning to produce results.

Historical context: communication

Mass communication and other communication forms have long been used to spread Islamic doctrine. Fathi (1979: 102) described Mohammed's need to gather his followers in a central place and at a specific time to communicate with them. So the mosque was built next to his house and Friday was settled on as the day when the congregation would gather for prayer. The mosque was also used as a centre for discussion of major political or social matters: 'in a major crisis or community dissatisfaction, the people flocked to the mosque to discuss the problem and to seek remedy or redress' (Fathi 1979: 103). Thus, throughout the history of Islam, the mosque has been the centre of numerous uprisings, revolts and social movements often led by popular preachers from the *minbar* (pulpit).

Sardar (1993) too is convinced that communication has been intimately connected with Islam from the first. 'That muslim culture is a culture of knowledge and communication is made clear in the first verses of the Qur'an revealed to the Prophet Mohammad.' He cites verses of Koranic scripture that:

> lay the foundations of a culture and society based on reading and writing, research and penmanship, communication and transmission of knowledge and information. Any society that does not demonstrate these traits cannot be said to be upholding the ideals of Islam.
>
> (Sardar 1993: 44)

The first paper brought to the Muslim world came from Samarkand in the eighth century. By the end of the tenth century many paper mills existed throughout the Middle East, while Europe had its first mill only in 1276. A ready supply of paper allowed for the creation of multiple copies of manuscripts and the proliferation of bookshops.

> The publication industry that dominated the length and breadth of the Muslim empire from the eighth to the fifteenth century, was an industry of mind-boggling complexity. But it was not just an industry; it was an institution central to the expression of Islamic culture – an institution with its own customs and practices, its own checks against fraud and misrepresentation and, above all, an institution that ensured that learning and books were not the prerogative of a select few but were available to all who desired them.
>
> (Sardar 1993: 50)[3]

Traditionally communication of important matters also took place in the bazaar, located next to the mosque. Sreberny-Mohammadi, writing about the locus of traditional communication in Iran, notes the historical role of this centre acting 'together with other traditional social groups in political opposition to kings and foreign encroachments' (1994: 95). The bazaar was connected through familial, financial and ideological ties with the religious establishment. Above all, the bazaar was an 'informal meeting-place where news, rumor, and gossip can be created and disseminated with remarkable speed. It is a locus of information as well as commodity exchange' (Sreberny-Mohammadi 1994: 80).

For the Turks, communication of Islam was more difficult than for many others. Until Ataturk adopted the Latin alphabet for the language, the script was Arabic, but the language was unrelated to Arabic, which was the language of the Koran. So most knowledge of the words of Mohammed needed translation, and this was a primary function of the Imam. Even the call to prayer was made in a foreign language in Turkey. Following the establishment of the Republic, a new divinity school, intended to serve as the centre for the modernised and scientific religious instruction, was established at the University of Istanbul. In 1928, a committee appointed by the faculty of that school examined the practice of Islam in Turkey with an eye to making reforms. The only one of the recommendations that was ever enacted, however, was the 'Turkicization of worship' (Lewis 1961: 409). There was strong opposition to the translation of the Koran and the traditions of the Prophet into Turkish, but the call to prayer was successfully translated and began to be used in 1932. However, when Adnan Menderes and his Demokrat Partisi came to power in 1950, he rolled back the stipulation that the call to prayer be in Turkish, in an appeal to the religious right.[4] The left-of-centre party went along with the proposal out of a fear of alienating voters.

Following the secularisation of the Turkish state in 1923, religious publications were not much in evidence. But during and after World War II, a religious press sprung up that published many periodicals devoted to religious topics and the propagation of religious ideas (Lewis 1961: 414). Toprak wrote that the increase in the publication of religious books and pamphlets following Menderes' election was unprecedented (1981: 81). For the illiterate believers, popular weeklies meant to be read aloud proliferated. Other publications aimed at intellectuals also thrived (Lewis 1961: 414–15).

At the same time, amplifiers were installed in mosques, Arabic texts appeared on the walls of cafés, shops, taxis and in the market – and were even sold on the street (Lewis 1961: 415). The Menderes government also brought the mass media into the religious scene with the sanctioning of Koranic readings on the public radio.

But the politicisation of religion and the propagation of Islam in the mass media slowed following the military coup of 1960 and the promulgation of a new constitution that forbade the use of religion for political purposes. However, politicians continued to appeal to the religious interests of the masses, and religious schools and publications increased in the years that followed. State radio and television (TRT) carried some religious messages, particularly during the month of Ramadan, and at the opening and closing of the broadcast day. Since private broadcasting did not exist until the 1990s, control of all broadcasting was in the hands of the party in power. That left opposition leaders, like Necmettin Erbakan, in a position to only criticise the content. Toprak (1981: 101) recalls an incident where the religious right tried to take legal action against the public television network for airing a documentary about Amazon Indians which showed elements of nudity. And on another occasion, criticisms were made about Western content on television, in imported films and in plays produced at Turkish theatres, alleging incompatibility with Turkish culture, meaning religious values. The National Salvation Party, one of the previously banned parties headed by Erbakan, called for more religious programmes on state radio and television (Toprak 1981: 103).

Though the state was able to control broadcast content, the press in Turkey is privately owned. Newspapers have always had a partisan perspective and one, in particular, has been associated with the several transformations of Erbakan's party. That paper is *Milli Gazete,* which has existed in Turkey since 1973. Readers in Europe today receive this newspaper only through mail subscription. Other religious publications exist, however. In a recent report from the military, the number of mass media under the control of Islamic organisations was estimated at 19 newspapers, 110 magazines, 51 radio and 20 television stations.[5]

One of the magazines, *Kadin ve Aile* ('Woman and family'), is a monthly that speaks to the traditional roles of women. Yeşim Arat (1995) has analysed the message of this publication in terms of 'Islamic feminism'. Begun in 1985, the magazine is aimed at 'housewives whose lives are sacrificed to the happiness of their families, children and husbands; their sacrifice sealed with religious benediction'. Arat also points to the magazine's connection between politics and religion, as it encourages women to have a more active social and political life and introduces them to the concept of individual rights (Arat 1995: 77).

Despite the myriad publications, broadcasting has had a greater impact on the political organisation of Islamic communities in Turkey and in Europe. The Turkish Radio and Television Corporation (TRT) held a monopoly over broadcasting until 1990. Though established as an independent state institution in 1964 following Article 121 of the 1961 Constitution, it has never been autonomous from government. But until this decade, TRT was the source of all national broadcasting in Turkish. In 1990, an upstart company called Magic Box began broadcasting via satellite from Germany on a new television channel, Star 1. Soon it was joined by other Turkish satellite broadcasters, all of whom claimed they broke no law since they were European companies, and therefore not violating TRT's monopoly status in Turkey. But of course, the footprint of the European satellites fully covered the Turkish land mass, causing the signal to be received by anyone with the appropriate satellite dish. Eventually, the widespread popularity of these channels led to the passage of a law in 1994 that permitted private radio and television stations to exist alongside the public stations.[6] Aksoy and Robins (1997: 1940–1) characterise the pre-private television era as the time of the 'dissemination of "official" culture', while the opening up of the system to private stations meant that 'real culture' could be broadcast to the people. Part of that 'real culture' included Islamic culture. And four national television channels went on the air to serve that audience. Samanyolu Television was established in 1990 by the highly influential Fethullah Gülen community; Mesaj TV was set up by the Kadiri community;

Kanal 7 was set up, first in Istanbul and then with full national coverage, by members of the Iskenderpasa group; and TGRT was launched by the large media group (Turkiye Gazetesi Radyo ve Televizyonu) founded by followers of Seyyid Abdulhakim Arvas of the Nakşibendi sect. Though Aksoy and Robins (1997: 1951) note that, once private broadcasting became legal, the 'media environment in Turkey has become more guarded and restrictive, less multivocal', it has still offered the opportunity for Islamic political and cultural views to be expressed openly and to be disseminated to people via cable and satellite all over Europe and the Middle East.

Öncu (1995) agrees that private broadcasting brought a wider diversity to broadcasting. And she also notes that it became more domestic because it added a number of local quiz and game-shows that were modelled on American and European originals, more local pop, classical and Arabesque music, and certainly a broader spectrum of political views. The combination of religious and political interests given voice on commercial channels allowed Erbakan's Refah Party to carry out a successful television campaign in 1991 and in succeeding elections.

> Its success hinged upon personalizing Islam's dark face, thereby rendering it simply ordinary. As packaged by marketing consultants for commercial television, Refah's constituents were not the turbaned women and bearded dark men of the imagination, but everyday people. The campaign presented closeups of a series of ordinary faces, encouraging the viewers to scrutinize them and use their own acumen to assess their honesty and sincerity.
>
> (Öncu 1995: 60)

In Öncu's terms, the televising of political messages in an Islamic context has allowed religion to be 'issue-tized' (1995: 53). Presenting Islam on public television, she said, allowed the public to understand a very complex subject because it was packaged in 'forms readily consumable by heterogeneous audiences' (1995: 54). Refah's media campaign was particularly successful because the theme was formulated as a kind of association between 'you' and 'us' – 'we know your problems', 'we are closer to you', 'we embrace all of you', 'we think alike', 'we are together', 'we are the same', etc.

This use of broadcasting media for political messages is not new for Americans, who have long been used to the appeals of candidates based on understanding voters' needs and fashioning themselves in the image of ordinary citizens. But it was new in Turkey. When TRT was in control of the political agenda, opposition candidates often complained about not getting access and being presented in an unfavourable light. Once religious groups were the owners of the stations, candidates had as much time as they wanted to create appropriate and appealing messages, and were free to frame their campaign messages in their own terms. So finally, with the arrival of commercial broadcasting in Turkey, Islam, politics and mass media came together in a way never seen before.

Indigenous television comes to the diaspora

Once these commercial stations were delivered by satellite, it was possible for them to be received anywhere under the satellite's footprint. Cable stations in many European countries carried TRT–INT (the international counterpart to the main TRT service in Turkey) since it was first transmitted abroad in 1990 (Sağnak 1996: 82). With the advent of private satellite television from Turkey, more than a dozen channels could be received on one or two small dishes, which could be attached to balconies or to rooftops. European Turks have been able to receive these stations since at least 1993. Before that time, print media, in the form of multiple newspapers and magazines, were available in Europe. Several Turkish newspapers have had European editions for more than a decade. *Milli Gazete*, the Milli Görüş daily, has been available through mail subscription for as long as it was available in Turkey, since 1973 (Sağnak 1996: 70). But it is television that has really opened the access to viewpoints with a conservative religious perspective in Europe. My interviews with more than sixty Turkish families throughout Amsterdam concluded that there is very little reading of the Turkish press on a regular basis, but widespread viewing of television from Turkey exists, even to the exclusion of Dutch television. With few exceptions, every home I entered had the television on and tuned to a Turkish channel.

The Milli Görüş Organisation

According to the literature distributed by the Avrupa Milli Görüş Teşkilatları (European National View Organisation), it became an official organisation in 1985 after several reorganisations with its headquarters in Cologne. It was considered the cultural and religious wing of the Turkish Refah Partisi (Welfare Party) until its banning in August 1997. Now it is affiliated with the party reorganised as Fazilet (Virtue) Party. According to Dassetto and Nonneman this conservative religious party grew out of 'efforts to merge three components: reference to Islam as a project of society; reference to the affirmation of Turco–Ottoman identity; and reference to technical and scientific modernity' (1996: 209). Though these authors claim that in Belgium and the Netherlands some thirty mosques are controlled by Milli Görüş, their data are at least four years old, and the organisation has grown in numbers and resources since that time. Milli Görüş claims about 160,000 members across Europe in 800 individual organisations. Though many migrants, who came to Europe as workers from small towns and villages in Turkey, had limited literacy skills, the second generation has somewhat more schooling. Many of these young people, who may have only visited Turkey on summer holiday, identify more with religion

135

than with their parents' home country, according to Nico Landman (Bousetta 1996). Or as Cem Özdemir, Germany's first ethnic Turkish MP, elected for the Green Party, said: 'There are two possibilities here [for those searching for an identity]: either to become a nationalist, a real Turk, or to become religious. Now a lot of people who never went into a mosque in Turkey have started to be religious' (Lebor 1997: 209). The Milli Görüş claims that 30,500 youth are affiliated, 2,300 of them enrolled in university. The organisation is said to be financed from its own resources, particularly through profit from goods sold from cooperatives (Dassetto and Nonneman 1996: 210). In most mosques in Amsterdam, the building serves as much as a cultural and community centre than as a house of worship. The compound generally includes a grocery store, a coffee house and restaurant, a place where young people can practice sports or take karate lessons, rooms for women's and youth's social activities, and a media room where the television is tuned to Turkish stations and newspapers for communal use are available.

The mass media controlled by the political party includes Kanal 7 television and several radio stations. *Milli Gazete* is the official newspaper of the group. In addition, several web sites are offered to members, both in Turkish and in European languages; German is the most extensively used European language on the web. In June 1998, the organisation announced plans to mount a school on the Internet that would replace the middle school educational programmes of Imam Hatip Okulları (Islamic Religious Schools for the training of Prayer Leaders and Imams) that were banned for the education of children through the eighth grade in Turkey. Those schools were closed in August 1997 out of fear that children who attended them were being politically indoctrinated at impressionable ages. The schools were allowed to continue training at high school level. According to the Milli Görüş web site (http://www.igmg.de/tr/kendimiz/frapor98), the organisation supports at least 25 weekend boarding schools, more than 125 summer camps (where students can stay at least a month), and many courses to help students with their secular school homework. Observers believe that political as well as religious messages are communicated through these courses.

The communication that occurs in youth groups has provided a sense of collective identity and belonging that has not been felt in relation to the host society. In a survey conducted by a team of German researchers among 1,221 Turkish youths in Germany, one-third of those interviewed said that Milli Görüş and/or the Grey Wolves (a Turkish nationalist group) represented their own views 'well' or 'fairly closely'. The researchers also noted that Turkish youth often associate with other Turks because of the similarity of religious values.[7] According to another report of this survey, half of the young people interviewed said, in so many words, that 'the future belonged to Islam and that all non-Muslims are infidels'.[8] My interviews among Turkish youth in Amsterdam reveal that they are closer to one another than to Dutch youth in their age group. And in travelling around Amsterdam on the tram, time and again I saw groups of young Turkish students travelling together – rarely mingling with Dutch friends, and conversing in Turkish sprinkled with Dutch phrases and words. Some of the young people I interviewed were religious, and closely affiliated to a neighbour-hood mosque. Others had no religious affiliation.

The media event

The very best example of the merger of sophisticated communication media, religion and politics takes place at the annual Peace and Culture Celebration of the Milli Görüş. Here, I will describe the event and analyse the ways in which the Islamic political organisation makes effective use of mass media and other communication forms.

For the first three years, this day-long event was held in Germany, but in June 1998 it was held in the new Amsterdam Arena, home to the Ajax soccer team. An estimated 40,000 people attended this event, which was broadcast live on Kanal 7 and transmitted to Turkey and Europe simultaneously. Large television screens on the field also tracked the events of the day. It was an unusually sunny and warm day in Amsterdam in a month when it rained nearly every other day. The conference organisers must have thought that Allah favoured their celebration. Participants and spectators came from all over Europe, many of them sleeping on the couches and floors of family and friends throughout the city. The women, most of the young boys and all of the girls sat in one half of the stadium, while the men and older boys were seated in the other half. The scene was a dramatic contrast to any other gathering ever held in this liberal Dutch city. Hundreds of large Turkish, Milli Görüş and Islamic flags – of the size that cheerleaders wave at American sports events – could be seen all over the stadium being raised at every emotional high point during the day. It was an incredibly colourful sight – the red and white of the Turkish flags, white with a green map of Europe for the Milli Görüş flags, and the green with Arabic script on the Islamic flags. Banners with the conference logo and announcement were hung around the stadium and advertising for Turkish Islamic businesses added to the scene. The field was adorned with still more banners, taking up more than half the space where soccer teams kick the ball about. Colourful scarves encircled the heads of the women in the crowd. Some of the young women tied red bands around the scarves. And all the women wore ankle-length coats or dresses, unusually colourful for the occasion. Even the Turkish men, usually dressed in grey and khaki clothing, wore bright coloured shirts. The crowd was stirred up at the onset with the entry of the Mehter takımı from Istanbul (a group of musicians who simulate – in dress and style – the old Janissary bands that thrived under the Ottomans until they were disbanded in the early 1800s). They marched slowly around the field, while the crowd rose to its feet and waved flags and cheered. The band not only served as a means to lift the excitement level, but also as a symbol of the Milli Görüş goal to return to the Ottoman style of government where religion and state were one. The Turkish national anthem, the 'Independence March', was another crowd pleaser. The words of the anthem also hark back to the days of glory. Other tactics were used to get the crowd emotionally involved. A singer from Kanal 7 welcomed the people on behalf of the television station, then sang as the crowd waved flags. Slogans were also used liberally throughout – 'To everyone justice and order', 'Our road is Allah's', 'The days of enlightenment are coming; they have come'. And poems were recited that came close to deifying Necmettin Erbakan, now banned from Turkish politics. It was indeed a spectacle meant to inspire; or, as Dayan and Katz (1988) would describe it, it was a media event to celebrate consensus.

In their analysis of the ritual and rhetoric of media events, Dayan and Katz refer to them semantically as proclaiming the charter of what is now called 'civil religion' (1988: 161). Since the Milli Görüş rally had as its foundation a celebration of religious as well as political consensus, it carries an even more powerful message than a civil religion. And its power is increased by the broadcasting of the event transnationally. Had this event been televised in the Netherlands or in Europe alone, it would have served to strengthen the commitment to Milli Görüş and its mission. But it becomes much more than that when it is carried live and uncut across the whole day to audiences throughout Turkey. Such events would not be staged so openly in Turkey, particularly after the banning of Refah Partisi and its leader, Erbakan, prime minister during 1996–97. Dayan and Katz maintain that the witnesses validate the event – those in the crowd and those watching on television. In this instance, the validation is being conducted across Turkey by those who believe that the religious/political message of this party will once again carry the day. These authors also claim that television plays an independent role in the process, that here television is a complicit part of the media event – part of the party structure itself. It is both actor in the event, and launcher and disseminator of the occasion. Crowd members are reassured of television's important role in bringing this message to their relatives, friends and fellow party members back in Turkey when they see themselves and the speakers live on the screen that looms large in the stadium complex.

In the analysis of Dayan and Katz, most of the events described are authorised by state authorities and meant to define consensus.

> Always grandiose, full of pomp, media events may be numbered among the major monuments of this part of the century. But they are ambiguous monuments because they do not only display and reaffirm an already established consensus. They are engaged, rather, in the business of defining a new consensus, either by proposing new symbols for an existing core of values, or, more profoundly, by modifying the nature of articulation of such values.
>
> (1988: 165–6)

In this case, the event is circumventing the state authority to define this new consensus. Very politically and media-aware, the organisers of the event appreciate the power they have to penetrate the Turkish borders with the message of change. That message was meant to reinvigorate those with 'religious right' political views to stay the course, despite the closure of Refah Partisi and despite the banning of their leader, the '*savunan adam*' (the defendant or man who defends himself). Before Erbakan arrives someone reads a poem about him, characterising him as the light of their faith, their heart and soul, their reason for pride.

Erbakan himself arrived at the event, full of symbolic power – if stripped of his real political power. Dayan and Katz refer to 'coronations' as one form of media event, where heroes are buried or come to power in actual coronation. Erbakan's arrival had elements of a coronation. He came into the stadium in a shiny green (the colour of Islam) BMW. Forbidden to give political speeches when banned from politics, Erbakan greeted the crowd and waved. It had the desired effect as they wildly cheered his arrival.

Unlike the Dayan and Katz view of the media event as a vehicle used in a democracy and sanctioned by state authority, this is a media event organised by a group seeking a legitimate voice. They seek legitimacy as an Islamic community on a par with Christian and secular European communities in the Netherlands, Germany, Belgium and other countries. At the same time they seek legitimacy as a political and religious movement in Turkey that wants to regain its democratic rights (the right for women to wear headscarves as workers in public offices and students in schools, for example).

If the Milli Görüş would like to institute Islamic law in Turkey and be able to live under it in their European communities, they are careful not to say this explicitly. It would be perceived as a revolutionary idea in both contexts. From my own interviews with members of the group, I conclude that there is no uniform opinion on this goal. Some believe that Islamic law should govern Turkey; others say the country should remain secular, but that there should be increased religious freedom in the country. In Turkey, people who have only suggested the possibility of merging religion with state have been jailed or had their publications closed. But the inability to openly state the desired goal of the organisation could work to the advantage of its leaders. As Gluckman (1963) and Kertzer (1983) have noted, the use of common symbols, and the performance of rituals like the annual meeting of the Milli Görüş, bind people together with a common purpose. But Kertzer argues that this is only possible through the ambiguity of the symbols used to accomplish this goal. The use of the Islamic flag, for example, means the followers are all Muslims, but it does not have to mean that they all subscribe to *Shari-ah*. The Mehter band reminds people of the glory of the Ottoman Empire, but it does not have to mean that followers want to return to the eighteenth or nineteenth century when church and state were one. That ambiguity of purpose was very clear to me as I spoke at length with Milli Görüş leaders, youth followers, housewives, student groups and men who were peripherally attached to the organisation. Some expressed the goals of Milli Görüş in a militant fashion, others were taken with the moral purity of the people who belonged, and still others were more attached to the group as purely a social affair. But all these people were dues-paying members who attended the rally in the stadium and probably felt exhilaration at the sights and sounds of the symbols. So whereas Dayan and Katz see the media event as reaffirming consensus, I am not so sure that such a consensus exists. Nor indeed does it have to exist. There could be a perceived consensus, but not a real one. One of the strengths of the religious conservatives in Turkey has been their patience in trying to achieve their objectives. As long as they have a growing number of enthusiastic followers, they can continue spreading their political and religious messages through whatever forms of media they can put to their personal use – and tolerate a great deal of ambiguity as to the ultimate outcome of the movement.[9]

Concluding summary

This chapter has argued that religion, politics and communication come together in Islam, perhaps in a more integrated fashion than the three strands do for other religions. My analysis has shown that for one group with a political agenda in Europe, the use of the symbols of a glorious past, when religion and state were combined, works very effectively – particularly when the mass medium of broadcasting is used to transmit the messages. And the group is perceived to pose an enormous threat to the country it would most like to change, a country where a parliamentary democracy has existed for nearly 75 years. Does that mean that Islamic groups cannot rest until *Shari-ah* is the law for all Muslims and there is no need to talk about politics, religion and communication as separate entities? The Milli Görüş may be a group committed to that goal. But that may not be their agenda, or the goal may change as time passes and the political environment changes. What is clear is that the Milli Görüş would like its members to live their lives in Europe according to Islamic teachings, and is doing all it can to make that happen.

NOTES

1   Bernard Lewis has been severely criticised for using historical examples of Islamic practice to explain current religious practice. Edward Said has been the most vocal in his attack on Lewis. In the introduction to the revised edition of *Covering Islam*, Said says:

> All of Lewis's emphases in his work are to portray the whole of Islam as basically *outside* the known, familiar, acceptable world that 'we' inhabit, and in addition that contemporary Islam has inherited European anti-Semitism for use in an alleged war against modernity. As I pointed out about Lewis in my book, *Orientalism*, his methods are the snide observation, the fraudulent use of etymology to make huge cultural points about an entire set of peoples, and no less reprehensible, his total inability to grant that the Islamic peoples

are entitled to their own cultural, political and historical practices, free from Lewis's calculated attempt to show that because they are not Western (a notion of which he has an extremely tenuous grasp) they can't be good.

(1997)

Here, I hope to be using Lewis for historical definition only. I do not mean to support his work in its totality.

2 Lewis would not agree that this was his intent. He wrote, 'The basis of Kemalist religious policy was laicist, not irreligious; its purpose was not to destroy Islam, but to disestablish it – to end the power of religion and its exponents in political, social and cultural affairs, and limit it to matters of belief and worship' (1961: 406).

3 In his 1993 article, Sardar also explains why Islam first promoted the spread of knowledge (*ilm*) until the end of the fourteenth century and then retreated from that position. Over the period of about 100 years *ilm* came to be associated only with religious knowledge and the *ulama* (religious leaders) eventually allowed only those people to communicate who had extensive knowledge of the Koran and of Mohammed's Traditions as well as a profound knowledge of science and Islamic law. The *ulama* also proclaimed that the Koran could only be understood by hearing it or by reading it aloud. So the distribution of printed material through the printing press was delayed for almost three centuries.

4 During the decade of Menderes' government, other signs of religious tolerance were exhibited. Dramatic increases in the numbers of people making the pilgrimage to Mecca, the number of visits to local shrines, the number of people wearing religious clothing in public, and the attendance at mosques were observed. Fifteen thousand new mosques were built and hundreds more were repaired. The total number of religious organisations increased from 95 to 5,104. Required courses in religion were made part of the school curriculum at this time too (see Toprak 1981: 80–2).

5 See M. Demir, 'Fundamentalist nepotism threatens secular Turkey', *Turkish Daily News*, 12 June 1998, online.

6 For a larger discussion of the efforts of these pirate companies to become legitimate see Aksoy and Robins (1997), Ogan (1992), and Sahin and Aksoy (1993).

7 See the report of this research by R. Grimm, 'In Germany, many Turkish youths avoid cross-ethnic friendships', Deutsche Presse-Agentur, Lexis Nexis, 28 May 1998.

8 See R. Schumann and H. Zimmermann, 'Allah's shadow over Germany', *Berliner Morgenpost International*, 5 April 1997, online.

9 The Dutch are also unsure of the political goals of the group. Tolerance is a Dutch cultural and legal characteristic, so the government has supported this group as they would all minority interests. But there is fear about its growing strength and size. The Dutch press covered the event in photo and print, calling the group 'radical' and 'fundamentalist' (*Trouw*, 22 June 1998: 6). The *Volkskrant* newspaper carried a large colour photo and a story about the event on its front page on 22 June. And Dutch television later aired a documentary detailing the activities of the group and the potential danger posed by the Milli Görüş organisation within Europe.

References

Aksoy, A. and Robins, K. (1997) 'Peripheral vision: cultural identities in Turkey', *Environment and Planning* 29: 1937–52.

Amiraux, V. (1997) 'Turkish Islamic associations in Germany and the issue of European citizenship', in Vertovec, S. and Peach, C. (eds), *Islam in Europe*, New York: St. Martin's Press.

Arat, Y. (1995) 'Feminism and Islam: considerations on the journal *Kadın ve Aile*', in Tekeli, S. (ed.), *Women in Modern Turkish Society*, London: Zed Books.

Bousetta, H. (1997) 'The political mobilization of Muslim minorities in Europe. A roundtable discussion with Talip Kuçukcan, Nico Landman, and Mohamed Tozey', *Merger* 4, 1: 10–12.

Dassetto, F. and Nonneman, G. (1996) 'Islam in Belgium and the Netherlands: towards a typology of "transplanted" Islam', in Nonneman, G. *et al.* (eds), *Muslim Communities in the New Europe,* Reading: Ithaca Press.

Dayan, D. and Katz, E. (1988) 'Articulating consensus: the ritual and rhetoric of media events', in Alexander, J. C. (ed.), *Durkheimian Sociology: Cultural Studies*, Cambridge and New York: Cambridge University Press.

Fathi, A. (1979) 'The role of the Islamic pulpit', *Journal of Communication* 29, 3: 102–6.

Gluckman, M. (1963) 'Rituals of rebellion in south-east Africa', in Gluckman, M. (ed.), *Order and Rebellion in Tribal Africa*, Glencoe: Free Press.

Jansen, G. H. (1979) *Militant Islam*, New York: Harper & Row.

Kertzer, D. I. (1983) 'The role of ritual in political change', in Aronoff, M. J. (ed.), *Culture and Political Change*, New Brunswick: Transaction Books.

Lebor, A. (1997) *A Heart Turned East*, New York: St. Martin's Press.

Lewis, B. (1961) *Emergence of Modern Turkey*, London: Oxford University Press.

—— (1993) *Islam and the West*, New York: Oxford University Press.

Ogan, C. (1992) 'Communications policy options in an era of rapid technological change', *Telecommunications Policy* 16, 7: 565–75.

Öncu, A. (1995) 'Packaging Islam: cultural politics on the landscape of Turkish commercial television', *Public Culture* 18: 51–72.

Sağnak, M. (1996) *Medya-Politik: 1983–1993 Yillari Arasinda Medya-Politikaci Ilikilei,* Istanbul: Eti Kitaplari.

Sahin, S. and Aksoy, A. (1993) 'Global media and cultural identity in Turkey', *Journal of Communication* 43, 2: 31–41.

Said, E. (1997) *Covering Islam*, New York: Vintage Books.

Sardar, Z. (1993) 'Paper, printing and compact disks: the making and unmaking of Islamic culture', *Media, Culture and Society* 15: 43–59.

Sreberny-Mohammadi, A. (1994) *Small Media, Big Revolution: Communication, Culture, and the Iranian Revolution*, Minneapolis: University of Minnesota Press.

Toprak, B. (1981) *Islam and Political Development in Turkey*, Leiden: E. J. Brill.

142

10

SATELLITE TELEVISION AND CHINESE MIGRANTS IN BRITAIN

Lee Siew-peng

This chapter examines the role of satellite television in engendering identity amongst Hong Kong Chinese[1] migrants in the UK. After a brief account of how this group first settled in Britain, I shall survey how they have been (mis)represented in the British media, and how their entertainment and information needs were met prior to the advent of satellite television. Then television viewing in general, and a specific 'television event' in particular, will be analysed in relation to how the processes and politics of identity formation have changed between and across generations. Original data were gleaned from participant observation at three sheltered housing schemes for more than 100 Chinese elderly in Nordentown[2] and a Chinese supplementary school in London between June 1997 and August 1998.

The Chinese in Britain

In the UK there is a tendency to speak in terms of the 'Asian community' as if they are one homogenous group, when in fact there are marked differences between regional, religious and linguistic groups coming from the different countries of the Indian subcontinent and Africa (see, for instance, Anwar 1998: 22). Likewise with the 'Chinese community' there are significant differences between the Chinese who originate from Hong Kong and those from Taiwan, between Taiwan and mainland Chinese, and even between those from Singapore and from Malaysia. It has been estimated by Chan (1989: 6) that 75 to 80 per cent of Chinese in Britain are of Hong Kong origin. More recent data from the 1991 British Census (Cheng 1997: 162) show that the largest proportion of the Chinese (34 per cent of the 156,938) was reported to be born in Hong Kong. The next highest proportion, 28 per cent, was born in the UK. Others were listed as from Malaysia/Singapore, China (including Taiwan), Vietnam and 'other parts of the world'. If only half of the 28 per cent of UK-born are taken to be of Hong Kong parentage, this would take the proportion of 'Hong Kong Chinese' up to 48 per cent. The real figure is possibly higher, as a large proportion of Chinese in the other categories are likely to be 'transients' – young overseas students and professionals without children who are in the UK for short periods of time and who are required to return to their own countries in due course (Li 1994: 38). Within this group, there are further and sometimes subtle divisions along the lines of language and educational attainment (Chan 1989: 7). Apart from the many who came to join the catering industry, there is also a group of intellectuals and professionals who came for further studies and then opted to stay after a minimum residence period (Taylor 1987: 35). Linguistically, it has been said that up to 70 per cent of the Chinese in Britain are Cantonese-speaking[3] while 25 per cent are Hakka speakers (Watson 1977: 185, 205). In my own fieldwork, however, I encountered a majority of Hakka speakers.

This chapter will focus on Hong Kong Chinese migrants who first arrived between the 1950s and 1970s. It is generally accepted that they came initially from the New Territories (NT) in Hong Kong on the basis of being British passport-holders[4] and were mainly involved in the catering business (see Baker 1968 and 1994; Ng 1968; O'Neill 1972; Taylor 1987; Watson 1975 and 1977). According to these authors, the NT rice farmers began to face competition from rice farmers in Thailand and vegetable farmers (refugees) from mainland China. A drop in rice prices coupled with a new demand for 'exotic foods' in postwar Britain caused many to leave for Britain in the hope of making a fortune before returning to their lineage villages (Baker 1994: 294; Watson 1975: 49, 131).

Watson has highlighted two important dimensions to this pattern of chain migration. First, new migrants were assured of a job and lodgings on arrival in Britain. Second, given the various attempts by the government to control this migration (from Hong Kong and other colonies) through the Commonwealth Immigration Acts, it was only those individuals who could find a sponsor – either a family member or fellow villager – who were able to enter Britain (Bauböck 1997). Initially it was only men who came but, with the 1968 Commonwealth Immigration Act which threatened to halt all further immigration, these migrants were quick to send for their wives and children. The 1971 Immigration Act, which required all Hong Kong-born and China-born potential immigrants to have work permits, only consolidated the pattern of emigrants joining the catering trade as this was the familiar way of finding a sponsor in order to obtain a work permit.

Unlike other immigrants coming to Britain during this same period who tended to congregate in certain major industrial and urban areas, the Chinese seemed unique in that they were willing to be dispersed across the country. Most of the new Chinese immigrants would stop initially in or around London or other big cities to get a taste of the trade and raise capital for their own businesses, before moving into the more remote areas of the country where they might run a viable Chinese food outlet. As we shall see, the nature of this scattered settlement has had a profound impact on the cultural identification of the younger generations.

Conceptually, there is a temptation to see the development of Chinese immigration as a sequential pattern, with a young man (married or single) as the typical first-generation migrant arriving on his own, going straight into a job, and sponsoring the arrival of his wife and children later on. These children have now grown up and their own offspring (grandchildren to the first immigrants) tend to be British-born. From my fieldwork experience, I have found it more meaningful to speak in generational terms: the grandparents and great-grandparents who tend to be aged 60 and over (some even in their 90s) as the 'older generation'; the 'middle generation' aged between 35 and 60 who came to this country as very young children, teenagers or young adults and who are now parents, sometimes grandparents, themselves; and the British-born 'young generation' who tend to be below 35 years of age. Many 'first generation migrants' (now aged 35 to 60) are in fact the 'middle generation'. They were the first in their families to establish a business here, sometimes with their British-born children. Grandparents (though a chronologically earlier or 'older' generation) tended to arrive only later, sponsored by these adult children. Several of my older women respondents (in their 70s and 80s) recalled how they came to assist their adult children in running their restaurants, usually in the 'tea room' making tea and coffee, and in washing up. During my fieldwork I also met several teenagers who are here without their parents, studying at private boarding schools. They are effectively 'first-generation migrants' without their parents. There are also other young people who have recently migrated here with their parents. I am therefore in agreement with Li (1994: 49) who asserts that the typology of 'first-generation emigrant/sponsored emigrant/British-born children' is not always isomorphic with 'parents/children/grandchildren'. Obviously, too, the age ranges I have given above are only approximate and while the assumption of such generational differences might be viewed as either too generalised or tautological (or both), I have found this to be a useful tool in facilitating further analysis.

The sojourner settles?

Many accounts maintain that the older Chinese had no intention of remaining in Britain. What they saw of British culture in the context of the restaurant business led them to think that Chinese culture is still 'infinitely superior' to European cultures (Chan 1989: 7; Watson 1975: 127). There was very little overlap in the worlds of the Chinese restaurant worker and the British customer and neighbour. As Baker (1994: 296) pointed out, for those who were 'trapped in the kitchen there was not even the opportunity to see a British person except in the few (unsociable) hours when they were not at work'. Social interaction was also hampered by the inability to speak English amongst many of the older generation. These were sojourners whose aim in coming to Britain was solely to make a fortune and retire back to Hong Kong (Baker 1994: 297; Skeldon 1994: 25).

The new immigration restrictions, however, encouraged reunion with their wives and children, and it was after this that the tendency to settle became more pronounced (Watson 1975: 130–1). With the prospective 'return' of Hong Kong to China, there was an even greater motivation to settle. To these, I would now add the category of 'new immigrants' coming into Britain on 'right of abode' packages (Skeldon 1994: 36), many of whom are not entirely settlers but 'modern sojourners' or 'astronauts' (*taai hoong yan*)[5] who seem to be merely spreading their risks by acquiring a British passport and then returning to Hong Kong to work (Skeldon 1994: 11). Amongst my older research contacts, many have tried resettling in Hong Kong, but found the pace of life and the weather rather more difficult to cope with now that they are physically less agile. Several also admitted to enjoying the privileges of the wel-fare/pension system in the UK, which far surpasses their entitlements back in Hong Kong.

Before satellite television

The information needs of ethnic minorities were first officially acknowledged in the Annan Report (1977) which recommended that the broadcasting authorities should provide programming which would introduce newcomers to the 'life and mores of this country', 'reflect their own [ethnic] culture', and which would additionally enable others to 'understand and appreciate these cultures' (see also Chan 1989: 47–8). In other words, there was a sense that the media could be used to help integrate ethnic minorities into the host commu-nity. Attempts by the broadcasting authorities to use television programmes or series for language instruction or to teach the 'English' way of life were considered patronising. It appears that while there might have been the will, there was not the expertise to produce programmes that were acceptable to the ethnic minorities.[6]

At the same time, there were many productions in English which stereotyped the ethnic minorities. Programmes like *Mind Your Language*, featuring migrants in an English language class, only emphasised the rift between the Sikh and the Hindu, and propagated the view that the Chinese lived by the sayings of Mao's *Little Red Book* and other similar myths. Then there were the *Fu Manchu* stories and films by Sax Rohmer in which the 'Yellow Peril incarnate' (Pan 1990: 89) is associated with drugs and debauchery. Later on, the genre of the Bruce Lee (or more recently Jackie Chan) films began to cast every Chinese (or simply 'oriental') person in the mould of a kung-fu fighter. Together these programmes reflected a situation whereby the images of the minorities were 'submitted to the decisions of a majority', resulting in messages which were 'conceived for that majority' (Dayan 1998: 105). So while the Chinese were enjoying a measure of economic success, they did not have the means of countering these dominant stereotypes.[7] It is true that, more recently, documentaries such as *Goodbye Chop Suey* (1985) and *Takeaway Lives* (1993), and programmes like *Orientations* have attempted to address the realities of the Chinese living in Britain (see Parker 1994), and religious, travel and food programmes have showcased aspects of Chinese culture. However, it is readily admitted by the broadcasting authorities themselves that most minority programming is produced with a (South) Asian and Afro-Caribbean audience in mind. Programmes designed specifically for Britain's Chinese community remain a noticeable absence in the broadcasting landscape.[8]

Where radio was concerned, Chan (1989: 16) found that amongst 30 BBC radio stations, only Radio Manchester and Radio Merseyside produced programmes to serve the Chinese community. It was only in December 1983 that the first bilingual programme, *Eastern Horizon*, was aired, for half an hour once a month. In 1988 this was increased to one hour a week. These slots consisted of an approximate 40–60 per cent split in Chinese–English content, reaching an audience of some 200,000 (House of Commons Home Affairs Committee 1985: lxxv). Until ten years ago London, which is home to the largest Chinese population in Britain, did not have any regular broadcast programme (Chan 1989: 92). Now Spectrum Radio broadcasts in Cantonese, but featuring many Mandarin songs, for an hour every evening.

The Chinese therefore continued to look towards their own home countries for news and entertainment. As Dayan (1998: 108) has observed, diasporic communication manifests itself through the development of 'community media such as daily, weekly or monthly newspapers'. *Siyu* and other geographically based community newspapers, usually with both English and Chinese articles, are periodically produced by cultural and community organisations for this purpose. For the literate Chinese, the daily *Sing Tao* is a major source of up-to-date news and pictures of events in China and Hong Kong as well as in Britain and around the world and is in much demand. However for the older genera- tion, many of whom are illiterate, Chinese-language newspapers cannot meet their information needs. It is in this context that many have turned to videotapes.

As Gillespie (1995: 77) found amongst her Asian respondents, most families have large video collections. This is true for the Chinese community as well. However, unlike the Sri Lankan Tamils in Denmark studied by Preis (1997), these are not videos of family events like birthdays and funerals.[9] Instead one finds a range of material – from old black-and-white Cantonese opera and movies to contemporary TV drama serials. The video hire shop in Nordentown was (and still is) an important establishment as Chinese from miles around trek here every week to get their week's supply of tapes. (A woman I interviewed noted how these weekly trips with her heavy rucksack of tapes were the cause of severe back pain and she therefore jumped at the opportunity to move into sheltered accommodation nearer Chinatown). With the advent of Chinese satellite television, however, the dependence on hired videotapes has been considerably reduced – at least for those with satellite access.

The satellite television in this chapter refers to the Chinese Channel which was launched in March 1997 as a subsidiary of the Television Broadcasting

147

Limited in Hong Kong (HK–TVB). It was the first digital satellite Chinese channel to provide day and night broadcasting services in the UK and its features range from costume and period drama to modern sitcoms and action series, feature films to classics and telemovies, as well as in-depth coverage of Asian news and news from Hong Kong.

Talking TV-watching

Gillespie (1995: 205) asserts that 'in order to understand how television is implicated in the remaking of ethnicity, or indeed in any process of cultural change', we must resort to ethnographic enquiry, and that television talk, 'though it may often seem esoteric and trivial, is an important form of self-narration and a major collective resource through which identities are negotiated'. I shall present three types of TV-watching 'events'. The first is based on secondary accounts of a researcher (Sham 1998), the second is culled from an assortment of TV-watching episodes with my research contacts, and the third is an analysis of how a major turning point in Hong Kong's history was celebrated, via television viewing, and then forgotten.

Takeaway television

Sham (1998: 82–120) has illuminated the phenomenon of video-watching amongst families who run takeaways – whether during their leisure time or whilst preparing food. At the point of service, BBC and ITV soaps like *Neighbours* and *EastEnders* are played for the benefit of customers waiting for their orders. However for their own viewing consumption, these families watch programmes taped from the Chinese satellite channel or hired from the Chinatown shop. Many young people complain that this preference prevents them from exchanging as 'communication fodder' the details of soaps watched by their schoolfriends. Nor are they comfortable with reading or speaking Chinese. One of Sham's respondents likened the spoken Cantonese in the videos to background music. Others, however, find the Hong Kong pop culture to be quite an attraction and even claim to speak better Cantonese as a result of watching these pop videos.[10]

Many are more familiar with Hong Kong film and pop stars than the British counterparts. The impact of the Hong Kong pop and entertainment culture on identity formation amongst British-born Hong Kong Chinese is an important area for further research (see Parker 1995). Indeed, so pervasive is the influence of pop culture transmitted on satellite television that I found that even older migrants are familiar with the top pop idols like the 'Heavenly Kings'.

Given the nature of the takeaway business, children tend to watch television and video in the company of their parents, either in a section of the shop, or at home on their 'off days'. The content of these drama serials is typically centred on family conflict and individual success (Sham 1998: 91). Sham has found that parents tend to use these story lines to reiterate family and cultural values, by reminding their children, for example, that they must not treat their parents like certain protagonists in the drama did. In this sense we could say that satellite television, through transmitting Hong Kong drama, is a platform of entertainment as well as a tool for the transmission of language and cultural values.

Television viewing amongst the elderly

I watched television at different times of the day with several of my older generation contacts, both individually in their own flats and with up to seventeen others in the communal lounge in a sheltered housing scheme. Like the elderly community in general, television viewing is a very significant part of the lives of elderly Chinese. Television provides the 'ambient noise' for many living alone and is a welcome companion to those suffering from insomnia. In this respect, the recent decision by the Chancellor of the Exchequer to reimburse the cost of the licence fee to the over-75s is a welcome move – and all the more so given the general lack of interest displayed by elderly Chinese for programmes on the British terrestrial channels. As such the Chinese satellite television company enjoys a virtually 'captive market' amongst these viewers and while the cost of satellite installation is high for those living in their own homes, the tenants in the housing schemes I studied were able to share the costs of subscribing to satellite television.

Their television diet usually consists of melodramatic serials that can run into hundreds of episodes. Some of these are repeats of very old drama serials, but they are still avidly followed (even by Hakka-speaking tenants who may understand little of the Cantonese used in these dramas). Documentaries are usually in Mandarin which even fewer tenants understand, but these also receive large and attentive audiences.

Significantly, though the drama series/soap operas are followed avidly by most, it was rare for me to overhear the story lines of these soaps being discussed in the common meeting areas. Instead, the most popular programmes for the older generation are the evening news reports and magazine programmes. While news broadcasts are always up to date, the 'gossip magazine' is transmitted some two weeks after its original broadcast in Hong Kong. I did not realise this was the case until one programme referred specifically to Christmas and we were nearing the middle of January! The tenants did not seem the least perturbed by this apparent time lapse in information. It did not seem to make a jot of difference whether they are two weeks behind (or two weeks ahead of) Hong Kong time. Instead, this temporal lag is compensated by a sense of their being in the midst of all that is happening in Hong Kong. This observation somewhat confounds the arguments of media theorists for whom it is the watching of events transmitted *simultaneously* that allows people of a nation to 'think their relationships to others across the spatial spread' (Tomlinson 1991: 82). In the case of these elderly Chinese, the communal spirit created by viewing an event in simultaneous time was subordinated to their greater need of identifying with an 'imagined community' (Anderson 1991), constituted by the space and place of Hong Kong. It was therefore not unusual for tenants to get quite excited about 'current' newsworthy events in Hong Kong – the weather, politics, health scares, etc. – even if these were two weeks late. More important than a sense of shared time with resident Hongkongers was the sense of spatial proximity and shared memories that older migrants conveyed as they identified locations shown on television, debated where these were in relation to their own ancestral villages of origin, their *laoxiang* or *xiangxia* (Christiansen 1997a: 15), or summarily dismissed the comments of those who had no inroads into this imagined space.

Ma (1999: 58, 176) has argued that television has become a 'ritual space' in which the Hong Kong audience regularly enters into communion with an imagined Hong Kong community. My fieldwork suggests that Ma's community has been extended, via satellite television, to those migrants now settled abroad. Though deterritorialised, these elderly Hong Kong migrants are now reterritorialised within a small physical space within sheltered housing, but despite these confines, and thanks to a shared television viewing experience, their sense of belonging to a larger imagined Hong Kong community is all the more heightened and intensified.

Wooi-gwai: 1997 and 1998

What is the nature of this reterritorialised identification? One way of opening out this question is to consider the most significant event for Hong Kong people in recent years: the 1997 'handover' (in the terminology of the British and European press) of Hong Kong to China, or, as far as the mainland Chinese (and many Hong Kong Chinese) were concerned, the 'return' (*wooi-gwai*) of Hong Kong to China. I had timed my visit to the sheltered housing scheme in Nordentown to coincide with this event. There, I was invited by the warden to join him and a handful of other tenants in the communal lounge to watch 'live' the proceedings of the *wooi-gwai* on satellite television. Most of the tenants from the housing schemes were following this event closely in their own flats. A number were also taping these programmes for their children who were at work. While I acknowledge that this is a limited sample from which to draw firm conclusions, there are none the less some suggestive hypotheses I would like to put forward concerning the processes of national and ethnic identification elicited by this television-viewing event.

The telecast ran from 10 a.m. to 7.30 p.m. The tenants were getting more and more excited with the arrival of the midnight hour (Hong Kong time), which was when the actual handing-over ceremony was to take place. Being Singaporean, I found it rather awkward when several viewers rose and saluted every time the Chinese national anthem was played. They even demanded the rest of us do the same. One of these viewers asserted that Hong Kong had always been part of China, that 'foreigners' had taken control, and that now that the Chinese were throwing them out, and independence was being restored, there was reason to celebrate! When Chris Patten's daughters were shown on the screen in tears, many derisory comments were made, suggesting that their grief was due to the loss of the privileges and wealth the Governor had enjoyed. Tung Chee Hwa, the new chief executive of Hong Kong as a Special Administrative Region, received more favourable comments, but leaders of the local democracy movement who were seen as acting in collaboration with the British government were given short shrift. One viewer commented: 'These are traitors. They will be arrested soon.'

Coverage then turned to the celebratory events held in London and other European cities, including interviews with Chinese – both mainland and Hong Kong – living throughout Europe. Everywhere the cameras focussed on smiling faces in a festive mood, giving *wooi-gwai* a decidedly positive slant. Pictures showed the People's Liberation Army soldiers being trucked into Hong Kong barracks and the crowds lining the streets to welcome them. Near midnight, police and other uniformed personnel were shown changing the badges on their berets from 'Hong Kong – British colony' to 'Hong Kong – Special Administrative Region'. In between the interviews, ceremony, fireworks and other scenes of celebration, Hong Kong pop and television stars performed in a combination of Cantonese *and* Mandarin Chinese.[11] As the British contingent led by the Prince of Wales left on HMS *Britannia*, attention was focussed on the swearing-in, in halting Mandarin, of the members of the new legislative assembly and top civil servants.

Having experienced the euphoria of the year before, I made sure I was back in Nordentown for the first anniversary of the *wooi-gwai*. I did not have access to satellite television this time and so had to keep asking the tenants and other contacts if there were any special programmes or celebrations on television. Their answer was negative. Sitting in the same hall as a group of Chinese women in a dressmaking class, I heard the following conversation:

'What is the date today?'
'Uh, the 30th. Oh, no, it's the 1st of July.'
'First of July? Wow! It's one year after *wooi-gwai*.'
'Oh, yes. It's already a year after *wooi-gwai*. Time really flies.'

The instructor and students went back to drawing their paper patterns.

The power of television

One year later, *wooi-gwai* was no more than a date that many had forgotten. Why then was there such euphoria amongst the Hong Kong Chinese in Britain just the year before? As a teacher at a Chinese supplementary school in London, I was surprised to learn that several teachers and parents had asked for leave in order to join their friends and family in Hong Kong to 'celebrate *wooi-gwai*'. There appears to be some inconsistency between the professed dislike for mainland Chinese by the younger Hong Kong Chinese in Britain and their action in returning to Hong Kong for the celebration. As Chow (1993: 22) notes, the Hong Kong Chinese share 'an identification with "Chinese culture" but a distantiation from the Chinese Communist regime'. Hong Kong is what it is today because the people there were determined to be distinguished from mainland China (Evans and Tam 1997: 3; Lau and Kuan 1988). From most available accounts the British-born Chinese are not keen to be identified with mainland Chinese. Parker's respondents (1995: 162–3, 169) confessed to being 'still prejudiced against mainland China', and to feeling insulted if so identified. Given the strength of these negative feelings, I would therefore suggest that satellite television has been a main force in galvanising a sense of 'belonging' to the new entity: Hong Kong/China.

Unlike other former British colonies in the Asia region, the 'return' of Hong Kong was a case of decolonisation without independence; Hong Kong was merely being transferred from being the subject of one power to another (Lau 1990).[12] I recall my first visit to Hong Kong in 1986, two years after the signing of the Sino–British Declaration, when the issue of the 'handover' was couched in terms of the '97 problem'. How has it come to pass, then, that in the interim, the 'handover' became a 'return' worth celebrating? Ma (1999), for example, has noted how in the 1970s the Hong Kong television stations produced melodramatic serials which portrayed mainlanders as outsiders who were backward, lazy and uncouth while the 'established Hongkongers' were seen as sophisticated, morally upright, and ready to climb the ladder of success through sheer hard work (see also Cheng 1997: 60). In the early 1990s, though, there was a sense of confusion as Hong Kong underwent politicisation and re-sinicisation in anticipation of the 'return' (Ma 1999: 45). The 4 June (Tiananmen Square) incident of 1989 also contributed towards the breaking down of the categorical distinction between 'Hongkonger' and 'Chinese' as the 'severance from China' in the postwar decades went into reverse (Ma 1999: 52–3).

By the time of my fieldwork in 1997, these television dramas appeared to have embraced their mainlander cousins quite effortlessly as story lines show protagonists flitting back and forth across the border to engage in all sorts of entrepreneurial ventures (as well as extra-marital affairs). In fact, by 1992, two-thirds of all foreign investments in China came from Hong Kong, and much of the booming commercial activities in the territory involved Sino–Hong Kong connections (Ash and Kueh 1993; Sung 1992). Hongkongers were certainly taking *economic* advantage of their new association with China and media images seemed to confirm this appreciation of the monetary benefits close association with China was in the process of generating. On these counts, Hongkongers do have reasons to celebrate.

The impact of *wooi-gwai* on identity

If the July 1997 celebrations were simply the result of media hype, does this mean that *wooi-gwai* had no substantial legacy at all? A partial answer can be gleaned by considering the impact of *wooi-gwai* on Hong Kong diasporic identity along generational lines (though given that my research focus was on the elderly, my broader hypotheses are necessarily speculative).

I have found that older migrants are quite happy to be physically 'home' in Britain where the 'English Queen' (social security) takes good care of their physical and medical needs. But in conversation it becomes evident that, emotionally, they still think of Hong Kong, or a specific area of the New Territories, as 'home'. For this generation, retirement and comfortable pensions now mean that their emotional 'home' is only a relatively inexpensive flight away.[13] Now that Hong Kong has reverted to China, they are quite comfortable with thinking of China as home, although it does not make any real or practical difference to them. In other words, their physical presence here does not automatically imply a sense of national belonging, and questions of politics or ideology, or of democracy or communism, which trouble other observers of Hong Kong/China, do not seem to figure in their perception of the 'return'.

For the 'middle generation' (aged between 35 and 60 and born in Hong Kong), however, these same questions of politics and ideology might have played a more significant role in negotiating their own relations to Hong Kong's changing status. Here we need to return to the specific experience of Hong Kong Chinese migration to Britain to explain the apparent contradiction between the negative images of mainland Chinese embraced by this generation and their professed desire to celebrate *wooi-gwai*. I would contend that this generation, although having enjoyed professional and economic success in Britain, have never really felt 'at home' in their Chinese/British identities. These were the children of those migrants who dispersed themselves through-out the country, thereby 'intruding' into homogenous 'white' British communities, with the subsequent sense of isolation and marginalisation that researchers in the 1970s have noted (Garvey and Jackson 1975; Jones 1979; O'Neill 1972). These children were the subjects of early studies measuring their (mal)adjustment to the language, school system, food and so on. The experience of being singled out for being Chinese in their formative years at school, and of having to help their parents in establishing businesses in their adolescence, has left this generation marked by a considerable ambivalence towards identifying Britain as their single or primary emotional 'home'. For many in this group, *wooi-gwai* provided the opportunity to reclaim and celebrate their Chinese identity 'at no risk' to the material and political securities they otherwise enjoy. And for the minority who have striven to rid themselves of their Chinese heritage (by not speaking the language, marrying non-Chinese, etc), *wooi-gwai* may have been a convenient platform to liberate them from a political identity they have no wish of maintaining.

Existing literature often refers to the Chinese born in Britain as being 'between cultures' (Watson 1977). However, while some of their forebears now in the 'middle generation' were in fact 'between cultures' in not being able to adapt linguistically or culturally, it seems more appropriate to describe some members of the current British-born generation as 'straddling cultures'.[14] These individuals, adept linguistically and culturally in a way their predecessors never were, have the resources to slip in and out of different cultural niches with great ease. They can speak Cantonese with their parents and, consistent with tradition, show respect for authority and family elders. At the same time, they are as British as any of their peers and can switch between cultural contexts and preferred identifications depending on the circumstances. For some of this generation *wooi-gwai* may have been used to 'lance' once and for all the Hong Kong/Chinese element of their hybrid identity. For others, *wooi-gwai* may have represented an occasion to reject their identities as former 'British Subjects' and to proclaim identification with a great Chinese civilisation, to revive their Chinese 'roots' in much the same way as some West Indian and South Asian children have reclaimed their 'roots' (compare Ballard 1979; Weinrich 1979). Whatever use they have made of *wooi-gwai*, one thing is certain for this generation: Britain is now more ethnically mixed than in the 1950s or even the 1970s, and the Chinese are no longer at the bottom of the pecking order of newer migrants (compare Van Hear 1998: 57).

On a wider front, it should also be noted that in the run-up to *wooi-gwai* many thousands of Hongkongers had secured passports to other countries like Canada, Australia, USA and Britain. In that sense they were like the Ugandan Asians who had learned to 'spread the risk' by placing family members in different countries (Van Hear 1998: 65, 199). This group of 'astronauts' has the best of both worlds: the political and economic security of a foreign passport and the emotional security which identification with an enlarged Chinese nation is providing. Meanwhile the new Chinese government has retained the New Territories Ordinance, which entitles British-born descendants of migrants from lineage villages to ancestral land (Christiansen 1997b). Thus, even if British-born 'Hong Kong Chinese' do not identify Hong Kong as 'home' after *wooi-gwai*, they still have an inalienable right to land in Hong Kong/China.

Conclusion

I have looked at three different types of TV-viewing activities amongst Hong Kong Chinese in the UK. In the first, TV-viewing was a means of transmitting language and cultural values to a younger generation. Second, I have suggested that TV-viewing amongst the older Chinese in sheltered housing plays a big part in reinforcing a sense of their belonging to an 'imagined community', and to their 'home' in Hong Kong. As for *wooi-gwai*, it seems to have been quickly forgotten by viewers who, a year before, had participated via television in its fervent celebration. My analysis tends to suggest, however, that if *wooi-gwai* celebrations are now a distant 'historical memory', their television coverage none the less played a decisive role in mediating new forms of identification for different generational groups who could trace their roots to Hong Kong.

NOTES

1 The focus in this chapter is on the 'Hong Kong Chinese' although this is sometimes simplified to just 'Chinese'.

2 This refers to a city in the north of England.

3 Traditionally the term '*Punti*' (meaning 'local') is used although I find the term 'Cantonese' much less confusing.

4 Up until just after the Communist Revolution in China, the population of Hong Kong was largely made up of transients, many of whom had come from mainland China, and therefore were not considered 'British'. In contrast the New Territories were ceded to Britain in 1898 and the inhabitants there were conferred the status of 'British Subjects' (see Evans and Tam 1997).

5 There is an interesting word-play here as the phrase is immediately translatable as 'astronauts', but *taai hoong* could also mean 'without a wife', which makes *taai hoong yan* to be 'people without wives'.

6 On 8 December 1999, the Broadcasting Standards Commission released a report which castigated television stations for 'failing to reflect the multicultural nature of the country'.

7 Gillespie (1995: 206) also noted how young Asians complained that there were too few images of 'Asian' style that they 'feel able to take as role models'.

8 In reply to my query to the Information Unit in December 1999, the BBC confirmed that, while they have a Multicultural Unit which offers programmes for ethnic minorities, they do not produce programmes specifically for the Chinese community in the United Kingdom.

9 One of the characteristics of older Chinese is that birthdays, especially of those aged under 60, are not celebrated at all, and funerals are not events that one would desire to record permanently on film.

10 Compare with Asian youngsters in Britain who claim that Indian films help them in learning Hindi (Gillespie 1995: 78).

11 It has been said that Hongkongers looked down on Chinese who did not speak Cantonese (Evans and Tam 1997: 27) and Hong Kong culture came into its own with the blooming of 'Canto-pop' (Cheng 1997: 60). Now these same Canto-pop artists seemed to be embracing the excitement of being fully mainland Chinese by singing in Mandarin.

12 A comparison however could be made with the case of Goa in India, and to Macau, which reverted to China in 1999.

13 Chinese satellite television constantly advertises cheap package fares, reflecting market strategies which are deliberately aimed at the Hong Kong Chinese in Britain.

14 This seems to be more evident in the South-East of England where many of the 'middle-generation' parents are involved in professional jobs, compared with those in the north who are still very much restricted to the catering business.

References

Anderson, B. (1991) *Imagined Communities*, London: Verso.

Annan Report (1977) *Report of the Committee on the Future of Broadcasting*, London: HMSO.

Anwar, M. (1998) *Between Cultures: Continuity and Change in the Lives of Young Asians*, London: Routledge.

Ash, R. F. and Kueh, Y. Y. (1993) 'Economic integration within greater China: trade and investment flows between China, Hong Kong, and Taiwan', *The China Quarterly* 136: 711–45.

Baker, H. D. R. (1968) *A Chinese Lineage Village: Sheung Shui*, London: Frank Cass & Co.

—— (1994) 'Branches all over: the Hong Kong Chinese in the United Kingdom', in Skeldon, R. (ed.), *Reluctant Exiles or Bold Pioneers: An Introduction to Migration from Hong Kong*, Hong Kong: Hong Kong University Press.

Ballard, C. (1979) 'Conflict, continuity and change: second-generation South Asians', in Saifullah Khan, V. (ed.), *Minority Families in Britain*, London: Social Science Research Council.

Bauböck, R. (ed.) (1997) *From Aliens to Citizens: Redefining the Status of Immigrants in Europe*, Aldershot: Avebury.

Chan, Y. M. (1989) 'Development of local radio for the Chinese community in England', Manchester: University of Manchester, M.Ed. thesis.

Cheng, S. L. (1997) 'Back to the future: herbal tea shops in Hong Kong', in Evans, G. and Tam Siu-mi, M. (eds), *Hong Kong: The Anthropology of a Chinese Metropolis*, Surrey: Curzon.

Chow, R. (1993) *Writing Diasporas: Tactics of Intervention in Contemporary Cultural Studies*, Indianapolis: Indiana University Press.

Christiansen, F. (1997a) *Overseas Chinese in Europe: An Imagined Community?* Leeds: Department of East Asian Studies, University of Leeds, Leeds East Asia Paper 48.

—— (1997b) *Overseas Chinese, Ancestral Rights and the New Territories*, Leeds: Department of East Asian Studies, University of Leeds, Leeds East Asia Paper 49.

Dayan, D. (1998) 'Particularistic media and diasporic communications', in Liebes, T. and Curran, J. (eds), *Media, Ritual and Identity*, London: Routledge.

Evans, G. and Tam Siu-mi, M. (eds) (1997) *Hong Kong: The Anthropology of a Chinese Metropolis*, Surrey: Curzon.

Garvey, A. and Jackson, B. (1975) *Chinese Children. Research and Action Project into the Needs of Chinese Children*, London: National Education and Development Trust.

Gillespie, M. (1995) *Television, Ethnicity and Cultural Change*, London: Routledge.

House of Commons Home Affairs Committee (1985) *The Chinese Community in Britain*, London: HMSO.

Jones, D. (1979) 'The Chinese in Britain: a minority's response to its own needs', *Trends in Education*, Spring: 15–18.

Lau, S. K. (1990) *Decolonisation Without Independence and the Poverty of Political Leaders in Hong Kong*, Hong Kong: Hong Kong Institute of Asia–Pacific Studies, Chinese University of Hong Kong.

Lau, S. and Kuan, H. (1988) *The Ethos of the Hong Kong Chinese*, Hong Kong: Chinese University Press.

Li, W. (1994) *Three Generations, Two Languages, One Family: Language Choice and Language Shift in a Chinese Community in Britain*, Clevedon: Multilingual Matters.

Ma, E. K. (1999) *Culture, Politics and Television in Hong Kong*, London: Routledge.

Ng, K. C. (1968) *The Chinese in London*, London: Oxford University Press.

O'Neill, J. A. (1972) 'The role of family and community in the social adjustment of the Chinese in Liverpool', Liverpool: University of Liverpool, MA thesis.

Pan, L. (1990) *Sons of the Yellow Emperor: The Story of the Overseas Chinese*, London: Secker & Warburg.

Parker, D. (1994) *The Chinese in Britain: Annotated Bibliography and Research Resources*, Birmingham: Department of Cultural Studies, University of Birmingham, Centre for Research in Ethnic Relations.

—— (1995) *Through Different Eyes: The Cultural Identities of Young Chinese People in Britain*, Aldershot: Avebury.

Preis, A.-B. S. (1997) 'Seeking place: capsized identities and contracted belongings among Sri Lankan refugees', in Fog Olwig, K. and Hastrup, K. (eds), *Siting Culture: the Shifting Anthropological Object*, London: Routledge.

Sham, S. Y. M. (1998) 'Cultural differences in teaching and learning styles – a case study of Chinese adolescents', Manchester: Manchester Metropolitan University, Ph.D. thesis.

Skeldon, R. (ed.) (1994) *Reluctant Exiles or Bold Pioneers: An Introduction to Migration from Hong Kong*, Hong Kong: Hong Kong University Press.

Sung, Y. W. (1992) *Non-Institutional Economic Integration via Cultural Affinity*, Hong Kong: Hong Kong Institute of Asia–Pacific Studies, Chinese University of Hong Kong.

Taylor, M. J. (1987) *Chinese Pupils in Britain: A Review of Research into the Education of Pupils of Chinese Origin*, Windsor: NFER-Nelson.

Tomlinson, J. (1991) *Cultural Imperialism*, London: Pinter.

Van Hear, N. (1998) *New Diasporas: The Mass Exodus, Dispersal and Regrouping of Migrant Communities*, London: UCL Press.

Watson, J. L. (1975) *Emigration and the Chinese Lineage: The Mans in Hong Kong and London*, Berkeley: California University Press.

—— (1977) 'The Chinese: Hong Kong villagers in the British catering trade', in Watson, J. L. (ed.), *Between Two Cultures: Migrants and Minorities in Britain*, Oxford: Basil Blackwell.

Weinrich, P. (1979) 'Ethnicity and adolescent identity conflicts', in Saifullah Khan, V. (ed.), *Minority Families in Britain*, London: Social Science Research Council.

11

'A SPACE WHERE ONE
FEELS AT HOME'

Media consumption practices among London's
South Asian and Greek Cypriot communities

Roza Tsagarousianou

Introduction

Diasporas are not novel phenomena; they have a long history virtually coextensive with the history of human geographical mobility. Having said that, diasporic experiences in late modernity have been markedly different from those of previous historical epochs. Premodern and early modern diasporas could be perceived as 'looser' translocal and transnational networks. However the intensification of relations that are instituted by time–space compression and the interlinking of remote locations introduces a new qualitative element in the character and practices of contemporary diasporas (Giddens 1990: 64; Harvey 1990: 240–2). In late modernity, global migration trends have produced diasporic groups related by culture, ethnicity, language and religion, not only in the sense of 'transnational dispersal' but also in terms of intense and constant interaction at a transnational level. The technological and socio-economic transformations that have fundamentally altered our experiences of time and space have undoubtedly been central in the transformation of diasporic experience.

Diasporas find themselves at the centre of sets of intersecting transnational flows and linkages that bring together geographically remote locations. In turn, diasporas contribute to the generation of transnational flows in the fields of population movement, finance, politics and cultural production. As a result, such diasporic phenomena are considered to be in the vanguard of the forces that deepen and intensify globalisation. An important position within the emerging diasporic *transnational* networks as well as of *local* migrant community activities is occupied by diasporic media which have also played an important role in the academic debate on transnational media (Karim 1998; Mohammadi 1998; Morley and Robins 1995; Murdoch 1992; Thussu 1998).

At the same time, little attention has been directed to the consumption practices of diasporic audiences as there seems to be an implicit assumption in the existing literature that these audiences would almost naturally turn to the recently emerged diasporic media and use them as their exclusive or virtually exclusive source of information, entertainment and raw material for identity building (Karim 1998).[1] In the absence of systematic research on diasporic audiences, researchers have often directed their research towards the *transnational* as opposed to the *local* dimensions of diasporic audience media uses – indeed the latter are often linked to the emergence of what Appadurai has called 'transnations' (Appadurai 1996), or others 'third space' (Bhabha 1994) or 'third cultures'. Usually the discussion has tended to stress at an abstract level the transnational, hybrid and 'cosmopolitan' character of diasporic experience without attempting to examine the ways in which this very transnational and hybrid character is anchored in, and reproduces, local contexts of everyday life.

This chapter attempts to revisit aspects of the debate on the development of diasporic transnational communities – in particular those aspects that link processes of globalisation to diasporic audiences in a rather uncritical and arbitrary fashion. I intend to do so by focusing on the media consumption practices of London's South Asian and Greek Cypriot communities. I explore the ways in which members of these diasporic communities utilise transnational media flows, in conjunction with local media products as resources, in the construction of everyday spaces where their experiences and identities are formed.[2]

London's South Asian and Greek Cypriot communities and the media

The arrival of migrants to the United Kingdom in the postwar period – especially, although not exclusively from Commonwealth countries – culminated in the formation of sizeable ethnic communities in Britain and has contributed considerably to the multi-ethnic and multicultural character of British society. However key institutions in British society, among them the British media, were slow to respond to the changing composition of the British population and the social, political, economic and cultural changes that post-World War II migration entailed. It is characteristic that the BBC's philosophy of addressing the needs of Britain's ethnic minorities, initially marked by a paternalistic-type ethos, was geared towards 'education' and 'acculturation' (Tsagarousianou 2001). Indeed when a second and third generation of British 'Asians', British Afro-Caribbeans and British of other ethnic origins entered in their turn the field of cultural consumption with the need and the right to have their 'Asian', 'Black' or other ethnic identity recognised and appropriately acknowledged,[3] it became clear that the provision of programmes for migrant communities and their descendants was in urgent need of rethinking by Public Service Broadcasting. Although British broadcasting – public and later commercial – did undergo some change, dissatisfaction, apathy and even alienation became more pronounced among Britain's diasporic audiences in the 1970s and especially in the 1980s (Tsagarousianou 2001).

It is in this context that the idea of media by and for specific ethnic communities developed. After several experimental or illegal attempts to establish ethnic media, the decisive impetus for the development of an ethnic media sector in Britain as well as for the operation of transnational diasporic media was given by the climate of deregulation in the late 1980s and early 1990s.[4]

South Asian and Greek Cypriot activists and entrepreneurs have both occupied a prominent place in the experimental, 'pirate' and in the commercial stages of the development of British ethnic media. As far as the media sector catering specifically for London's South Asian diaspora is concerned, at the time of writing, there is one London-wide FM radio station (Sunrise Radio) and a number of Asian television broadcasters, notably Zee TV Europe (satellite formerly operating as TV Asia), Asianet (cable), Sony Entertainment Television Asia (satellite and cable), Namaste TV (satellite) and more recently Bangla-TV, a broadcaster targeting exclusively Bangladeshi viewers in the UK. Plans for a limited terrestrial Asian television service in Northern England have recently been approved by the ITC, whereas digital broadcasting has provided more 'space' for further Asian television services such as the Asian film channel B4U launched by Sony Entertainment Television Asia. Spectrum International, a London-wide AM radio station, broadcasts South Asian language programmes and music as part of its overall multicultural programme, while a limited local licence has been granted in the past few years to Ramadan Radio, an East London-based station, to broadcast to the local Muslim – largely Bangladeshi – community during the month of Ramadan. The Greek Cypriot community, for its part, can tune in to London Greek Radio, a North London-based FM radio station, and Hellenic TV, a cable television programme provider in the London area.

In contrast to the past, it is obvious that London's South Asian and Greek Cypriot communities today have access to a considerable array of media ranging from mainstream Public Service Broadcasting and commercial provision to local and transnational radio and television targeted at ethnically specific and diasporic audiences. In the remainder of this chapter I shall examine the ways in which these communities use this diverse media available to them.

Methodological notes

The empirical material that will be used in this chapter has been collected in the course of a research project on diasporic media focusing on London's South Asian and Greek Cypriot communities, the diasporic media that they have at their disposal and the way these communities use the media available to them. The material drawn upon here is from 45 audience interviews and 24 focus-group sessions conducted between June 1998 and February 2000 by the author

(Greek Cypriot audiences) and by the author and Hasmita Ramji (South Asian audiences).

Initial plans to select interviewees and focus-group participants from respondents to an extensive questionnaire-based survey[5] of members of the communities in question had to be modified when it became apparent that older South Asians and Greek Cypriots with little or no literacy skills would as a consequence be considerably under-represented. What is more, given the potentially intrusive character of such an investigation, identifying and approaching potential interviewees and focus-group participants necessitated the adoption of a flexible strategy of selecting respondents. The method employed could best be described as being premised on the 'snowball' sampling principle whereby initial respondents or other contacts suggested further interviewees and focus-group participants. In addition, several selected ethnic community welfare, cultural, religious, social and professional associations were approached; this facilitated further contact with potential respondents and helped to ensure the greatest possible sample diversity in terms of gender, age, class, education and ethno-religious identity. This strategy enabled the interviewers to overcome feelings of mistrust and other obstacles that an unsolicited approach might entail.

Focus groups and interviews took place in a variety of settings which were as familiar as possible to the respondents (community association premises, community schools, temples, mosques and, on three occasions, in accordance with participants' preferences, London and Harrow campuses of the University of Westminster). Most discussions were conducted in the native language of the respondents and (where this was not English) transcribed and interpreted by the interviewers. At all times respondents were made aware of the purposes of the research and were guaranteed anonymity and access to transcripts of the sessions should they wish this.

Audiences and diasporic media

Commenting on the availability of diasporic media, members of both the South Asian and the Greek Cypriot communities, especially those born outside the UK, stressed the importance of diasporic media and the links they provide with their country of origin or with their respective cultures and politics. According to most older respondents, this contact is vital because it reduces the sense of distance – physical as well as emotional – from their country of origin. Bangladeshi respondents stressed the importance to them of the daily Bangladeshi news slot on Spectrum Radio late every evening and described the almost ritualistic preparation for this unique moment which, for many, provided the only means of daily contact with their country of 'origin'. Similarly, Greek Cypriot respondents acknowledged the opportunity they now have to keep up-to-date with what happens in Cyprus and Greece through radio and TV news bulletins. Some also expressed a great interest in London Greek Radio's link programmes with Cypriot, Greek and diasporic radio and television stations in other parts of the world:

> It is somehow comforting and interesting to hear other Greeks from the edges of the world talking about their lives in foreign lands. I myself have relatives in Australia and South Africa and whenever there is [a link of London Greek Radio with their local Greek stations] we send greetings and wishes to each other. It is moving.
>
> (female, 49; Greek Cypriot)

> I like these programmes very much. I have made friends from many parts of the world through these [phone-in] programmes. We now correspond as well.
>
> (female, 56; Greek Cypriot)

Even people with no kin relationships or friends in other destinations often admit they find these programmes intriguing to tune into and some even phone the station to send wishes to the unknown fellow-Greeks who are also tuning in. Such testimonies indicate the attraction that diasporic media have, not only because they provide a link with countries of origin or because of their cultural familiarity, but also because, on occasion, they recognise and assert a common diasporic experience. Such media are well placed to allow their audiences to establish connections – virtual or actual – with other parts of their diaspora and to find in the active or passive contact that ensues an experience that is consoling, pleasurable or rewarding. In many ways, one could argue that by constructing together a common frame of diasporic experience, these audiences are participating in the process of 're-imagining' their national community at a deterritorialised, transnational level (Morley and Robins 1995: 37–42).

However, tension and contestation regarding the nature and intensity of the transnational links established and reproduced by diasporic media are also in evidence. Muslim South Asian respondents, for example, have accused Sony Entertainment Television Asia, Sunrise Radio and, to a lesser extent, Zee TV of pro-Indian sympathies and anti-Muslim bias. In quite passionate responses they presented these media sources as culturally threatening. Greek Cypriot community members have also expressed anger and a sense of betrayal; they perceive London Greek Radio, or 'their radio station' as they often call it, as being transformed into a station increasingly catering for audiences from Greece and focusing too much on this country and its political and cultural life as opposed to Cyprus and the London Greek Cypriot community. Diasporic audiences may, therefore, regard diasporic media not only as a resource but as a threat to the extent that they reproduce relations of power prevailing in the larger political context.

Diasporic media and the construction of a space where one 'feels at home'

The relationship between audiences and diasporic media, I have suggested, is not exhausted by the linking of diasporic communities with their 'countries of origin', but extends to processes in which transnational flows combine with 'local' resources to construct spaces and contexts within which everyday diasporic experiences become intelligible to their audiences.

Not surprisingly, older people express more readily their appreciation of diasporic media:

> For many years after we arrived [in Britain] you could rarely hear your language being spoken. I knew some English, but this was not important. We were lost. I was like a crazy woman. We did not have these things then [Greek radio and TV].
>
> (female, 60; Greek Cypriot)

> For me Sunrise is a daily companion. ... It gives me the music I enjoy and up-to-date accurate news. All in a way that makes sense.
>
> (female, 50; Indian)

> I find the programmes entertaining because I can understand the language and relate to the ideas that I can appreciate, having been raised in India.
>
> (female, 45; Indian)

For these older consumers, diasporic media provide a framework in which individuals can relate to and render intelligible the context of their everyday life. Comments such as 'it's a daily companion', 'I no longer feel lonely' and 'it is like having someone keeping you company' were common in interviews and in focus groups as several quotes confirm:

> I can really feel at home. I can listen to people talk in my language, music that I understand, and I can keep up with the news from Greece and Cyprus.
>
> (female, 55; Greek Cypriot)

> When I first came here I missed home very much. It seemed so far away that I could not bear it. But all this changed when the Greek radio was established. Now you can listen to the news from back home, you can listen to people like you talk, and you can listen to the music you like. Thanks to the radio, you feel you've never left home.
>
> (male, 60; Greek Cypriot)

These media provide a structure of support for people who might otherwise feel physically or psychologically isolated because of linguistic constraints, cultural distance or disability. Stark expressions such as 'I was like a crazy woman' articulate, very dramatically, the *aporia* and the intensely felt *subaltern position* which many recent immigrants to Britain experienced.[6] When prompted to elaborate on what being 'crazy' meant, respondents identified a number of conditions or states among which were the inability to relate to or make sense of the new place of settlement and the inability to overcome feelings of 'emptiness'. To draw upon de Certeau's (1984) contribution to an anthropology of everyday life, I would argue that diasporic media can offer older people who may lack the cultural, linguistic or emotional resources to adapt to an initially alien environment the framework that enables them to turn the meaningless and 'empty place' of settlement into an intelligible and 'lived space'.[7]

At first sight audiences seem to be split overwhelmingly along generational lines regarding their responses to diasporic media. It is often assumed, with different degrees of caution (Gillespie 1995; Karim 1998), that younger people are more 'cosmopolitan' and therefore critical of diasporic broadcasting, in contrast to older people who are thought to be more homesick and culturally introverted and therefore more appreciative of the availability of diasporic media offering them products in their own language and related to their own ethnic culture. My own research reveals a more complex situation which questions notions of cosmopolitanism and the assumption that younger people are more cosmopolitan than older ones. Young people of South Asian and Greek Cypriot origin tend to reject either the lack of professionalism or the low quality of what is offered to diasporic audiences. But, in addition, they rebuke this sector for failing to address the different needs of the second-generation audiences:

> I don't listen to Asian stations. It would be [*sic*] breakfast shows on Heart, Capital FM. Just mainstream. I used to listen to Sunrise Radio a very, very long time ago and there were just too many ads. And they spoke in languages I did not understand. I mean, I know they were trying to cater for the whole South Asian group. But if I don't understand it, I'm going to switch it off. I think there was the Bhangra hour and I think they tried to make it too varied. Maybe they should have different stations for different communities.
>
> (male, 24; Indian origin)

> One of the major problems with Sunrise is the quality of sound. There is no point in listening to it for Indian music that you can buy on tapes with a 100 per cent better quality of sound. The tapes are dirt cheap anyway.
>
> (male, 26; Gujarati Hindu origin)

Sunrise is irrelevant. They have so much advertising in their programmes and they do not care about community. And in any case I, as
a Muslim and Bangladeshi, cannot relate to Sunrise. It is so anti-
Muslim [approving nods from all group members].

(female, 24; Muslim Bangladeshi origin)

Older respondents, although overall more appreciative, appear also to be in a
position to adopt a critical attitude towards diasporic media and indeed they do
so. Their arguments often echo younger audiences' complaints about low
quality:

The quality of the image is not at all good. And these movies are so
old – we have seen them again and again. ... If one is to pay a lot of
money in order to have Hellenic TV, one expects more.

(female, 62; Greek Cypriot)

Many arguments also target the increasing commercialisation of diasporic
media, especially radio, perceiving it as betrayal of community:

I am not happy with Sunrise at all. I think there is far too much advertising [all focus-group members nod with approval]. There are not
enough quality programmes available.

(female, 62; Indian origin)

They [the station management] have turned their back on the community that nurtured them and supported them. They do not want to
know us any more; it is profits now that they are interested in.

(male, 64; Greek Cypriot)

Now they do not consider people of our own [i.e. Greek Cypriots]
good enough for the station. They have brought all them students
[from Greece] as presenters and DJs because they think they will bring
profits.

(male, 65; Greek Cypriot)

Although for the majority of the people who expressed an opinion commercialisation is considered unavoidable and indeed, according to some, a price worth
paying in exchange for having community-specific media, respondents often
expressed disillusionment with the fact that radio stations put their sponsors'
interests above the interests of the community.

However, despite a sense of diffuse and widespread dissatisfaction, audiences
do seem to appreciate the existing diasporic media available to them. A young
critical listener of Sunrise attests:

Yeah. It is the only one on my stereo. I listen to it while cooking, but it's only the music. ... On Sunday they have a really good show, 'Back-chat', I think. Those are very good. When these forced marriage things were on the news and became really big, they had a discussion. Young Asian women calling in and ... it was a really good format. And that is good. I like that. ... But in the comedies, there's a man on in the morning and he cracks a joke and then it sounds like he's pressed 'play' and there is this whole bundle of audience laughing and then he presses 'stop'. It's such a fake laugh and that kind of thing is quite in-sulting. And I think, why am I listening to it?

(female, 26; Gujarati Hindu origin)

Many respondents confirmed that 'phone in' and 'talk' shows are especially attractive to younger and older audiences alike, as they deal with issues that are of interest to them, such as marriage, racism, gender relations etc. – issues which are not addressed in many other spaces. Again, in this context, respondents appeared more willing to overlook the tensions and divisions within the South Asian and Greek communities and to treat issues they identified as of common interest as a unifying factor.

A final important criticism by both communities concerns the failure of diasporic media to recognise how these audiences are differentiated from those of the 'country of origin'. In their effort to address the largest audiences possible or due to financial constraints, diasporic media (satellite television as well as local cable TV and radio) often treat their audiences as a mere extension of the 'homeland' or as undifferentiated audiences that just happen to live in different countries. In contrast to this, a desire for emphasis on and respect for the local dimension of the diasporic community and its needs were present in many audience responses – even among older audiences that largely offer a positive evaluation of diasporic media. A complex interpretation of the transnational character of their diasporic condition is discernible in their narratives:

They keep showing old Greek movies. They do not understand that we are not the people who left [our countries]. We want something different.

(male, 52; Greek Cypriot)

They [Hellenic TV] keep on showing us political discussions, talk, talk, talk. We are not interested in the parliament, we are not living in Cyprus or in Greece anymore. They do not see that we have other needs here.

(female, 60; Greek Cypriot)

Why don't they show us something more interesting? Always the same old movies. There is that much of it that one can see. They think we do not need more? We have different interests too. We live here, we have our families here but they do not understand this.

(female, 56; Gujarati)

Such responses are very common and indicate the audiences' awareness of their diasporic status and specificity. Contrary to what satellite media strategists assume, diasporic audiences resent being treated as appendages of a 'home audience' and express demands for more locality-specific programming that addresses their needs and their interests. Respondents made it clear that they expect to be treated in a way that acknowledges and accepts the fact that they are living in a different place (physically and socially) and are attempting to negotiate their inclusion into the national community as well as affirming their commonality with fellow-nationals living in their home countries or in other diasporas.

The realm of intimacy

As has been already pointed out, Muslim South Asians have been critical of Asian TV and radio broadcasts on the grounds of their perceived anti-Muslim bias. They also rejected the description of Sunrise Radio as a community radio on the grounds of commercialism. By contrast, many of those residing in East London expressed their appreciation of a local, limited-licence station, Ramadan Radio, which operates every year during Ramadan in the Borough of Tower Hamlets. Apart from the non-commercial character of this station, they introduced another set of reasons for preferring Ramadan Radio:

> Ramadan Radio is much nicer to listen to. It offers you the opportunity to feel you are a member of a community. For one, you listen to people you know personally. You hear their voice on the radio and then when you ring them at home you say 'I heard you on the radio you know ... '.
>
> (female, 21; Muslim, Bangladeshi origin)

> Yes and you can listen to programmes from the local hospital, and you know the people who work there too. ... And then it's the prayers ... there is something for everyone.
>
> (female, 23; Muslim, Pakistani/Bangladeshi origin)

Generally, listeners of Ramadan Radio expressed a sense of intimacy with the people working for the station and the station as a whole and expressed a desire for it to be granted an ordinary licence. I would argue that, in its current form, Ramadan Radio operates at what one might call the 'intimate' level, not only because of the explicit relation with the intimate realm of religion that its name denotes, but also because it constitutes a very local medium that promotes personal interaction in a relatively small community. Indeed, East End Asian respondents stressed primarily the 'community spirit' and the 'feeling of membership' as the main measure of the success and popularity of Ramadan Radio, and only secondarily – if at all – the role of religion. Although religion undoubtedly constitutes a central element of Asian community life in East London, it is precisely part of a broader vernacular and culture which Ramadan Radio celebrates and integrates into its operation and identity as a community medium. The station's emphasis on familiar contexts of everyday face-to-face interaction and the rather 'extraordinary' character that its restricted licence gives it, effectively turns Ramadan Radio into something resembling an annual festival of plebeian culture for the East End Asian community.

A sense of intimacy was also evident in the responses of several members of the audience of London Greek Radio and, to a lesser extent, Hellenic TV. They consistently referred to persons involved in the operation of the radio and television station (not only DJs and presenters but also managers and editors) by their first names or even by affectionate nicknames, both on air (during 'talk in' shows) and during interviews and focus-group sessions. The discourse of these respondents was one of membership, or even 'ownership'. Indeed, during my visits to London Greek Radio, listeners were ringing for information or even for a chat, or dropping in to talk to the staff at the reception and sometimes even in the studio.

Referring to the establishment and reproduction of modern nation-states, Michael Herzfeld has argued that 'cultural intimacy' provides the infrastructure for collective self-representation. He has argued that although states often shun the field of the intimate, everyday and vernacular culture, their existence depends upon this sphere. To demonstrate this, he shows how the official is incorporated into the vernacular, and how the modern nation-state and its paraphernalia intrude into everyday life contexts of intimacy (Herzfeld 1997: 74–88). Along parallel lines I would argue that, through audience expressions of intimacy such as the ones discussed above, Ramadan Radio as well as the Greek community media are incorporated into the vernacular and everyday culture of the communities in question and are occupying an important role in the processes of the communities' collective self-representation. Through incorporation into the domain of intimacy, these media become a crucial, local element of what I identified earlier as 'home'. Moreover, through this process of incorporation, diasporic media play an important role in sustaining what Herzfeld has called 'structural nostalgia' (1997: 109–38), a nostalgia which invokes images of a harmonious community. But in contrast to the conventional sense of the term, nostalgia here does not necessarily refer to an historic ideal of community to which members of the diasporic communities in question would aspire to return. In fact, this nostalgia is for a *topos* that may have never existed, a *topos* embodying the promise of its realisation in the future. In other words, I would argue that the structural nostalgia mobilised by diasporic media and audience strategies is marked by a yearning for the warmth and solidarity of an idealised community.

In the case of Ramadan Radio, listeners expressed an affection for the station because it invoked this ideal of a harmonious community during a limited period every year. The possibility of it being granted a regular licence only fuelled the expectation of this ideal coming true. In its current state, Ramadan Radio possibly represents a peculiar, liminal moment or event[8] within the annual calendar during which the solidarity and the intimate dimensions of the Muslim community manifest themselves. Similarly, in the case of the Greek media, intimacy evokes a sense of harmony and closeness among members of their audiences and these media and incorporates them into the web of community practices and institutions that members of the Greek Cypriot community have grown to associate with 'home'.

Home is ... From aporia to cultural citizenship and beyond

Respondents of all ages were overwhelmingly critical of what they perceive as their lack of representation within Public Service Broadcasting provision. It is interesting to note that audience discourses, however inarticulate, tend to formulate a particular perception of *cultural citizenship* and a corresponding feeling of being disenfranchised.

> I do not think that we will ever reach the point where they will be giving us 5 per cent of their air time although we are contributing 5 per cent of the country's revenue from the TV licence.
>
> (female, 27; Punjabi origin)

> They do not have adequate provision of programmes for people like us although we are licence [fee] payers. We are living in this country and we are contributing too.
>
> (female, 56; Greek Cypriot)

Some of the responses show clearly the frustration of audiences with mainstream broadcasting:

> It's like that *Goodness Gracious Me* sketch. You can have a 10-minute slot on Sunday morning. At 7.00 in the morning who the hell's going to be watching? It's at 11.00 am now but still marginalised. We are getting there, but we're still not there. Things like *Bollywood or Bust* [a Zee TV programme] are good and professionally done. Why can't we have them from, let's say, BBC1 or even BBC2? They are better than a lot of other crap ... like *Airport*. Who watches that?
>
> (male, 26; Gujarati Hindu origin)

169

In many ways, a feeling of under-representation and exclusion, similar to the feeling of *aporia* identified in my earlier discussion of the isolation experienced by newly arrived immigrants, was prevalent in audience responses. Although these are expressed in varying ways depending primarily on generational differences, they are nevertheless premised on a broadly shared pessimism and, at the same time, demands and expectations. Generally audience discourses on this issue are linked to expectations of recognition of the particular contribution to 'Britishness' that their diasporic condition brings about.

The *discourses of cultural citizenship* that have emerged in focus groups and interviews were also complemented by discursive strategies of overcoming tensions and fissures that may characterise the South Asian and Greek communities in other everyday contexts. Whereas the majority of South Asian respondents would opt for narrower or more inclusive definitions of their identity than the one denoted by the term 'South Asian' (e.g. Gujarati, British-Punjabi, or Muslim), when they discussed issues of rights and of cultural citizenship, they would often adopt the idiom of *South-Asianness*, possibly as they consciously or subconsciously linked the latter to the politics (both cultural and conventional) of the South Asian community in Britain as well as to the way state and local authority perceived them in the context of service provision and policy implementation. In a similar vein, the discourse of *Greekness*, as opposed to the customary emphasis on their Greek Cypriot specificity, was often activated by Greek Cypriot respondents in discussions pertaining to issues of cultural citizenship.

Conclusion: strategies of belonging

This chapter has focused on diasporic audience practices that attempt to overcome cultural *aporia* and establish a sense of 'belonging', a space where one feels 'at home' and where diasporic identity can be negotiated. Literature on transnationalism and diasporas has tended to be enthusiastic regarding the rootlessness and mobility of diasporas and, by extension, their transnational experiential horizons. In their otherwise stimulating book *Nations Unbound*, Linda Bash and her co-authors talk about the ability of certain diasporas to live 'transnationally', to 'transfer themselves from one place to another' (Bash et al. 1994: 4–7), but they ignore the fact that transnationalism should rather be seen in conjunction with the construction of 'locality', and the processes of domestication and translation that the diasporic audiences examined in this chapter are practising in their everyday life contexts. Diasporic media in their current form are a relative newcomer in transnational communications. Reflection on them offers us valuable insights concerning global and transnational media flows in an age of intensifying transnationalisation and globalisation of communications and the social relations that these entail.

NOTES

1 The most notable exception is that of Marie Gillespie's path-breaking research on Southall youth in the late 1980s and early 1990s (Gillespie 1995).

2 The empirical research upon which this chapter is based has been funded by the Centre for Communication and Information Studies of the University of Westminster.

3 My own audience research with 'South Asian' and 'Greek Cypriot' audiences confirms overwhelmingly the simultaneous expectation of the recognition and acknowledgement by British Public Service Broadcasting institutions of their existence and a widespread sense of resignation to the rigidity and lack of responsiveness of the mainstream television and radio stations.

4 For more details on the process of emergence of ethnic media in the UK, see Tsagarousianou (1999 and 2001).

5 The survey comprises 613 returned questionnaires from South Asian and 420 from Greek Cypriot respondents.

6 For an extensive discussion of issues relating to the concepts of *aporia* and *subaltern position* see Spivak (1988: 271–313).

7 For the definitions of 'place' (*lieu*) and 'space' (*espace*) that I am adopting in my analysis, see de Certeau (1984: 117–18). In summary, space is a practised, lived place, produced by flows, operations and practices which situate it and temporalise it, give a meaning or meanings to it.

8 For the concept of *liminality* see Turner (1967: 93–111, 1969: 95–7, 1974: 231–300).

References

Appadurai, A. (1996) *Modernity at Large: Cultural Dynamics of Globalization*, Minneapolis: University of Minnesota Press.

Bash, L., Glick Schiller, N. and Szanton Blanc, C. (1994) *Nations Unbound: Transnational Projects, Postcolonial Predicaments and Deterritorialised Nation States*, Amsterdam: Gordon and Breach.

Bhabha, H. K. (1994) *The Location of Culture*, London: Routledge.

de Certeau, M. (1984) *The Practice of Everyday Life*, Berkeley: University of California Press.

Giddens, A. (1990) *The Consequences of Modernity*, Cambridge: Polity.

Gillespie, M. (1995) *Television, Ethnicity and Cultural Change*, London: Routledge.

Harvey, D. (1990) *The Condition of Postmodernity*, Oxford: Blackwell.

Herzfeld, M. (1997) *Cultural Intimacy: Social Poetics in the Nation-State*, London and New York: Routledge.

Karim, H. K. (1998) 'From ethnic media to global media: transnational communication networks among diasporic communities', Working Paper Transnational Communities Series, WPTC-99-02.

Mohammadi, A. (1998) 'Electronic empires: an Islamic perspective', in Thussu, D. K. (ed.), *Electronic Empires: Global Media and Local Resistance*, London: Arnold.

Morley, D. and Robins, K. (1995) *Spaces of Identity: Global Media, Electronic Landscapes and Cultural Boundaries*, London: Routledge.

Murdoch, G. (1992) 'Citizens, consumers and public culture', in Skovmand, M. and Schroder, K. C. (eds), *Media Cultures: Reappraising Transnational Media*, London: Routledge.

Spivak, G. C. (1988) 'Can the subaltern speak?', in Nelson, G. and Grossberg, L. (eds), *Marxism and the Interpretation of Culture*, London: Macmillan.

Thussu, D. K. (1998) 'Infotainment International: a view from the South', in Thussu, D. K. (ed.), *Electronic Empires: Global Media and Local Resistance*, London: Arnold.

Tsagarousianou, R. (1999) 'Gone to the market? The development of Asian and Greek-Cypriot community media in Britain', *Javnost/The Public* 6, 1: 55–70.

—— (2001) 'Ethnic community media, community identity and citizenship in contemporary Britain', in Jankowski, N. and Prehn, O. (eds), *Community Media in the Information Age: Perspectives, Findings and Policy*, New Jersey: Hampton Press.

Turner, V. (1967) *The Forest of Symbols*, Ithaca: Cornell University Press.

—— (1969) *The Ritual Process*, New York: Aldine de Gruyter.

—— (1974) *Dramas, Fields and Metaphors*, Ithaca: Cornell University Press.

12

'BLACKPOOL IN THE SUN'

Images of the British on the Costa del Sol

Karen O'Reilly

Introduction

During the 1980s, increasing numbers of British people began migrating to Spain's coastal areas. Attracted by the warmth, the cost of living and the potential for a leisured lifestyle, and aided by portable pensions and capital gained during the property boom of the 1970s, they were the outcome of a phenomenon which began in the 1960s with cheap air travel and mass package tourism. By the late 1980s the British migrants to Spain had attracted the attention of the British mass media as well as the general public, to the extent that, at the time I decided to research this migration in the early 1990s, it seemed everyone had something to say about the British in Spain.[1] Media images and representations abounded and many were derisory, negative or sensationalist. An overriding impression was that many of these migrants now wished they could return home, but were trapped in homes they could not sell, or had 'burned their bridges' in other ways. Yet I had visited the Costa del Sol on several occasions and had never met British migrants who wanted to go home. It seemed important to me that these images of the British in Spain should not be accepted uncritically, but should be viewed for what they were: media constructions which interacted with common knowledge to create a unifying set of representations which had some basis in reality but which were essentially stereotypes.

An important reason for viewing such stereotypical representations as constructions is that, as social scientists, we are supposed to question the taken-for-granted. It is crucial to explore the sources of, and meanings behind, such media constructions, which often tell us more about the society which constructs them than about the phenomenon they pretend to describe. The same is true of the British in Spain. As we explore these collective representations we note that migration tends to be depicted in a negative way but that this migration is associated with tourism, and since mass tourism is often considered frivolous, this migration and its migrants must also be trivial and silly. We note that it has been popular to denigrate the British abroad (especially working-class

British people) and that this has been extended to the British migrants in Spain. The migrants are assumed to be elderly and therefore perceptions of them draw on images of and assumptions about ageing and retirement. But a further reason for seeing the images as distinct from the object they pretend to describe is that, as discrete phenomena, we can observe their effects on the object of our inquiry. The British in Spain felt the media representations of them depicted them in a bad light. First of all they did not want to talk to me at all for fear that I, too, would misrepresent them. When I gained their trust, and they began talking to me about their lifestyles, they often constructed their stories in opposition to the view they believed I must have of them.

The emergence of a phenomenon

During the 1980s the mass migration of Britons to Spain's coastal areas began to attract the attention of the mass media. By the early 1990s these migrants had become something of a phenomenon in Britain, as newspaper journalists wrote about them, television dramas and comedies were based on them and people talked about them. Everyone I spoke to about my proposed research was familiar with the topic and most had something to say: an opinion to express, a question to ask, an assumption to challenge. Much of the talk was derogatory, but at times the comments seemed tinged with envy. Most thought the phenomenon would make a fascinating research topic, and viewed the behaviour and attitudes of the expatriates in terms of a problem; it was assumed they do not integrate, do not learn the language, spend too much time doing nothing, and drink too much. It was implied that they take no interest in Spain or the Spanish way of life, that they spend most of their time in British bars, and that they buy British goods whenever possible. 'They have practically colonised the place, haven't they?' one woman asked. 'You should do some undercover work for the police while you are there', suggested a man who assumed that many of the British in the area are ex-criminals. 'It's one long round of beach parties and cocktail parties; I couldn't stand it for long', reported a woman whose friend lives in the Costa del Sol. These were quite obviously a set of collective representations about the British in Spain which had been fed by the media and which had become 'common knowledge' for the majority of British people.

Academic researchers had shown little interest in this new migration trend. Some academics had written on the topic as it impinges on or articulates with other issues such as ageing (Victor 1987), British home-owning in France (Buller and Hoggart 1994) and European migration (King and Rybaczuk 1993; Misiti *et al.* 1995). Others had begun to identify British migration to Spain as part of a larger and interesting phenomenon worthy of serious research; a phenomenon they labelled International Retirement Migration or IRM (cf. Champion and King 1993). But the hypotheses, assumptions and conclusions made by academics prior to systematic research both mirrored and consolidated the collective representations addressed above to become part of the body of 'knowledge' about Britons resident in Spain. Prior to his team's recent detailed research on IRM,[2] Warnes (1991) drew on 'casual observation, impressionistic newspaper, radio and television accounts, and personal contacts' and on inferences made from studies of retirement migration within Britain, France and the US, to suggest that migrants to Spain are attracted by the weather, the leisure opportunities and cheap property, and by the fact that British tastes and customs are catered for and English is often spoken by officials and locals. Drawing on 'common knowledge and general observations', Champion and King (1993: 54) concluded that, 'aided by portable state and private pension schemes and by the general growth in wealth, increasing numbers of older people in Europe are moving on either temporary or near-permanent bases towards the Mediterranean sun-belt' and furthermore, that 'the elderly migrants do tend to cluster in purpose-built tourist and residential complexes with many services ... very close by'. Champion and King accepted that, although they call the phenomenon retirement migration, younger Britons also migrate to provide services for this older migrant community. The same authors suggested that many British migrants in Spain never learn the language, do not assimilate the local culture, and end up in quasi-ghettos. Assumptions such as these complement the 'collective representations' cited above of generally older British migrants, living in ghettos or colonies, speaking little Spanish, and, having been attracted by weather, leisure and low costs rather than by anything inherently Spanish, showing either disdain or disregard for Spain, its people and its culture (cf. King and Rybaczuk 1993).[3]

And the construction of a stereotype

Media images tend to be negative, stereotypical, and to select some stories and emphasise those, while ignoring other facets of life; the focus is on problematic social reality and the result is the framing of an event or a type in the public imagination (Hall *et al.* 1978). It is important not to accept such emotionally charged images uncritically; they are social constructions, and for the research I proposed, they were both part of and distinct from the phenomenon of interest. The British in Spain and the popular representations of them are not one and the same. The representations provide the context and 'thin description' of the phenomenon; they have the potential to affect outcomes and especially the behaviour of the migrants; but even more, as social constructs, they provide a window onto the society which constructs them. But media power does not work in a social vacuum; ideas are exchanged between friends, relatives and neighbours and draw on experience as well as current ideas (cf. Eldridge *et al.* 1997). Emile Durkheim's notion of 'collective representations' allows us to include all general, popular, non-scientific, non-analytical ideas, notions, images, assumptions and stereotypes about a group of individuals who are so often treated as one homogenous group, and to treat this set of images as a unitary object for research (see Lukes 1982). It is, therefore, useful to view the media phenomenon of the British in Spain as a set of collective representations which have come together from various, often unreliable, sources and which combine with other forms of communication in a process of broad dissemination and interpretation. Crick (1989: 308), writing during the early stages of the development of an anthropology of tourism, said:

> It may seem derogatory to speak of collective social science represen-tations rather than analyses. I do so to raise the issue of whether we yet have a respectable, scholarly analysis of tourism, or whether the social science literature on the subject substantially blends with the emotion-ally charged cultural images relating to travel and tourists.

I now raise the same issue in relation to British migration to Spain, which, as a pursuit, is so bound up with the hedonism of tourism it has lacked serious attention. When I initially told colleagues of my intention to research this topic it almost invariably provoked laughter or derisory comments such as 'oh, that's a good excuse for a year in the sun'. As was once the case with the study of tourism, ambivalence, stereotypes and sweeping generalisations surround discussion about 'the Brits in Spain'. But, as Hammersley and Atkinson (1995) argue, there is no reason to completely discard common-sense knowledge about the world, just as there is little justification for treating it as unquestioningly valid 'in its own terms'. This common-sense knowledge is all that we have and it should be worked with and examined in the light of new information. It is not possible to examine a phenomenon objectively until we face our precon-ceptions head on. For this piece of research, these representations were all I 'knew' about the phenomenon under study before I studied it and as such were part of the research.

The sources of the images

It was therefore important to locate the various sources of images about the British in Spain, and to identify what was being said where, how and by whom. The mass media have been crucial in this process for the British in Spain. During the early 1990s, as noted earlier, the British in Spain appeared on British television screens in documentaries, holiday programmes, dramas, comedies and soap operas, and in a range of newspaper reports and articles. A soap launched on British television at the time became more famous for its huge costs (£10 million was spent on the set alone) and its failure than for its content. *Eldorado* (a name which conjured images of a golden, fantasy world) ran from June 1992 to July 1993, was set in the Costa del Sol, and depicted a British community of people who spent most of their time in each other's company, speaking little or no Spanish, drinking, socialising, and eating British food. The programme featured a former (but still active) criminal, a suffering alcoholic, British bar owners, and a rather untalented entertainer amongst its migrant Britons. It was set in a complex of houses, shops, bars and a beach, apparently isolated from the rest of Spain.

In July 1992 Channel Four presented a two-part documentary entitled *Coast of Dreams*, which was shown again in August 1994. The programme reported on the experiences of British expatriates living in southern Spain. Both young and older couples were seen to be moving to Spain in search of their dreams. Newcomers to Spain appeared hopeful, excited, happy; they believed they had found the answer to life. More settled Britons appeared quite satisfied with the move and were aware of the envy of friends and relatives back home; but the younger ones, running bars in Spain, were having to work very hard and were not making their fortunes. They saw little of the sun and the beach and had little time for each other in their new lifestyles. Women, especially, seemed dissatisfied and disappointed. Older expatriates were depicted in the documentary as living alongside other migrants, knowing little of the Spanish way of life, language or culture, and not wanting to know more, and spending their days drinking and socialising. An interpreter from a local hospital talked of the way the British residents in Spain live in their little communities, dependent on each other for company and support, not speaking any Spanish and experiencing huge difficulties when faced with hospitalisation or illness. 'They forget when they come here that they will get older, that a partner may die and they will be left alone, that they may want to go home but they can't because they have sold everything there', she explained. A Spanish doctor spoke of the terrible problems these people have with alcoholism and liver disease: 'they live in ghettos, they have no idea of Spanish life, they just visit each other and drink'. The programme also focused a little on the British tourists, who merely wanted a 'Blackpool in the sun'; everything that Britain can offer plus the sunshine. Little distinction was made between this attitude and that of the expatriates: 'they come here, they want to make their own little England in Spain', reported a Spanish woman. Retired Britons were shown socialising together, some speaking in crisp English accents, drinking gin and tonic, while Britons who had bought bars in Spain were shown spending time with tourists, enjoying the holiday atmosphere, the wine and the beer, and British food. The two programmes together shared a general theme, depicting the difference between dreams and reality. They were individually titled 'Paradise in the Sun' and 'Paradise Lost', and featured, simultaneously, the growth and decline of tourism, the development and subsequent disfigurement of the Costa del Sol, and the settling and unsettling of British expatriates. For the producers of the programmes, these were clearly meant to be interpreted as associated concepts.

The British expatriates in Spain, and especially in the Fuengirola area of the Costa del Sol, have often featured in newspaper reports in Britain. In the *Sun*, the area has variously been labelled Costa del Bonk, Costa del Crime, and Costa del Cop. Reports once focused on the number of criminals and, later, ex-policemen who live in the area. One report told how the bar owned by the famous bank robber Ronnie Knight is frequented by an ex-policeman who once worked on his case. Some newspaper reports portrayed the British expatriates in southern Spain as better-off rebels who had chosen an escapist life in the sun. They were said to be living colonial lifestyles: 'First came the hardened expats, the colonials. … They liked the look of Spain's sunshine coast: hot, relaxed, cheap, giveaway booze, close to the banks and shops and other home comforts of Gibraltar', reported the *Guardian* (Crampton 1993). Later 'news' depicts the British in the coastal areas living in ghettos, speaking very little or no Spanish, watching satellite television, shopping in Gibraltar for British goods, and drinking too much alcohol. In the *Independent on Sunday*, Ian MacKinnon (1993) described Britons living in ghettos, speaking no Spanish, buying fish and chips and British beer, and having little to do with the Spanish. John Hooper (1993), writing in the *Guardian*, said 'the real-life inhabitants of Eldorado are forced to depend on satellite television for their home entertainment' since the guy who used to sell pirate video tapes has been caught; another article in the *Guardian* on the same day reported that the expats 'have colonised the coast so much that the shops now sell Oxo cubes and British meat'.

Two reports which were published at around the same time, from Help The Aged (Mullan 1992) and Age Concern (1993), focused on the health and financial problems experienced by some elderly expatriates living in the coastal areas of Spain. At the time of the reports the peseta was strong against the pound, effectively devaluing British pensions and savings held in sterling accounts: 'times are particularly hard for those people surviving on basic pensions', the Age Concern report argued (1993: 6). These reports were concerned that those who had moved to Spain several years ago were now older and possibly more unhealthy. They had discovered that the Spanish health service was lacking in home care and nursing provision, the system traditionally depending to a great extent on the family in times of need. With the British government refusing to pay supplementary or hardship benefits to expatriates, some were struggling to cope. The reports suggested these problems were exacerbated by factors such as the language barrier, isolation and boredom. Newspaper journalism reflected and exaggerated these reports. Headlines appeared such as, in the *Daily Mail*, 'Life in the sun is not so hot for elderly' (Fletcher 1994) and, in the *Times Magazine*, 'Costa del Sunset' (Crampton 1993). The accompanying reports portrayed an elderly population for whom the dream of retirement in Spain had become a nightmare. 'If it weren't for the sun we'd go home tomorrow', agreed one elderly couple of whom the journalist said, 'They do not speak Spanish and have had endless trials with local bureaucracy. They miss their seven grandchildren. They have been shocked by the cost of living. The interest on their savings from the sale of their house has fallen. The fall in the value of the pound (has) hit their pensions hard. And, worst of all, their flat is not worth what they paid for it' (Crampton 1993). Furthermore, the expatriates themselves are implicitly to blame for their problems; it is suggested that they did not 'go in with their eyes open' (Beard 1994), or that they 'fail to realise that a life in the sun cannot make up for illness, disability, bereavement and isolation' (Fletcher 1994). While newspaper reports focused on hard-up and unhealthy older expatriates, books written for people intending to visit or move to Spain's Costa del Sol warned readers to 'beware criminal Britons lying in wait for unsuspecting newcomers' (Hampshire 1995); and to avoid the pitfalls experienced by older, isolated and lonely Britons who thought life could be an extended holiday (Baird 1995; Fodor 1994; Voase 1995).

Reports about 'the Brits in Spain' continue to appear in national newspapers and on television screens in Britain, though perhaps with less frequency now than in the early 1990s. Nevertheless, the image remains of either upper-class, colonial style, or lower-class, mass-tourist style expatriates searching for paradise, living an extended holiday in ghetto-like complexes, participating minimally in local life or culture, refusing to learn the language of their hosts, and generally recreating an England in the sun. The images may not be unitary but combine to construct a phenomenon with the above stereotype. In 1999 Channel Five, for example, ran a docu-soap called *Viva España*, which featured British expatriates living and working in Fuengirola. Radio One held its 1999 road show in Ibiza, where the British Consul has expressed shame at the behaviour of his fellow-nationals and where the cutting edge of the European party scene seems now to be located (see Thompson 1999). Occasional stories are told of wealthy celebrities living in the Marbella area, the 'California of Europe'; and Costa del Sol criminals are still caught from time to time, as reported in the press. Soap operas and drama series like *The Bill* continue to feature criminals escaping to Spain, even though an extradition agreement has been in place for some time.

Images have their basis in real experiences

The content of media images, as with much 'common knowledge', has some basis in reality. If not, since the power of the media does not work in a social vacuum, it would never be accepted by the audience. It has been suggested that interpersonal communication is influential in the absorption of information from other sources (McNair 1996), and so individuals' experience of migrant friends or relatives, and shared stories of these, reinforce the media images to aid the construction of a set of collective representations. And it is true to say that the British in Spain do *not* integrate well into Spanish society; many never manage to learn the language (I met a woman who had lived in Spain thirty years who spoke about five words of Spanish). There *are* elderly migrants who are poor, lonely and suffering ill health, there *are* criminals, and there *are* those who sit around in bars all day. There are those who are working very hard to make a go of the businesses they bought, and therefore have little time to enjoy Spain. The Britons do seem to spend a lot of time in each other's company and they do buy British (as well as Spanish) goods (King *et al.* 1998; O'Reilly 2000a; Rodríguez *et al.* 1998). And there are a few who would go home if they could.

But the representations discussed above neither give the whole picture, nor accurately represent reality. For a start, British migrants to Spain are not simply expatriates or tourists. There are many other forms of mobility whereby people migrate to Spain for part of the year, move backwards and forwards peripatetically, or go back 'home' for part of the year (O'Reilly 1996). The representations of them not only conflate these forms, they often even blur the boundary between tourist and expatriate to produce 'the Brit in Spain'; part-tourist, part-expatriate. The representations tend also to present an elderly population, but while many of the migrants are older and many are not working, they are not all elderly or retired and those who are older do not have the same experiences of old age as are attributed to them. The British in Spain are certainly not all poor, miserable and wanting to come home. They do not integrate but they are not living in ghettos or enclaves. Though they obtain certain British goods and draw on symbols of Britishness in the construction of a community, they are not trying to recreate a little England, and they also share Spanish goods and symbols of Spanishness. Though many are not working, they are not all lazy: lots of settled migrants work very hard at making life in Spain successful for themselves and for others like them. Many are involved in voluntary work in the numerous clubs and societies which provide leisure and welfare for the tourists and the migrants. Many are spending a great deal of their time creatively building support networks and exchange relationships; community-building work which is both active and positive. Many positive aspects of life in Spain were revealed during my research but were not picked up on by the media (O'Reilly 2000b). There were elderly people who told me they felt a sense of place and belonging since moving to Spain, which they had not felt at home. Working-class people told me they felt 'richer' in life as well as in money. Single women believed they were more accepted than in their own country, and parents felt their children were safer and happier. So why, if we are only being told part of the story by the media and the collective representations they influence, are we seeing this particular set of images and not others?

Images have currency

What happened with the Brits in Spain was in some ways to do with real events and real experiences of migration, and in some ways to do with other concerns which had currency at the time, so that audiences were more receptive to a particular interpretation of events, created in order to sell papers and make good television. What was new was, first, the massive migration of many Britons to Spain and, second, the financial hardship some of them were experiencing. Such was the extent of in-migration to Spain that during the 1980s it went from being a country of emigration to a country of immigration (King and Rybaczuk 1993). Although numbers are very difficult to obtain and to trust (cf. O'Reilly 1996; Williams *et al.* 1997), we know that the most substantial groups of legal foreign residents in Spain in the late 1980s were from (in order of importance) the United Kingdom, Germany, Portugal, France, USA, Argentina, Morocco, the Philippines and Venezuela. In 1989 there were 73,535 immigrants from the UK (as far as anyone could measure) and two-thirds of Spain's foreign residents were Europeans (King and Rybaczuk 1993). The effect on local areas was substantial. In the municipality of Mijas (in the Province of Málaga) for example, in the last census in 1991, European migrants accounted for over 11 per cent of the population and for almost a third of those aged over 55 (Rodríguez *et al.* 1998). Eventually, commentators in Spain began to express concern about the effects of these influxes of 'visitors' on water consumption, the treatment of waste, and the demands placed on natural and cultural environments (Jurdao 1990).

This was not all that was happening to trigger the media interest. At the height of the spate of media reports and documentaries discussed above, the peseta was in a strong position against the pound sterling, and people who had retired to Spain on British pensions or on money held in sterling accounts were finding it difficult to cope. Financial difficulties tend to exacerbate all other hardships, and so problems which can now be managed seemed then to be overwhelming. But there was another, quite dramatic event that affected many of the migrants and triggered a string of media and personal reports and exchanges: the BCCI crash. According to Kochan and Whittington (1991) many British pensioners who had retired to Spain had deposited their small nest-eggs with the Bank of Credit and Commerce International (BCCI). They were attracted by tax-free offshore banking, higher than average interest rates and a friendly service, but their combined savings of £83 million were wiped out overnight when BCCI was closed amidst allegations of huge fraud. While I was in Fuengirola this topic was energetically discussed amongst migrants, many of whom had invested in the bank or knew someone who had. Lots of people had lost their life savings and were now dependent merely on a state pension; some had to return to the UK because they had insufficient funds to stay in Spain. News images are often negative because negative makes better news, and so it was perhaps understandable for the newspapers and documentaries to focus attention on the hardships and suffering and on those wanting to come home – and there was some truth to their reports. What is essential is that we should avoid taking these images to be representative of a group or a phenomenon. Although migration can be a positive thing, it is rarely viewed as such by the mass media, and there are no popular channels to correct the unbalanced view.

Media images as a window on the society that constructs them

But it is not just news that makes news; news is made up of new events wrapped in old meanings (Hall *et al.* 1978). The collective images of the British in Spain have been motivated by stories which come directly from the migrants themselves, but these images are coloured by general views of the abnormality of migration. Generally migration tends to be viewed as something negative and problematic rather than as a positive, natural, exciting event which can offer advantages for both the hosts and the migrants. Migration has been a fact of human history since hunter–gatherer communities migrated to new pastures; yet, in European society at least, migration is seen as a deviation from the norm of stability and migrants are viewed as deviant individuals bringing instability and flux. As Benmayor and Skotnes tell it (1994: 4):

> Against all evidence, there is a strong tendency, especially in the 'advanced' countries, for observers and 'opinion-makers' of all sorts – journalists, politicians, scholars – to treat migrations, no matter what their scale, as isolated, random events, outside of the central thrust of social development. Massive population movements are viewed de facto as accidents of history, the result of unusual circumstances, catastrophes, deviations from the norm.

Since the mid-1980s interest in migration has been revived within Europe, with the main triggers of concern being the fall of the Iron Curtain and political and economic disruption in Eastern Europe, both threatening an influx of immigrants into Europe; and 'racial' tensions within Europe which question the harmony of ethnic pluralism and implicate persistent ethnic discreteness as a cause of conflict (Fassman and Munz 1994). Events in the former Yugoslavia have made the spectre of ethnic cleansing all too familiar, along with the subsequent flight of refugees to 'Western' shores. Individual governments are concerned that massive influxes of immigrants into their countries will compete for capital and over-stretch resources; for many, 'migration' has become synonymous with 'social problems' (Anthias 1992; Collinson 1993; Fassmann and Münz 1994). As a result, and as spelled out in more detail in earlier chapters of this book (see especially Chapters 1 and 4), newspapers tend periodically to be filled with negative scare stories of immigrants and refugees 'invading our shores', while governments regularly react to peaks in inflows of refugees with new and tighter legislation.

Media images are received and interpreted by audiences through a filter of their own experiences or 'knowledge' of their world, so that certain framings of an event, a group or an activity are more likely to work than others (Eldridge et al. 1997). A lot depends on which ideas have currency within a society at the time of reporting. Not only is it commonplace to view migration as a negative event, it was also not a new idea at the time to criticise the British abroad. They had received bad press in previous years as football supporters had been thrown out of countries for violent behaviour and package holiday makers (especially those in Spanish resorts such as Torremolinos and Benidorm) had reportedly misbehaved under the influence of too much alcohol. There was arguably a moral panic in the 1980s as these British representatives of 'our once-great nation' were considered to reflect decadence in British society as a whole.

British people at the time became familiar with images of Brits abroad in Union flag shorts and knotted handkerchiefs. Many Britons now apparently try to dissociate themselves from these images of lower-class British tourism, with its superficiality, lack of respect for local culture and hooligan mentality.[4]

At the same time the term 'tourist' was increasingly being used as a derisive label for someone who seemed content with 'obviously inauthentic experiences' (Crick 1989: 307). As we move beyond the age of mass package tourism, the tourist has become associated with commercialism, the trivial, the buying of signs rather than reality; tourism itself has become linked in the mind to the destruction of culture, the loss of the 'real', and the spoiling of the natural environment. Once fêted for offering travel opportunities to the working-class masses, holiday packaging is now denigrated as lacking the lure of the real and natural (Urry 1990). Commentators began to suggest that all package tourism did was relieve tourists of the burden of decision-making; providing them with an 'environmental bubble' to prevent confrontation with anything alien or unfamiliar (Crick 1989: 327). The image of this sort of traveller, now, is of someone who is not concerned with the culture of the people or the area to which he or she is travelling, but is hell-bent on hedonism, spending, freedom and indulgence. This view of the tourist as narrow-minded, as opposed to the 'traveller' who wants to explore and to become immersed in the culture and real environment of the unexplored 'other', is summed up by Paul Theroux (1992) when he says 'Tourists don't know where they've been. ... Travellers don't know where they're going.' But it is not just tourists that we cannot take seriously; the whole phenomenon of tourism is so bound up with hedonism and pleasure that even sociologists and anthropologists have in the past found it difficult to take the subject seriously. When Valene Smith (1978), now an established anthropologist of tourism, expressed her research interests, colleagues attempted to dissuade her. More recent researchers in the fields of geography, social policy and sociology have only been able to approach the topic since it became defined in terms of the elderly, retirement, tourism and the environment, or in terms of migration and poverty; in other words they were able to approach it as something serious as opposed to the frivolous and trivial.

Mass tourism and its tourists are now all bound up with images of over-development, exploitation, pollution and decay, as intellectuals, religious organisations, radicals within the countries themselves and, more recently, sociologists and anthropologists draw attention to tourism's adverse socio-cultural consequences. This has been picked up by the mass media and reports have appeared depicting crowded beaches, high-rise blocks and construction sites, pollution and decay.[5] Tourists themselves are directly associated with bad behaviour; 'the behaviour of so many tourists is ... deeply offensive to the people among whom they stay', says Crick (1989: 328).

It was not difficult to see where the British migrants to Spain's coastal resorts would fit in to all this. They appear to have turned tourism into a way of life and they have done it in areas which were previously associated with sun, fun, sex and alcohol. With such images of the British abroad and of Spain as a site for package tourism to draw on, it was easy to believe they were frivolous and hedonistic, eschewing the real authentic experience of travel to a foreign country for the unreal, fun experience of long-term tourism.

It was a small step from this to imply a class relation, at least in terms of tastes and aspirations if not of occupations (cf. Urry 1990). Class in Britain continues to be ubiquitously tied up with notions of superior breed and intellect and therefore of 'high culture', as well as with the traditional occupational and wealth classifications. The major division, between the growing middle and service classes and the lower or working classes, persists in the popular mind despite the attempts of successive governments to disguise it, including John Major's aspirations towards a classless society and Tony Blair's pronouncements that the class war is over. This major division is represented most articulately in the national newspaper industry, with the more left-wing and intellectual *Guardian* newspaper directly contrasting the (more) right-wing, anti-intellectual and working-class *Sun* newspaper. While the *Guardian* accuses the British migrants of living in a bubble, of not integrating, of regretting their poorly planned decision to move to Spain, the *Sun* identifies with these fun-loving nationals, sensationalising their liminal status as criminals, cops or sexy sun-seekers. At the same time as the *Guardian* represents the intellectual and discerning traveller, the multiculturalist, anti-racist individual, the *Sun* represents the 'naturally' nationalistic, touring, fun-loving British masses. Recent reports in the media have picked up on Thomson Holidays' dual attempt to market Majorca to the lower class of traveller in terms of sun, sea, sand and sangria and to the higher (or wealthier and more discerning) class of traveller as Mallorca, island of tranquil scenery, mountain villages and cosmopolitan resorts.[6] The implication is that different classes of people choose different classes of resort. The British in Spain's mass tourist areas are therefore lower class.

The construction of the 'Brit in Spain' has conflated images associated with retirement and old age with images of worklessness to draw conclusions about a way of life and health which are only minimally true. Popular attention has brought preconceptions about migration generally to suppositions about the British in Spain in particular. Immigrants to Britain have generally been labour migrants, who retain a myth of return to the homeland. Expatriates from Britain have been imperialists or upper-middle-class professionals. Since Britons in Spain cannot be attributed the status of labour migrants or expatriates in the modern sense, and since it is assumed they do not work at all, they are, therefore, classified as 'retired'. This reflects a basic division in British culture between work and leisure, and work and retirement. Other constructions are built upon and associated with the notion of retirement: older age, poverty, loss of status, loss of power (cf. Vincent 1995). Other things are then tagged on as associated with these concepts: ill health, boredom, dependence – a problem.

For example, Alden Speare (1992: 57) concludes of the elderly in general that 'most ... do not work, most are dependent upon either their children, the country of residence, or public transfers ... elderly persons have a much higher incidence of chronic illness and disability than the general population'. Retirement is, therefore, when talking about British migration to Spain, associated with elderly people, some of whom are living old colonial lifestyles, but others of whom clearly suffer problems associated with poverty and ill-health, loneliness and isolation, and who could become a burden at any time in the future.

Things change

If journalists and scriptwriters trade on current concerns and contemporary ideas then, as these change, so will the reports and media images that get produced and reproduced. What was considered newsworthy changes, as do dominant ideologies. Now, since the late 1990s, the British media have all but lost interest in their expatriates in Spain. This is due to a whole array of reasons, but no one is suffering there to the extent that they were. The pound is very strong and the migrants are feeling comparatively wealthy. The events have had their coverage and are no longer worthy of attention while there are other things of interest to report, and nothing new is happening to trigger fresh interest. However, some of the collective representations remain powerful. Drama programmes and news reports in Britain continue to depict criminals escaping to Spain, and working-class people holidaying there. Reports of wealthy media stars buying up apartments and villas as holiday homes in the Marbella area, and of drug barons who 'make a killing' in Ibiza, continue to hit the headlines occasionally. These 'stories' ensure that many of the images of the British migrants remain intact.[7]

The stereotype and the people

Finally, it is important to consider the effects of the images on those described. The migrants I met in Spain could not help but be affected by these images. They felt betrayed by reporters and scriptwriters who they believed depicted them negatively and found it difficult to trust me to do anything different. At the outset of my research I found people less than willing to tell me their stories until I had reassured them thoroughly that I was not a reporter, a journalist or a scriptwriter. They felt that there were sufficient images and stories of them which depicted their lives in a bad light and they did not want to give me the chance to produce more! Several people I met had been interviewed for a television documentary or a radio programme and felt their feelings and words had been misinterpreted or misrepresented. One woman told me at length about how she had agreed to appear on an early morning show called *Kilroy*, which she believed was an honest discussion programme, and had been shocked to be told what to say. 'They didn't want to hear about life here really', she told me, 'they just wanted to hear the bad stuff.' Another man told me he had been interviewed by a journalist who had obviously decided what he was going to write before the interview; and a woman was very angry about the programme *The Coast of Dreams*, in which she had appeared. She told me it had shown her working all the time and this just was not true.

However, having reassured people that I was not wanting to produce yet another media report and that I was looking for their side of the story, the media representations of them continued to provide a marker against which to argue their case. Their stories were constructed as refutations of what they assumed I believed and, as a result, the picture I built up of life in Spain from interview data was very much in opposition to the one presented by the collective representations discussed above. Older people enthused about how full and active their lives are, and about how healthy they feel. Younger people reminded me that not every British migrant is old and retired, and assured me that they get a lot of pleasure out of life in Spain. Several people told me warmly of the Spanish friends they had made. Some insisted 'we're not like them lot, that sit around in bars all day and drink'. Some told me of criminals they knew, but stressed that 'we're not all like that, you know'. Everyone was very enthusiastic about their lives and almost everyone said, more than once, that they never want to go home (and see King *et al.* 1998; Rodríguez *et al.* 1998). Several older people assured me that they did not even want to be buried back home. 'This is home now', one man told me. Indeed the insistence, on the part of the majority of British migrants, that they never want to go home was so powerful that I began to view it as a symbol of the group's identity; certainly it had the power of inclusion and exclusion (cf. Cohen 1985). But the question remains: to what extent was this a reaction to a stereotypical representation of their lives?

NOTES

1 I carried out fifteen months' fieldwork in Fuengirola on the Costa del Sol for my doctoral thesis at the University of Essex; for a published version of my thesis see O'Reilly (2000a).

2 For some results of this research see King *et al.* 1998; Williams *et al.* 1997.

3 This was more true in the early 1990s than it is now, for reasons which will become clear later.

4 As I was writing this, a radio presenter on my local radio station announced the results of a survey of what the British like to do abroad. One recurring response was that they like to pretend not to be British!

5 Modern tourist brochures and travel programmes suggest travellers look inland for the 'real' Spain. Spain's own tourist board, meanwhile, is trying to encourage visitors back to its shores and its rural areas by changing its now negative package holiday image.

6 See the *Guardian*, 2 September 1999. Thomson are catering for the elitist snobbery that assumes that mass tourist sites are not suitable for the discerning traveller, suggested the Consumer Association, in the same report.

7   See, for example, the *Guardian*, 3 February 1999 ('Pass notes: Majorca') and Thompson (1999).

References

Age Concern (1993) *Growing Old in Spain*, London: Age Concern England.

Anthias, F. (1992) *Ethnicity, Class, Gender and Migration*, Avebury: Aldershot.

Baird, C. (1995) *Spain: The Versatile Guide*, London: Duncan Peterson.

Beard, R. (1994) 'The cost of keeping a home in paradise', *Daily Mail*, 17 August.

Benmayor, R. and Skotnes, A. (1994) 'Some reflections on migration and identity', in *Migration and Identity. International Yearbook of Oral History and Life Stories, Vol III*, Oxford: Oxford University Press.

Buller, H. and Hoggart, K. (1994) *International Counterurbanization: British Migrants in Rural France*, Aldershot: Avebury.

Champion, T. and King, R. (1993) 'New trends in international migration in Europe', *Geographical Viewpoint* 21: 45–57.

Cohen, A. P. (1985) *The Symbolic Construction of Community*, London: Routledge.

Collinson, S. (1993) *Europe and International Migration*, London: Pinter.

Crampton, R. (1993) 'Costa del Sunset', *Times Magazine*, 28 August.

Crick, M. (1989) 'Representations of international tourism in the social sciences: sun, sex, sights, savings, and servility', *Annual Review of Anthropology* 18: 307–44.

Eldridge, J., Kirtzinger, J. and Williams, K. (1997) *The Mass Media and Power in Modern Britain*, Oxford: Oxford University Press.

Fassmann, H. and Münz, R. (eds) (1994) *European Migration in the Late Twentieth Century*, Aldershot: Edward Elgar.

Fletcher, D. (1994) 'Life in the sun is not so hot for elderly', *Daily Mail*, 6 May.

Fodor (1994) *Fodor's Spain*, New York: Fodor's Travel Publications.

Hall, S., Critcher, S., Jefferson, T., Clarke, J. and Roberts, B. (1978) *Policing the Crisis: Mugging, the State and Law and Order*, London: Macmillan.

Hammersley, M. and Atkinson, P. (1995) *Ethnography. Principles in Practice*, London: Routledge.

Hampshire, D. (1995) *Living and Working in Spain*, Harmondsworth: Penguin.

Hooper, J. (1993) 'A hard lesson in Spanglish', *Guardian*, 4 June.

Jurdao, F. (1990) *España en Venta*, Madrid: Endymion.

King, R. and Rybaczuk, K. (1993) 'Southern Europe and the international division of labour: from emigration to immigration', in King, R. (ed.), *The New Geography of European Migrations*, London: Belhaven Press.

King, R., Warnes, A. and Williams, A. M. (1998) 'International retirement migration in Europe', *International Journal of Population Geography* 4, 2: 91–111.

Kochan, N. and Whittington, B. (1991) *Bankrupt: The BCCI Fraud*, London: Victor Gollancz.

Lukes, S. (ed.) (1982) *Emile Durkheim, The Rules of Sociological Method and Selected Texts*, London: Macmillan.

MacKinnon, I. (1993) 'A place in the sun loses its shine', *Independent on Sunday*, 23 May.

McNair, B. (1996) *News and Journalism in the UK*, London: Routledge.

Misiti, M., Muscarà, C., Pumares, P., Rodríguez, V. and White, P. (1995) 'Future migration into Southern Europe', in Hall, R. and White, P. (eds), *Europe's Population. Towards the Next Century*, London: UCL Press.

Mullan, C. (1992) *The Problems of the Elderly British Expatriate Community in Spain*, London: Help the Aged.

O'Reilly, K. (1996) 'A new trend in European migration: contemporary British migration to Fuengirola, Costa del Sol', *Geographical Viewpoint* 23: 25–37.

—— (2000a) *The British on the Costa del Sol*, London: Routledge.

—— (2000b) 'Trading intimacy for liberty: British women on the Costa del Sol', in Anthias, F. and Lazaridis, G. (eds), *Gender and Migration in Southern Europe*, Oxford: Berg.

Rodríguez, V., Fernández-Mayoralas, G. and Rojo, F. (1998) 'European retirees on the Costa del Sol: a cross-national comparison', *International Journal of Population Geography* 4, 2: 183–200.

Smith, V. (ed.) (1978) *Hosts and Guests*, Oxford: Basil Blackwell.

Speare, A. Jr (1992) 'Elderly migration, proximity of children, and living arrangements', in Rogers, A. (ed.), *Elderly Migration and Population Redistribution*, London: Belhaven Press.

Theroux, P. (1992) *The Happy Isles of Oceania*, London: Hamish Hamilton.

Thompson, T. (1999) 'British drug barons overrun Ibiza', *Guardian*, 15 August.

Urry, J. (1990) *The Tourist Gaze*, London: Sage Publications.

Victor, C. R. (1987) *Old Age in Modern Society*, London: Chapman and Hall.

Vincent, J. A. (1995) *Inequality and Old Age*, London: UCL Press.

Voase, R. (1995) *Tourism: The Human Perspective*, London: Hodder and Stoughton.

Warnes, A. M. (1991) 'Migration to and seasonal residence in Spain of Northern European elderly people', *European Journal of Gerontology* 1: 53–60.

Williams, A. M., King, R. and Warnes, A. M. (1997) 'A place in the sun: international retirement migration from Northern to Southern Europe', *European Urban and Regional Studies* 4, 2: 115–34.

INDEX

189